SERIALS IN LIBRARIES

SERIALS IN LIBRARIES

Issues and Practices

Steve Black

A Member of the Greenwood Publishing Group

Westport, Connecticut • London

Library of Congress Cataloging-in-Publication Data

Black, Steven, 1959–
    Serials in libraries : issues and practices / by Steve Black.
      p.   cm.
    Includes bibliographical references and index.
    ISBN 1-59158-258-X (pbk. : alk. paper)
    1. Serials librarianship—United States. I. Title.
    Z692.S5B55 2006
    025.17'32—dc22   2006023751

British Library Cataloguing in Publication Data is available.

Library of Congress Catalog Card Number: 2006023751
ISBN: 1-59158-258-X

First published in 2006

Libraries Unlimited, 88 Post Road West, Westport, CT 06881
A Member of the Greenwood Publishing Group, Inc.
www.lu.com

Printed in the United States of America

The paper used in this book complies with the
Permanent Paper Standard issued by the National
Information Standards Organization (Z39.48–1984).

10 9 8 7 6 5 4 3 2 1

Table of Contents

Acknowledgments

Many thanks to Maggie Horn, not only for patiently helping me improve this text at several stages in the process, but also for being a fine guest speaker for the serials course I teach. Her phenomenal knowledge and experience with serials combined with her generous willingness to help me are deeply appreciated. Special thanks to Jean Hirons for her generous investment of time and energy to correct my mistakes and make helpful suggestions for improving the chapter on cataloging. I am also delighted that she agreed to create the cover art for this book. Thanks to Les Hawkins for critiquing the chapter on remote access serials, aggregation, and consortia. Any remaining errors are mine alone, and exist despite the wise and patient counsel of Maggie, Jean, and Les.

An anonymous reviewer's thoughtful and perceptive constructive criticism of my manuscript was enormously helpful. Thank you, whoever you are. Acquisitions editor Blanche Woolls' thorough close reading of my manuscript and beneficial corrections and suggestions are greatly appreciated. Thank you, Blanche.

I wish to thank Paula Gresen, the bindery supervisor and organizational wizard of the College of Saint Rose Library's periodicals for her consistently excellent day-to-day management of the collection and for her valuable feedback on Chapter 4.

Mary Lindner, my wife, has been not only patient and understanding, but also a perceptive critic. Her helpful feedback led to many improvements. Thanks, Mary!

I welcome and encourage feedback and questions from you, the reader. Please feel free to e-mail me at blacks@strose.edu or send a note to Steve Black, Neil Hellman Library, College of Saint Rose, 392 Western Ave., Albany, NY, 12203-1419.

Introduction

Serials present some of the most interesting challenges in librarianship. The challenges arise from various sources including changes to how serials are published, new expectations of patrons, technological advances, and budgetary pressures. *Serials in Libraries: Issues and Practices* is designed to introduce library students and librarians with little experience in serials management to the principal themes and challenges of selecting, acquiring, receiving, and maintaining serials in libraries. Best practices will be introduced in areas where they exist. In areas where best practice is currently in flux, available choices will be described.

The origin of this book is the authors' notes for a course in serials he teaches annually in the Master of Science in Information Science program at the University at Albany. The notes built upon two excellent books that became outdated because the serials environment is evolving so rapidly. Marcia Tuttle, Luke Swindler, and Frieda B. Rosenberg's *Managing Serials* (Greenwich, CT: JAI Press, 1996) and Thomas E. Nisonger's *Management of Serials in Libraries* (Englewood, CO: Libraries Unlimited, 1998) still contain valuable information, but the two books do not address some important issues and practices. Remote access to serials and new business models for providing online access have profoundly affected serials librarianship in ways impossible to predict in the 1990s.

The present book is designed to introduce the reader to current issues and practices. The author has sought to accurately and economically introduce the scope of issues facing serials librarians in a readable style that is neither too academic nor too informal. Sources are cited as needed to properly recognize authors, but the goal of this book is not to review the literature on serials. The suggestions for further reading at the end of each chapter point the reader to appropriate entry points in the literature for more in-depth study.

The author wrote this book with two audiences in mind. One audience is library and information science students, particularly those taking a course on serials, but also for students taking courses in library management, issues in librarianship, and reference. Since serials comprise a large portion of libraries' budgets and are crucial sources of information in almost every discipline, better awareness of issues surrounding serials in libraries can benefit any librarian. The second audience is experienced librarians who move into serials management from some other type of library work. This book's concise introduction to the complex challenges of serials is intended to provide a helpful overview for those who find themselves suddenly responsible for serials in a library.

Serials in Libraries: Issues and Practices is not a training manual. This book will introduce the issues a librarian will face with managing serials and suggest sources for learning detailed practices, but it cannot teach all one needs to know. Much of the required knowledge can only be learned locally, based on the library's policies, integrated library system (ILS), and cooperative agreements. Proper cataloging practice exceeds the scope of this work. Main themes concerning the bibliographic control of serials are introduced, but the reader is referred to other sources for appropriate training.

The book begins with a broad survey of the serials environment, including definitions, an introduction to the serials crisis, and acknowledgement of the stakeholders in serials. Chapter 2 discusses several issues surrounding the online delivery of remote access serials. Characteristics and types of online serials and ways to provide access to them is presented early in the book to highlight their important role in current library practice. Chapter 3 introduces the practice of working within a budget and choosing which titles belong in a serials collection. Some emphasis is placed on the duty of collecting appropriate data and writing reports, as reporting is a job requirement for many serials librarians. Chapter 4 addresses the prosaic tasks of managing a print serials collection. Despite increased emphasis on online delivery of serials, proper management of print serials is still needed, and requires knowledge of best practices.

Bibliographic control of serials is the topic of Chapter 5. Guidelines for cataloging are introduced with discussion of ongoing issues surrounding cataloging practice, options for displaying holdings in catalogs, and ways to link patrons to online journals. The next two chapters shift the focus from what happens in libraries to issues affecting serials in general. Chapter 6 introduces economic principles as they apply to the serials marketplace and discusses the serials crisis in more depth than was introduced in the first chapter. The applicability to serials of the economic concept of public goods is discussed in some detail. Chapter 7 presents issues surrounding the production and dissemination of the content of scholarly journals, including benefits and criticisms of peer review, motives for scholarly publishing, and alternatives to traditional subscriptions such as Open Access. Chapter 8 investigates the use of serials and introduces practices librarians can employ to measure and analyze use. Finally, Chapter 9 explores an area not addressed in other books on serials management, means and strategies of teaching patrons to efficiently and effectively find and use serials.

Chapter 1

The Serials Environment

This chapter introduces the serials environment and basic management of serials. Definitions are provided with an introduction to the fundamental concepts and important organizations involved in serials. The environment includes the conditions or forces that influence or modify the things in the system, and the conditions of the serials environment considered here are definitions of terms, historical context, and standards. Forces affecting serials discussed in this chapter include the current crisis in pricing, organizations that establish cataloging rules and other standards, descriptions of the stakeholders, types of libraries, and the various groups who have a stake in the system of serials publishing, acquisition, and long-term access. Because the serials environment is evolving rapidly, a common set of definitions is helpful.

DEFINITIONS

This section includes definitions for serials and periodicals as defined in authoritative sources. They are both functional and operational.

1

Serial

Functional definitions of the word "serial" may be found in various authoritative sources, including dictionaries and glossaries of library and publishing terms. A functional definition describes what something is, but does not define how this term is used in practice, while an operational definition offers this. *Webster's Third New International Dictionary* (2002) provides a functional definition of "serial" as a publication issued as one of a consecutively numbered and indefinitely continued series.

Two acceptable operational definitions of a serial are provided. The first, by the International Organization for Standardization (ISO) Technical Committee 46, developed for the purpose of assigning International Standard Serial Numbers (ISSNs), is based on the principle that one serial gets one ISSN. Therefore, "a serial is defined as a publication in print or nonprint form, issued in successive parts, usually having numerical or chronological designations, and intended to be continued indefinitely" (Bowker 2001). The second definition is from the National Serials Data Program (NSDP).

The NSDP, assigning ISSNs to serials, uses the following definition. While it is similar to the ISO definition, this one includes examples: "Serials are print or nonprint publications issued in parts, usually bearing issue numbers and/or dates. A serial is expected to continue indefinitely. Serials include magazines, newspapers, annuals (such as reports, yearbooks, and directories), journals, memoirs, proceedings, transactions of societies, and monographic series" (National Serials Data Program 2003). Based on these definitions, there are three primary characteristics that distinguish a serial from other types of publications:

- Successive parts (necessary)
- Numerical and/or chronological designations for each part (typical but not absolutely necessary)
- No planned termination date, it is a continuing resource (necessary).

A related but different type of publication issued in successive parts is a series.

Series

Monographic series, like serials, are successive publications. Each volume or issue in a series typically has a common subject matter, publisher, and format. The CONSER Cataloging Manual defines a series as "a group of separate items related to one another by the fact that each item bears, in addition to its own title proper, a collective title applying to the group as a whole" (Hirons, Module 12, 7, 2002). The key to this definition is that each volume or issue has a unique title. Series may or may not have a planned termination date. If termination is planned by the publisher in advance (e.g., the volume in hand includes the statement "volume 1 of 20"), the publication is clearly a series and not a serial. A multi-volume reference work published over a span of years is an example of a series published over time, but with a planned termination date.

Unfortunately, the line between a serial and a series is frequently not so clear. Monographic series, annuals, and other series can and do meet the ISSN three-part definition for a serial. A volume in a series can carry both an ISSN for the series and an ISBN (International Standard Book Number) for the volume. Volumes in series with no planned end date present a special challenge for catalogers, since these continuing resources can be handled as serials or as monographs. Edited scholarly books with a volume title that appears above or before the series title are also usually considered as series. Publishers have great leeway in how they choose to designate the volumes and issues in series and serials, and the variety of methods they employ are a testament to publishers' creativity. It seems that every possible way of grouping and numbering series has been employed.

Periodical

A periodical, a name including newspapers, popular magazines, scholarly journals, and trade magazines or trade journals, is a serial intended to be published on a regular schedule. Publishers can and do choose some quite inventive schedules, but common schedules are quarterly, monthly, biweekly, or weekly. But just to keep things uncertain (this being a discussion of serials, after all), some periodicals have a stated publication pattern of "irregular." Note that by definition periodicals are "intended" to be published on a regular schedule. One of the challenges of managing serials is that periodicals often deviate from their intended publication schedules. Popular magazines tend to come out before their cover dates. That does not create a problem, especially since the lead time is usually pretty consistent. In contrast, scholarly journals almost never come out ahead of their intended date, and they are quite often late. Publication delays of months after the intended date are common, and it is not unheard of for journals to be published years behind schedule. When long delays occur, publishers may combine or skip issues to get the journal back on a current schedule. But serials with planned publication schedules are considered periodicals even if intended patterns are disrupted by delays and irregularities.

While it is usually fairly obvious to a librarian which type of periodical one has in hand, there are no sharp, clearly defined differences between newspapers, magazines, scholarly journals, or trade journals. Newspapers are generally printed on newsprint, unbound, and have a daily or weekly publication pattern, but other types of publications may also have those characteristics. Popular magazines tend to be glossy, bound, and have extensive advertising. Prices of magazines tend to be low, because most or all of the cost of production is typically covered by advertising. Since advertising rates are based largely on circulation, it behooves the publishers to set a low price in order to maximize sales. Subscriptions can be even lower when information from the subscriber database is sold to marketers.

Scholarly journals may also contain some advertisements, but their primary distinguishing feature is the peer review process through which most of the articles pass before publication. While some content of scholarly journals, such as letters to the editor or book reviews, may not be peer reviewed before publication, the process of experts critiquing research articles before publication distinguishes scholarly journals from other periodicals. In some cases, critiques before publication are made only by an editor, but typically several peer reviewers are involved. Scholarly journals are aimed at readers with specialized knowledge, and the articles published within them typically include references or works cited. The characteristics of scholarly journals hold true for print and online versions, but it may be more difficult for patrons to determine whether a source is scholarly when individual articles online are viewed independently from an issue of a journal.

Trade magazines or trade journals are geared toward specific audiences with knowledge and expertise on the topic of the publication, but the articles are not peer reviewed before publication. No sharp lines distinguish popular, scholarly, and trade periodicals from one another. While it may be obvious that *People* is a magazine, *Library Quarterly* is a journal, and *Aviation Week and Space Technology* is a trade publication, other periodicals may not fit neatly into the three categories.

BUDGETARY CHALLENGES FOR SERIALS LIBRARIANS

Publishing successive parts under one title is a logical way for individuals or groups to disseminate information. Readers benefit from readily recognizing that a publication is from a familiar source. The publishers benefit from readers' familiarity if the publisher has established a positive reputation. So library patrons naturally expect their libraries to collect serials relevant to their interests. A few of the most important trends that have impacted the place of serials in libraries' collections and budgets in recent decades include rapid inflation of subscription prices and the proliferation of serials being published. The "serials crisis" is a term commonly used to describe the high inflation rates and proliferation of titles that have characterized scholarly journal publishing since the 1980s.

Popular Magazines

The challenge of rapidly inflating subscription prices has affected the collection of scholarly journals far more severely than the collection of popular magazines. Prices of magazines have remained fairly stable or decreased when adjusted for inflation. For example, a subscription to *Business Week* cost $7.50 in 1932, which is equivalent to $85 today. *Business Week* cost $46 in 2004, so its price has gone down in real dollars. Like scholarly journals, popular magazines proliferate into niche markets, but their prices are relatively modest. But a challenge to collecting popular magazines is their tendency to fail. Some venerable titles like *Time*,

National Geographic, Harper's, and *Atlantic* endure for decades, but 60 percent of newly started magazines never publish a second issue, and only 20 percent remain in business after ten years of publishing (Husni 2004). Roughly 700–1,000 magazines are launched in the United States each year, and the trend is toward ever more specialization with titles such as *Step-by-Step Beads, Luxury Pool,* and *Montana Golf* (Husni 2004). Deciding which special interest magazines to include in a collection depends on the library's budget and requests from local patrons. Making these choices can be a challenge, but they do not constitute what is known as the serials crisis. The serials crisis is the result of subscription price inflation exceeding the general rate of inflation combined with a proliferation of serial titles being published.

Scholarly Journals

The roots of the serials crisis lie in the recent history of scholarly publishing with its proliferation of scholarly journals and subscription price increases. Before World War II, most scholarly journals were published by professional societies, usually at prices intended to just cover costs. The list of periodicals indexed in the *International Index* (covering scholarly journals in the humanities and sciences) for 1931–1934 shows that the expensive journals sold for $5–7 (comparable to *Business Week*), and many cost only $2 or $3 per year. Seven dollars in 1931 is equivalent to about $73 today. Scholarly journals used to cost about the same as popular magazines, but now they cost far more. According to the 2003 Periodical Price Survey (Van Orsdel and Born 2003), the average price of a general interest magazine is about $50. The average of all periodicals, including scholarly journals, is over $300. Business journals average $178, psychology journals average $420, chemistry and physics journals average $1,626. What happened?

The years following World War II saw extraordinary growth in higher education in the United States. Immediately after the war, the federal government fed money into academic institutions through the G.I. Bill (tuition grants for military veterans) and research grants. During the Cold War years, high priority was placed on educating scientists to stay technologically ahead of the Soviet Union. State governments heavily subsidized the cost of attending public colleges because politicians agreed that well-educated citizens were good for society and the economy. In the 1970s, the baby boom led to a sharp increase in the number of college-age students, and an array of social trends increased peoples' expectation of access to a college education. Money flowed into college budgets, more research was conducted, more professors were hired, and more students attended college. These developments increased the demand for journals to publish the rapidly expanding corpus of research. Professional societies, the traditional publishers of scholarly journals, did not increase their production at a comparable rate.

Professional societies such as the American Chemical Society and the American Institute of Physics were perceived by some as not expanding their journals fast enough to handle all the research worthy of being published. Recognizing an opportunity in the market for scholarly journals, commercial publishers like Elsevier, Pergamon, Plenum, and Springer-Verlag launched new journals and became competitive rivals to the scholarly societies. Many libraries, especially those at research universities, went through a phase of having funds available for almost any worthwhile journal. Successful commercial publishers delivered products meeting consistently high standards. Some of them charged more than societies' similar titles, but libraries could pay and there was demand for the journals. This demand-pull inflation caused some rise in journal prices, but before about 1980 these increases roughly paralleled the overall inflation rate.

Since private companies are designed to make a profit, commercial publishers naturally brought out new journals and raised subscription prices to the degree the market could bear, and they still do. Some nonprofit societies also seek revenue exceeding their costs of production in order to support their organization's interests and activities. But many librarians believe, based on published comparisons of journal prices, that commercial publishers have been primarily responsible for taking advantage of demand-pull inflation.

Library Budgets Unable to Keep Pace

The phase of having funds available for just about any worthwhile journal ended in the 1980s, when the typical library budget experienced much smaller annual increases for materials than had been experienced in the 1970s. Most libraries consequently slowed their efforts to add new serials to their collections. Demand-pull inflation may still occur in particular disciplines, and many publishers continue to raise prices as demand allows. But since about 1990, cost-push inflation has become a more apparent cause of increased subscription prices. Production cost increases include more pages published per volume, printing and paper costs, and expenses for peer review and editing processes.

These stagnant acquisitions budgets, higher subscription rates, and new journals combined to create hard times for libraries and the serials crisis. The average subscription price increases of 8 to 10 percent per year exceeded most libraries' annual budget increases. The gap between prices and budgets made libraries unable to maintain existing subscriptions. To add worthwhile new journals, other subscriptions had to be cut. Articles published in 1988, comparing the cost of science journals produced by society and commercial publishers and quantifying some libraries' cancellations, brought greater awareness of the crisis. In the context of this sense of crisis, the Resources and Technical Services Division of the American Library Association launched the *Newsletter on Serials Pricing Issues* (Tuttle 1989–2001). Superbly edited by Marcia Tuttle until it ceased in 2001 with its 257th issue, the newsletter kept readers up to date on the state of the crisis.

Library cancellations created more cost-push inflation. One could logically surmise that as demand drops, prices will also drop to attract more subscribers. This did not happen. Rather, as fewer subscriptions sell, publishers raise the price of the remaining subscriptions to cover production costs. Cancellations and price increases have thus fallen into a vicious cycle. As of 2005, the serials crisis of too few dollars to pay for rapidly increasing subscription rates for the journals needed by researchers has become the status quo. Round after round of subscription cancellations has become dishearteningly commonplace at many academic and special libraries.

Ongoing proliferation of disciplines and sub-disciplines needing outlets for their research exacerbates the serials crisis. As specializations rapidly advance, scholars need new journals to publish their research. The hard reality for libraries is that journal subscriptions cost more, the need to add journals continues unabated, but that need exists in the context of budgets growing more slowly than journal subscription inflation. Not only are librarians unable to buy all the titles desired by its patrons, budgets often do not allow librarians to maintain current subscriptions. It becomes difficult or even impossible to add new titles.

SERIALS COLLECTION DEVELOPMENT

Library acquisitions budgets typically allocate funds for various types of materials, including books, periodicals, manuscripts and archival materials, microforms, and databases. Allocations for serials (including monographic series) vary among libraries because the portion of literature published as serials varies among areas of interest. For example, while fiction is published in both books and periodicals, a great majority is acquired by libraries in book format. Literary magazines are important venues for expression, but they are rightly famous for being operated on a shoestring and having low circulation. In contrast, many of the sciences place high value on the currency of information, and thus place great emphasis on periodical literature. As a general rule of the thumb, the higher the value of currency of information, the more emphasis is placed on periodical literature over books. Differences also exist between types of libraries.

Contrast between Public and Academic Libraries

According to the *Bowker Annual Library and Book Trade Almanac* (Bowker 2002), public libraries in the United States spent 6.41 percent of their total acquisitions expenditures on serials. This represents 4,203 libraries spending almost $70 million. These public libraries devoted 43 percent of acquisitions for books, spending about $467 million on them. So public libraries' expenditures on serials are about 15 percent of what they spend on books. While the *Bowker Annual* table of serials expenditure data lists serials as "periodicals/serials," librarians reporting data to Bowker make their own interpretation of whether serials other than periodicals count as serials or books with any variation in reporting unlikely to affect the percentages very much.

In contrast, according to the *Bowker Annual* (Bowker 2002), academic libraries spend about 43 percent of acquisitions on serials, and 21 percent on books, more than twice as much on serials ($711 million) as on books ($350 million). Note that while all public libraries together spend more on books than academic libraries spend, academic libraries spend ten times more on serials than public libraries do. This explains why the literature on the serials crisis never mentions public libraries.

Another big reason for much higher academic library spending on serials is that the average price of popular and general-interest magazines is much lower than the average price of scholarly journals. According to the 2003 U.S. Periodical Price Survey (Van Orsdel and Born 2003), the average price of popular and general-interest magazines is approximately $50. Scholarly journals in some disciplines are only slightly more expensive than that. The average subscription price for arts is $65, for literature $71, for history $80. But the average title in education costs $160, psychology $419, medicine $847, and chemistry and physics a whopping $1,626. A public library can purchase 32 magazines for what an academic library is paying for a single chemistry journal.

Carnegie Classification for Academic Libraries

Although averages are useful for understanding the big picture, individual academic libraries' mixes of books and serials vary to meet local needs. Academic institutions are by no means all alike. The Carnegie Foundation first devised a classification system for institutions of higher learning in 1973. The Carnegie Classification system is often used in higher education in the United States to group colleges and universities into categories of institutions with similar functions and similar characteristics of students and faculty members. In broad terms, the classification system is based on categories of doctoral/research universities, master's colleges and universities, baccalaureate colleges, associate's colleges, and specialized institutions (Carnegie Foundation for the Advancement of Teaching 2006).

These classifications correlate with serials collection development policies, as the sizes of collections naturally grow with academic patrons' needs to do research. How librarians meet the needs of patron populations in institutions described by the Carnegie classification is described in *Guidelines for the Formulation of Collection Development Policies* (Perkins 1979). The *Guidelines* are for all types of materials, including manuscripts. Only the parts applicable to serials development will be summarized here. Although the Carnegie classification system is primarily used for institutions of higher learning, the principles of the *Guidelines* also apply to public and special libraries.

Several levels of collection development exist, including comprehensive, research, and advanced study levels, initial study level, and basic study level. The first two, comprehensive and research, are assigned at doctoral/research institutions. At the comprehensive level, the collection is one in which the librarian endeavors, so far as possible, to acquire all significant works of recorded knowledge, in all applicable languages. This would mean every serial published in a subject area, with the goal of obtaining and maintaining an exhaustive collection within the defined field.

Research Level collections include the major journals required for dissertations and independent research. This means having a very extensive collection of journals and the indexes or databases needed to support their use. A research level collection will include many serials published in languages other than English. It would include subscriptions to all (or virtually all) journals covered in the indexes and databases important to a discipline. For example, a research level collection for psychology would include ongoing subscriptions to all, or almost all, the journals indexed in PsycINFO.

Doctoral and research universities, including the 123 institutions represented in the Association of Research Libraries (ARL), will typically strive to support research level collections for doctoral degree programs. Comprehensive collections are exceedingly difficult to afford, both in terms of dollars and in terms of collection development effort. Exhaustiveness means going way beyond simply using standard collection development tools, and is thus an arduous, time-consuming, expensive task. For this reason, even at large research libraries, comprehensive collections can be maintained in few disciplines.

Far more common in academic libraries are collections at the advanced study level. This means a collection that is adequate to support the course work of advanced undergraduate and master's degree programs, or sustained independent study. For serials, this requires a selection of representative journals and adequate indexes and databases to effectively use them. This level of serials collection development may also be found in large public libraries and in research facilities' libraries. The study level collection described in the *Guidelines* is similar to the advanced study level. In fact, the wording for both advanced study level and study level is "a selection of representative journals." Whether a library's journal collection meets the "advanced study" or the "study" level is apparently subject to a fair amount of interpretation. Either level is appropriate to serve undergraduate and graduate degree granting programs, but not doctoral programs. A portion of an entire serials collection can be at a research level to serve the doctoral programs offered, and the rest of the collection at one of the study levels. Unfortunately for the faculty working at institutions with collections in their discipline at the study level, journals that they need for their own research may not be available on campus. Fortunately, the combination of online journal packages and interlibrary loans can go a long way toward filling that gap. Librarians at research facilities typically use document delivery services to supplement their library's serials collection.

Library collections intended for undergraduate use are at the initial study level. Collections at this level have a selection of the major review journals for the disciplines taught at the institution. Review journals are those that report on other research and/or contain reviews of books in the discipline. The initial study level does not require journals with original research. While there is a relatively small and somewhat fuzzy step down from advanced study to study levels for journals, there is a significant step to the fewer titles required for initial study. A fairly small collection of journals in each discipline can suffice. However, as colleges often include many disciplines in their undergraduate programs, maintaining even an initial study level of journals can require a major allocation of the materials budget.

The basic study level is a highly selective collection, which serves to introduce and define the subject and to indicate the varieties of information available elsewhere. It only requires a few major periodicals in the field. The minimal study level for a subject requires even fewer titles, perhaps only a single journal. The *Guidelines* use the term "out of scope" for no collection at all on a subject.

Collection Development in Practice

Librarians at each of the Carnegie Classification types of higher education institutions decide for each program offered which level of collection they desire and can afford to achieve. Consideration for patron's needs is not the only reason to do this. Accreditation bodies assess library collections and expect journal subscriptions to be adequate for the degrees being offered. If a college adds a major, or a master's degree, or a new doctoral program, there are significant ramifications for the library's budget. These ramifications are not always considered by faculty and administrators in advance, so librarians need to be, whenever possible, proactively involved in planning processes while adding new programs.

As will be discussed in some detail in the chapter on journal use, journals relevant to each academic discipline are concentrated in a core of heavily used titles. If librarians choose to collect at the study level, they might decide that the journals accounting for 50 percent of citations in the discipline's literature will suffice. In most disciplines, half the citations will be covered by about two dozen journals. The advanced study level might be defined as the journals covering 80 percent of the citations. This would likely require several dozen subscriptions, representing a far greater financial commitment than what would be required to subscribe to journals covering half of the citations. Beyond the 80 percent level, it can require ten or more subscriptions to cover each 1 percent of citations in the literature. So, if a library chose to define the research level as one that covers 90 percent of the relevant literature, it would cost more than twice as much to subscribe to the periodicals as it would to collect the titles covering 80 percent of citations. Striving for comprehensiveness is thus an exceptionally expensive undertaking.

In academic settings, faculty expectations drive collection development policies in the disciplines. In general, the higher the degree being sought by students, the higher are the expectations by the faculty for the students to be comprehensive in their pursuit of journal literature. Dissertation committees insist on it, pounding the necessity of exhaustive searching into the brains of Ph.D. candidates. But faculty teaching introductory undergraduate courses often emphasize critical thinking and writing skills, allowing students some discretion in how comprehensively they search for journal articles. When wide latitude in choice of articles to refer to is given to students, a less comprehensive collection can suffice. Collecting at the study level thus makes sense for undergraduate work, particularly for students not majoring in the topic. Conversely, doctoral students expected to perform comprehensive searches need the journals required to meet that expectation. Faculty expectations alone should not drive collection development, though, in part because faculty members tend to overlook general-interest periodicals. Libraries with policies that emphasize faculty input often have a "general" fund to meet patron desires for those types of serials.

The *Guidelines for the Formulation of Collection Development Policies* are a starting point for each library to develop goals for their entire collection, including serials. Each librarian interprets and applies the *Guidelines* according to local needs. However, other areas of serials work require genuine standards that apply uniformly to all.

STANDARDS

This section will focus on the ISSN and the data standard Serials Item and Contribution Identifier (SICI). Standards for identifying serials at the time of publication are vital for accurately ordering, cataloging, indexing, receiving, and linking. Other standards such as cataloging rules make cataloging and managing serials much less difficult because they provide standard ways to describe, identify, and categorize serials. These cataloging rules, including Anglo-American Cataloguing Rules, 2nd ed. (AACR2) for serials and Machine Readable Cataloging Record (MARC) bibliographic and holdings formats, will be discussed in the chapter on cataloging, and an overview of the OpenURL standard will be covered in the chapter on remote access serials. This discussion begins with the ISSN.

International Standard Serial Number

The basic and most widely used standard for serials is the ISSN. The fundamental concept behind the ISSN is that one eight-digit number represents one serial title. The ISSN can thus serve as the key field for a serials record in any database. How the ISSN began is best described by quoting from Bowker's *Ulrich's International Periodicals Directory*: The implementation of the ISSN system started with the numbering of 70,000 titles in the serials database of R.R. Bowker (*Ulrich's International Periodicals Directory* and *Irregular Serials and Annuals*). The next serials database numbering was the *New Serials Titles 1950–70* cumulation listing 220,000 titles . . . published by R.R. Bowker in collaboration with the Serials Records Division of the Library of Congress. These two databases were used as the starting base for the implementation of the ISSN (Bowker 2001).

The ISSN standard was codified in 1975 by the International Organization for Standardization (ISO) in document ISO 3297. ISSNs are assigned by over 50 national centers. In the United States, the NSDP assigns ISSNs. Their website http://www.loc.gov/issn/ includes a concise and informative FAQ and full information about how a publisher can get an ISSN for a serial, including information about title changes, where the ISSN should appear, and the relationship of ISSNs to ISBNs.

The NSDP response to the publisher's rhetorical question, "Where and how do I print the ISSN?" is "The preferred location for printing the ISSN on a printed serial is on the upper right-hand corner of the cover. Other good locations are the masthead area, the copyright page, or in the publishing statement where information about the publisher, frequency, and other publication facts are given. On a nonprint serial, the ISSN should be printed, if possible, on an internal source, such as on a title screen or home page" (Serials Section of ALCTS 2000). While this gives librarians a good indication of where to look for an ISSN on a serial, it also leaves publishers quite a lot of leeway.

The answer to the question "Can a publication have both an ISSN and an ISBN?" is yes. They explain that "[T]his situation occurs most commonly with books in a series and with annuals or biennials. The ISBN identifies the individual book in a series or a specific year for an annual or biennial. The ISSN identifies the ongoing series, or the ongoing annual or biennial serial" (Serials Section of ALCTS 2000).

Possible Changes to ISSN

Electronic journals are forcing reconsideration of the ISSN standard. To adapt to publication of journals online, an ISSN working group of the ISO is exploring possible changes to the ISSN system, carefully considering the ramifications of each scenario. Possible changes being considered were summarized by Pat Harris, Executive Director of National Information Standards Organization (NISO), in a memo forwarded in an e-mail to the SERIALST discussion group on April 5, 2004:

The four scenarios that are being considered are:

1. SCENARIO A: ISSNs are assigned to each different *medium* (e.g. print vs electronic; online vs offline; CD vs DVD) but not to each different *format* (e.g. HTML vs PDF; SGML vs XML). This is the current situation, although not all publishers follow it.
2. SCENARIO B: ISSNs are assigned to a serial publication at the *title* level, to cover all versions. This is essentially making the ISSN a Work identifier.
3. SCENARIO C: A "base ISSN" is assigned to a serial publication at the title level (i.e. as for Scenario B), but standardized suffixes are used to identify each media version (e.g. ISSN 1234-5678.dvd) and possibly each format (e.g. ISSN 1234-5678.htm).
4. SCENARIO D: A "master ISSN" is assigned to a serial publication at the title level and separate "secondary ISSNs" are assigned to different media and/or

format versions (e.g. ISSN 1234-5678 is assigned to title, 2345-6789 to the CD version, 3456-7891 to the online version, 4567-8912 to the print version, etc.). Each ISSN would be "dumb" so a database will be needed to link secondary ISSNs to master ISSNs.

Where all this will end up is an open question. Reasonable minds differ on the relative merits of each approach, and it will take time to reach a conclusion. Changes will impact serial cataloging and linking to remote access serials. As the merits of proposed changes are discussed, the perennial question of whether it is best to use successive or latest entry cataloging (addressed in the chapter on cataloging serials) will probably be debated again, as well.

Serials Item and Contribution Identifier

The Serials Industry Systems Advisory Committee (SISAC) standard for SICI includes standards for encoding SICI data in barcodes. SICI barcodes identify issues of a journal and can also identify individual articles. It enables a librarian who has entered the SICI-compliant serials data for acquisitions to check in print issues of serials by simply scanning the SICI barcode. The SICI standard barcoded data on individual articles is helpful to document delivery services. Unfortunately, SICI barcodes were never uniformly adopted by publishers of serials. Interest has now turned to means of identifying issues and articles online, using digital object identifiers (DOI) or other means that will be discussed in the chapter on online journals. SICI barcodes are still used, albeit inconsistently. The work that went into developing the SICI standard should be helpful as new standards are developed.

STAKEHOLDERS

The various individuals and organizations that create, organize, maintain, and use serials each have a stake in the efficient production and dissemination of this type of literature. The primary stakeholders are authors, publishers, indexing services, vendors, libraries, institutions of higher learning, professors, students, and the general public. These groups of stakeholders have different goals, needs, and economic incentives, which sometimes overlap, or are not sharply defined; therefore, it is best to think of these as perspectives, rather than as autonomous groups. The purpose of listing and briefly discussing each group of stakeholders is to promote awareness of the existence and importance of every group's needs.

Authors

Authors need outlets for their work, whether they publish in popular or scholarly serials. The authors of newspaper and magazine articles need remuneration and the satisfaction of seeing their work in print. Authors of scholarly research are not paid for publishing reports of their research, but they need the prestige of publication to be recognized for tenure and promotion. All authors need adequate support from their publishers, including expert editing to help make their work suitable for the publication. It is in an author's interest for the serials their work appears in to be readily available to their intended audience.

Publishers

Publishers need to sell enough subscriptions and/or advertisements to pay the bills. To do this, they have to build a reputation that attracts authors to submit their works, and readers (or their libraries) to pay for the publications. Building and maintaining a reputation requires not only good editors, but also staff adept at producing, marketing, and distributing serials. Publishers add value to authors' works through these processes, and they have to recoup costs through sales revenue, advertising, or by subsidizing costs with membership dues, foundation grants, or other funding.

Indexing Services

Indexing services add value to journals by making articles more accessible to readers. Indexes used to be only in print format, but now most are sold as online databases. Sales to libraries comprise most of the market for indexes. In order to sell sufficient copies of their indexes or databases to libraries to cover costs, the serials indexed must be of interest to library patrons. Library collection development criteria for serials typically include index and database coverage. Because of the importance of database coverage for libraries, publishers of scholarly journals are keenly interested in having their titles covered by indexes. So indexing services are not only dependent on having desirable serials to cover, but they also act to raise the prestige and accessibility of serials.

Vendors

"Vendors" is a general term for a rather loosely defined category of companies that package journal and/or index content, provide databases, serve as agents between publishers and libraries, or manage serials subscriptions. Database vendors take citation data they or others produce, add a search engine and user interface, and license the product to libraries. Selling individuals access to databases was a hot topic during the dot.com rage around 2000, but it never caught on. Many vendors also license and package full text articles with their databases. The costs database vendors need to cover include the costs of indexing, full text (if offered), servers, Internet connections, and computer professionals.

Serials subscription vendors help librarians manage the process of ordering and claiming serials. The value of their function will be discussed in the chapter on work flow. A good overview of what they do may be found at http://www.subscription-agents.org/, the site of the Association of Subscription Agents and Intermediaries. Their basic goal is to use economies of scale to offer cost-effective management of serial subscriptions. The fee they charge the libraries for this service is less than the cost to libraries of handling each individual subscription directly with the publishers. The subscription vendor typically also gets revenue from publishers, as grouping billing and claims is cheaper for publishers, too. The subscription vendors thus have incentives to satisfy both libraries and publishers, and have a stake in the ongoing financial health of both.

Libraries

Librarians work for their libraries to select, pay for, and provide access to serials for the benefit of their patrons, for today and for the future. They have a stake in having worthy serials to collect at prices they can afford. They also have a stake in predictability and stability in serials (e.g., titles, publication patterns, dates of receipt), to reduce processing costs and make the access to them less confusing for patrons. Librarians operate a gift economy. That is, they pay for serials, indexes, and the costs of maintaining them for the benefit of patrons. A consequence of this is that patrons are typically unaware of these costs to libraries. So patrons may ask for and expect journals without sufficiently considering their cost. This puts a particular spin on the law of supply and demand, as will be discussed in the chapter on the economics of serials. In any case, librarians have incentives to control the cost of serial subscriptions, control the costs of acquiring and maintaining serials, and maximize their patrons' access to desired serials.

Institutions of Higher Learning

Institutions of higher learning have a stake in reputable outlets in which their researchers can publish at subscription prices their libraries can afford. Institutions of higher learning financially support the research activities reported in scholarly journals in several ways. Authors, editors, and peer reviewers of scholarly journals work for very little pay (if any) beyond their faculty salaries. Research projects may be funded by grants, but colleges and universities pay for them, too. Since they pay for many of the costs in the chain of scholarly publishing, research institutions have a major stake in high-quality serials sold at reasonable prices.

Professors and Researchers

Professors and other researchers publish in, read, and base some teaching processes on serials. They have a stake in having sufficient outlets for their work and timely access to literature in their fields for themselves and their students. Their immediate incentives are for the prestige and recognition needed to gain tenure or promotion, which translates into personal financial returns. Professors and researchers tend to be somewhat insulated from the cost of serials because their libraries' budgets tend to be out of sight and out of mind. A significant issue in serials management at colleges and universities is how to effectively raise awareness of costs and engage professors in collection development.

Students

Students need timely and convenient access to the serial literature they are expected to use in their course work. Their expectations and patterns of journal use are different from those of their teachers. As discussed previously, many college students tend to perform less comprehensive searches for serial literature than their professors would prefer, and they tend to be somewhat bewildered by serials. Reasons for this and strategies for addressing this issue will be discussed in the chapter on teaching patrons to use journals. Nevertheless, students have a stake in convenient access to the serial literature that their teachers expect them to read.

General Public

The general public has a direct interest in having a choice of high quality, trustworthy, affordable serials available to them in personal subscriptions, or at the library. The public has an indirect interest in a system of scholarly publishing that helps further knowledge in all fields of endeavor. Since many of the costs of scholarly journal publishing are indirectly subsidized by public funds, an efficient system ultimately affects everyone's pocketbooks. The demand for scholarly journal articles among people outside of academe is only rarely considered, and has not been measured. Ready access by the general public to scholarship can benefit society.

Effectively and efficiently recording and preserving knowledge in serial literature is thus important to everyone. Among the stakeholders, serials librarians have the special role of selecting, providing access to, and preserving this literature for the public good. Their training, ethics, and professional standards put serials librarians in a unique position to support the interests of all stakeholders, including those with no direct financial interest in serials.

This chapter has described important aspects of the environment in which serials librarians work. Some aspects are universal, such as the definition of a serial and the ISSN standard. Inflation of subscription prices is a fact of life for all librarians responsible for serials, but the serials crisis has affected some libraries' budgets more than others. The Carnegie classification is most helpful for collection development in institutions of higher learning, but the concept of choosing a level of serials collection comprehensiveness can be applied to public, school, and special libraries, as well. The needs of stakeholders will be emphasized differently in the policies of various libraries, depending on their missions and patrons. But awareness of broad trends and needs makes one a better serials librarian. The next chapter will demonstrate the increased importance of a broad perspective in to-day's interconnected and rapidly evolving serials environment.

SUGGESTIONS FOR FURTHER READING

The ALCTS Serials Section Education Committee published *Unraveling the Mysteries of Serials* in 1996, a brief but authoritative and readable FAQ about serials on the ALA website at http://www.ala.org/ala/alctscontent/alctspubsbucket/webpublications/alctsserials/unravelingthemys/unravelingmysteries.htm.

An overview of the history of serials with extensive references to additional sources may be found in Thomas Nisonger's *Management of Serials in Libraries* (Englewood, CO: Libraries Unlimited, 1998), chapter 2. For the history of specific serials, see Robert V. Hudson, *Mass Media: A Chronological Encyclopedia of Television, Radio, Motion Pictures, Newspapers, and Books in the United States* (New York: Garland, 1987). Despite the exclusion of "magazines" from the title, this chronological treatment of media includes annotated lists of magazines and newspapers published in the United States from 1638 through 1985 and has a wealth of information about the people and organizations responsible for prominent serials published in the United States.

Among the many treatments of the serials crisis, one would be well served to begin with Walt Crawford and Michael Gorman's *Future Libraries: Dreams, Madness & Reality* (Chicago: American Library Association, 1995). Crawford and Gorman describe the broad context of the serials crisis and also directly address how libraries can cope. Commentary on and analysis of the serials crisis as it unfolded may be found in the *Newsletter on Serials Pricing Issues* (1989–2001) archived at http://www.lib.unc.edu/prices/. The 257 issues are an excellent repository of news about publishers, prices, and how librarians struggled with subscription price increases. *Library Journal's* annual periodicals price survey is published each April under a different article title expressing a theme characterizing periodicals publishing. The ALA/ALCTS Library Materials Price Index Committee now publishes the annual U.S. Periodicals Price Index data in *Library Resources and Technical Services*. The Index was formerly published in *American Libraries*, and still also appears in the *Bowker Annual* and may be found online at http://www.ala.org/ala/alcts/alctspubs/pubsresources/resources.htm.

Full descriptions of the Carnegie Classification system and discussion of work in progress to revise the system may be found at the Carnegie Foundation for the Advancement of Teaching at http://www.carnegiefoundation.org/Classification/index.htm. A good entry point to the literature on serials collection development is Thomas E. Nisonger, *Evaluation of Library Collections, Access, and Electronic Resources: A Literature Guide and Annotated Bibliography* (Westport, CT: Libraries Unlimited, 2003).

The best source of information about International Standard Serial Numbers is the ISSN website at http://www.issn.org. This site includes a thorough FAQ and up-to-date links from the home page to news about modifications of ISSN. SICI and other standards are also addressed in the FAQ.

REFERENCES

Carnegie Foundation for the Advancement of Teaching. 2006. *Category Definitions.* Stanford, CA: Author, http://www.carnegiefoundation.org/classifications/.

Hirons, Jean, ed. 2002. *CONSER Cataloging Manual.* Washington, DC: Library of Congress, Cataloging Distribution Service.

Husni, Samir. 2004. A bumper crop. *Folio: The Magazine for Magazine Management* 33(4): 26–29.

National Serials Data Program. 2003. *ISSN Is for Serials.* Washington, DC: Library of Congress, http://www.loc.gov/issn/issnbro.html.

Perkins, David L., ed. 1979. *Guidelines for the Formulation of Collection Development Policies.* Chicago: Collection Development Committee, Resources and Technical Division, American Library Association.

R.R. Bowker. 2001. *Ulrich's Periodicals Directory,* 40th ed. New Providence, NJ: Author.

R.R. Bowker. 2002. *Bowker Annual Library and Book Trade Almanac.* New Providence, NJ: Author.

Tuttle, Marcia. 1989–2001. *Newsletter on Serials Pricing Issues.* Chapel Hill: Academic Technology and Networks at the University of North Carolina at Chapel Hill, http://www.lib.unc.edu/prices/prices.html.

Van Orsdel, Lee, and Born, Kathleen. 2003. Big chill on the big deal? *Library Journal* 128(7): 51–56.

Chapter 2

Remote Access Serials

Online delivery of serials from locations remote from the library has created challenges and opportunities for librarians and publishers. The topic of remote access serials is being presented before other topics within serials management to emphasize the importance of remote access serials to the evolving work of serials librarians.

This chapter will describe remote access serials, introduce various issues concerning the types of delivery and costs of remote access serials, and discuss practices that librarians are implementing to manage serials online including joining library consortia. It further discusses the future of remote access serials and its promise of expansion with the addition of multimedia formats to enhance patron access to information.

Libraries provide remote access serials via networks to their patrons. How access is provided to authorized users (and only to authorized users) requires implementation of systems beyond those used for print serials, a major difference being license negotiation as an important component of serials management. Terms of license agreements are based on two things. The first is the cost to publishers who publish the serials and the second is the cost to librarians who wish to purchase these remote access serials. These two costs powerfully influence the terms and conditions of the license agreements. To help control costs, publishers have created aggregations of full-text serial content, and librarians have formed consortia to mitigate the escalating costs of serials.

The development of these cost-saving aggregations and consortia has led to new ways to provide patrons access to serials. Thus, the means of providing access to remote access serials, the costs of producing and providing access to them, and the efforts to control costs are intertwined issues in the practice of managing remote access serials. Other considerations have to do with the debate between access and ownership, ensuring long-term archival access, and broader consideration of the true costs to libraries to purchase online serials and the costs for publishers to create them. Finally, librarians must face problems caused by the consolidation of publishers. To better understand these issues, one should begin with the characteristics, formats, and future possibilities of remote access serials.

CHARACTERISTICS OF REMOTE ACCESS SERIALS

In this section, characteristics of remote access serials will be presented with their present and possible future formats as well as responses to challenges in providing remote access. These challenges include moving into multimedia formats and whether the traditional practice of designating issues with enumeration and chronology will continue. Certainly, the ability of a publisher to update or correct content presents interesting possibilities.

The Cooperative Online Serials Program (CONSER) distinguishes two types of electronic serials, direct access and remote access. Direct access electronic serials are those acquired in a physical medium, such as a CD-ROM, diskette, or DVD. Direct access electronic serials, while fairly common in the late 1990s, are rarely found in libraries in 2005.

The second type of electronic serials, remote access, are delivered to users over any network, including the Internet, a network within a library building, or college campus-wide network. CONSER uses the AACR2 defined term "remote access" to describe all online delivery of serials via a network. This definition has the distinct advantage of encompassing any type of network delivery, so is unlikely to become outdated by wireless or other new technologies.

Formats

In 2005, most remote access electronic serials are delivered over the web in Hypertext Markup Language (HTML) or Portable Document Format (PDF). HTML is adequate for viewing text on screen, and it allows the inclusion of graphics. PDF allows images to be transmitted over a network so the exact appearance of a printed page can be reproduced on a reader's printer. Some remote access serials have Extensible Markup Language (XML) features and metadata. Other formats being used to publish serials include Standard General Markup Language (SGML), used by publishers for typesetting, or TeX, the markup language favored by mathematicians. For most remote access serials, HTML and PDF are the current *de facto* standard formats for online delivery.

These standard delivery method(s) may change in the future. Neither HTML nor PDF take full advantage of the web's capability to deliver information. HTML gives relatively little control over fonts, layout, and special characters. HTML is sufficient for text and hyperlinking to images within documents and provides the ability to deliver multimedia content. But page layout is crude, original pagination is lost, and illustrations must be embedded as separate files. Image files embedded in a HTML document may require additional software to view. The software may not be installed on a user's computer, and images saved in GIF or JPG format may not have adequate resolution for detailed images.

PDF files can reproduce pages that look the same as an original print version. However, if the PDF file is generated from a scan, rather than saved directly with Adobe Acrobat as a PDF file, the resolution may be fuzzy and difficult to read. A potential drawback to documents saved in PDF is that the files can require several megabytes of memory. Periodical articles stored as large PDF files can take a long time to download and print. File size is becoming less of an issue because each new generation of networks, computers, and printers are faster and have more memory. But the size of some PDF files remains a problem for users with older equipment or dial-up Internet connections.

Potential for Multimedia

A basic limitation of both HTML and PDF formats is that they are best suited for conveying information in print. One of the great attractions of the web for serials publication is the ability to transmit information with animated images, sound, and interactive features. Periodical articles could include audio files of people speaking rare languages, videos of surgical procedures, or excerpts of stage performances. It is also possible to provide searchable data sets that can be manipulated by the end user. Many data sets are available on the web, but including the data upon which research articles are based has not yet become a widespread practice. It will be very interesting to see how extensively researchers will use the new Google Base (http://base.google.com) service to post data sets, and how that will affect scholarly journals. Information conveyed by animation, sound, and interactive databases is being included in some online serials, but text and static graphical image content still predominates in serial literature. The potential benefit of fully multimedia serial publications is far from being achieved, and HTML and PDF may prove inadequate to achieve this potential.

A significant problem with creating multimedia serials is the lack of standard software for delivering multimedia content. Many brands of software are capable of playing audio, or video, or manipulating data on Macs or PCs running Mac OS, Windows, or Linux. The variety of software and systems can create interoperability problems. Remote access delivery of content presents a significant technological challenge to publishers because no single standard software is used to store, play, and manipulate the files on all systems. Since many types of software are used by potential readers, whichever software a publisher chooses may limit who can "read" the serial.

Download times for users not on high-speed networks are also an issue. Finding the best way to provide audio, video, and data in serials content may take several years of experimentation to develop and adopt *de facto* standard file formats.

Enumeration and Chronology

An open question as remote access serials evolve is whether the traditional practice of designating issues with enumeration and chronology will continue. A printed journal or magazine needs to be physically issued in successive parts so each issue can be produced and delivered to readers. However, with online serials, there is no technical reason why a journal or magazine cannot be a continuing integrating resource. That is, publishers can simply add content to the publication's website as it becomes available. In theory, having an author, article title, and serial title would be enough to locate the article. A publisher could choose to give each article an accession number and not use volumes or issues. Page numbers are not strictly necessary either, since the find feature in browsers and Acrobat Reader can be used to easily locate passages of text. The issue of path dependency is a factor in enumeration and chronology.

Path dependency, continuing a practice even though the original reasons for adopting the practice no longer apply, can be powerful. The classic example of path dependency is the QWERTY keyboard. The standard arrangement of keys was designed to minimize jamming of mechanical typewriters, not to maximize typing speed, and we no longer have technical reasons to have keyboards arranged to prevent keys from jamming. However, many people are so used to the QWERTY arrangement of keys that changing the pattern would be too disruptive to be worth it. Path dependency may similarly cause serial enumeration to continue for many decades. No technical reason may exist to have volumes and issues associated with each article, but people are accustomed to that way of organizing the serial literature. Enumeration and chronology add legitimacy to online journals, and scholars expect articles to be marked with volumes, issues, and page numbers. Standard citation styles still require references to include volumes and page numbers, as well. So for the foreseeable future, publishers are likely to issue remote access serials in enumerated, successive parts. When they do not, their publications will need to be cataloged as continuing integrated resources instead of as serials.

Updates and Corrections

Another new possibility with remote access serials is publishers' ability to make updates and corrections to published works. In print, updates and corrections are made with notes published in subsequent issues. In contrast, corrections to articles published online can be made to the original article. This opens a can of worms.

Should an author, editor, or publisher be allowed to change something after it is published? What if a scholar cites the original version of an article, and then a reader tracks down the citation and discovers the cited information is different from the current version of the article? The reader may not be able to discern whether the citing author made a mistake or the article was altered. Perhaps the scholarly record should display the mistakes and dead ends that are natural to intellectual progress. Workable solutions may be found for this problem. Corrections can be kept distinct from the originals so that both original and corrected information is available. Whether and how corrections to articles online will be recorded is an issue to be determined by publishers, hopefully with ample input from affected stakeholders.

TYPES OF DELIVERY OF REMOTE ACCESS SERIALS

Individual remote access serials have not only the characteristics described previously, but they also have features based on how the titles are delivered to subscribers. While the mode of delivery does not affect content, it does affect patrons' paths of access to serials. The delivery methods each have their strengths and weaknesses. The four categories of delivery are: direct subscription to an individual title, publisher packages, platform providers, and index- and abstract-based aggregation.

Direct Subscription to Individual Titles

With the direct subscription mode of delivery, the subscriber pays for an individual serial title (not for a package of titles). The content one receives with a direct online subscription to an individual serial title varies. In many cases, the online version has exact duplicates of the print pages plus valuable supplemental content. Since publishers have strong incentives to make the online version of a print serial attractive to subscribers, direct subscriptions to individual serial titles are usually good substitutes for print. The caveat is that online subscriptions are typically a leasing of content. With most licenses, if the subscription is not continued, access is lost. Patrons' issues with the speed of downloading articles, the quality of printouts, and the cost of printouts are factors to consider when contemplating replacing print subscriptions with online only. To make the transition less difficult, many publishers price print plus online subscriptions at approximately 10 percent more than print alone. While librarians do not save money with print plus online, patrons gain the convenience of remote access and librarians can assure archival access.

Publisher Packages

Publisher packages provide the same type and quality of remote access serials as individually subscribed serial titles. The difference is that the serial titles are sold as a bundled group, where one price is paid for access to multiple serial titles. Publishers selling their packages in bundled groups include societies as well as commercial publishers.

Societies that sell their online journals in bundled packages include the Association for Computing Machinery (ACM), the American Chemical Society (ACS), the Institute for Electrical and Electronics Engineers (IEEE), and the American Psychological Association (APA). Librarians may have some options in choosing which serial titles will be included in the package. Since most individual members of these societies are comfortable using computers, the online format has been well accepted by subscribers. Except for the important caveats concerning long-term access and network and printing needs, societies' bundled packages provide acceptable substitutes for print subscriptions. Their packages also save significant shelf space when the publisher package replaces print subscriptions. Among the four delivery methods, society publishers' packages probably represent the greatest advantages and least risks of converting from print to online serials.

Packages of online serials provided by commercial publishers also have accurate reproductions of print pages coupled with valuable search capabilities, and may also provide added content. Elsevier's *ScienceDirect* package provides an example of added content in that articles are posted online before the print issues are published. Publisher packages often include backfiles of issues going back many years, sometimes at an additional charge.

A key difference between society and commercial publisher packages is diversity of topics covered by the serial titles in the package. The ACM, ACS, IEEE, and APA publish journals within single disciplines, albeit diverse disciplines with many sub-disciplines. In contrast, commercial packages include serials covering broad ranges of disciplines. Since some disciplines will be of more interest to a library's patrons than others, some publishers allow libraries to subscribe to the serial titles in their packages individually or in topic groupings. Publishers who do not allow libraries that level of control in their "Big Deal" packages have been criticized for unduly restricting librarians' choice, as is discussed in some detail later in this chapter.

Platform Providers

Platform providers are intermediaries who load content on servers and control access to the content (unless the content is Open Access). They facilitate online delivery for publishers who are too small to provide remote access on their own. The distinguishing characteristics of platform providers are that they provide access to serials published by entities other than themselves, and they do not originate from an existing index or database. Publishers who use platform providers negotiate contract(s) to have their journal(s) offered online on the providers' servers. Examples of platform providers include OCLC's Electronic Collections Online, JSTOR, HighWire Press, Project MUSE, BioOne, and Ingenta. The business models of these platforms and their specific relationships with publishers vary a great deal. Access to the serials is by licenses signed between subscribers and publishers, but some platform providers act as aggregators of licenses.

How well online content for serials delivered via platform providers can substitute for print subscriptions varies by provider. The diversity of business models, policies, and delivery methods among platform providers makes generalizations about this type of remote access delivery method difficult. OCLC's Electronic Collections Online emphasizes archival storage of content. The BioMed Central platform is exclusively for Open Access publications. JSTOR provides high-quality PDF files of every article going back to volume one of each serial, but has a "moving wall" of no content from the most recent three to five years. JSTOR is thus a good substitute for back issues but is not a substitute for current subscriptions.

Index and Abstract-based Aggregations

Index and abstract-based aggregations are at once the most tempting and most risky substitutes for print subscriptions. These are online bibliographic databases that include the full text of periodicals from a variety of publishers. The attraction of subscribing to aggregated full-text packages offered by EBSCO, Gale, Lexis-Nexis, ProQuest, WilsonWeb, and others is that a wide variety of full-text content is seamlessly wedded with citations and abstracts. The packages of aggregated full text make it easy for patrons to link directly from a citation to complete articles. They provide articles from hundreds or thousands of serials at a fraction of the cost to libraries of subscribing to each title. Since libraries do not have to process or shelve any issues, nonsubscription costs of providing these titles are very low (nonsubscription costs are described in the next section on costs, "Costs to Libraries of Remote Access Serials"). While the search interfaces are not created equal, some are quite powerful and user-friendly. The one-stop shopping offered by these databases is very popular with patrons.

When these products were first developed, the content in the databases was presented as a supplement to print subscriptions. Publishers were encouraged by the aggregators to provide the content of their serials for relatively modest fees, since the titles would get increased exposure in return for a little extra revenue. The aggregators and the publishers expected, or at least hoped, that libraries and individuals would continue subscribing to their periodicals. One reason that many did continue print subscriptions had to do with lost illustrations. Many full-text articles were text only, without the graphics, charts, or other illustrations of the original typeset printed pages. Library and patron demand have increased the percentage of articles reproduced in PDF, but some articles in aggregated databases are still HTML text files. A further reason for continuing print is the need for the archived record.

An essential fact about index and abstract-based aggregated databases is that there is absolutely no guarantee of future availability of content. The librarian subscribes to the package as a whole and has access to the content currently available. Aggregators work very hard at maintaining content, but publishers have the last say. Unfortunately for the publishers, serials content was made available in these aggregated full-text databases at the same time library budgets continued to be pinched. Full text in aggregations was intended by the vendors and publishers to supplement print subscriptions, not replace them (EBSCO Publishing 2005). But when faced with the choice between canceling titles available in full-text databases or titles only available in print, many librarians have chosen to not renew the print subscription for titles available online. Librarians do this even when fully and painfully aware of the risks of relying on aggregated full-text databases. Just how many institutional subscriptions are being dropped in lieu of access via aggregations is an important but thus far unanswered question.

Some publishers have responded to cancellations by withdrawing their content from the full-text databases. Because aggregators try hard to maintain publishers' content, one practice used to entice publishers to stay on board is for articles to be embargoed. An embargo is a period of time between when an issue is published and when it appears in the full-text database. Typical embargoes are six months or a year, but they vary depending on publishers' agreements with aggregators. When a title is embargoed, patrons using the database will see the citations and abstracts for recent articles from a serial, but not have the links to the recent articles.

Other reasons that full-text aggregated databases are not fully equivalent to print were explored in depth by Sprague and Chambers (2000). Their systematic appraisal of full-text journal articles in databases was built around four criteria: currency, coverage, graphics, and stability. They found that 45 percent of full-text articles were not as current as print subscriptions, and 17 percent of major articles in print were missing in the databases. Many graphics were missing from the articles, and 140 of 3,393 titles were dropped from the full-text databases over a six-month period (Sprague and Chambers 2000). Delayed and missing content mean that index- and abstract-based full-text databases must be regarded as fundamentally different from a collection of individual subscriptions. When selecting how these aggregated databases fit into the serials collection, their overall convenience and broad (but faulty) coverage must be compared against the quality and long-term predictability of other means of accessing serials, including subscriptions to serials in print, individual online subscriptions, and publisher packages. Whether it is worth giving up control over the selection of individual titles is a major consideration with publisher packages and index- and abstract-based aggregations. The key is providing patrons access.

PROVIDING PATRONS ACCESS

Most libraries now have a mix of print and remote access serials. As described earlier, remote access serials can be provided to patrons with various blends of individual subscriptions, publisher packages, titles accessed via platform providers, and aggregated full-text databases. Providing patrons access presents the librarian with challenges. A variety of means of full-text access is available on the database where a patron is searching and on a database other than the one the patron is using. The ways publishers limit access to their databases to paid subscribers can create challenges. To deal with these challenges, librarians must understand how to link sources.

Full Text

Patrons experience the easiest access to articles when the full text is available within the database they are searching. When a library offers access to articles in full text from a source other than the database the patron is searching, the patron may be confused or might not know that it is available. For example, a patron could be searching in the PsycINFO database and find a citation to an article from the journal *Psychological Science*. Depending on which database vendor the library uses for PsycINFO, there may not be a link from the citation to the full text of the cited article. If the library has full text access to *Psychological Science* through a different database, the patron will not know it is available to them when no link appears in the citation. The challenge to librarians is finding ways to provide convenient access to every serial the library is paying for, and the challenge to publishers is to control access to authorized users.

Publishers need to control access only to authorized users, and in the case of libraries, the patrons of libraries with paid access to the content of their database. If just anyone was allowed to link into full-text content from anywhere, the publishers and vendors could not ensure proper payment. To control access, publishers and vendors can use either logins or Internet Protocol (IP) address recognition. If logins are used, librarians are responsible for restricting distribution of user names and passwords only to registered patrons.

With IP address recognition, the librarian registers the IP addresses with the publisher or vendor. A patron using a computer with a registered IP address seamlessly connects with the database. Some vendors' license agreements limit access to a certain number of IP addresses; perhaps only one. Such limits have become uncommon because librarians and their patrons do not like being able to use only one or a very limited number of computers to access a database. Licenses for access from only one or a few IP addresses are still offered by some vendors for libraries seeking a lower price for products that receive infrequent use. But license agreements now typically allow the librarian to register the IP addresses for all the computers on the institution's network. Institution-wide access by IP address recognition works well, is relatively easy to administer, and is popular with users.

When IP address recognition is used on college campuses, students can connect from their dorms and professors can connect from their offices just as if they were sitting at a computer in the library. But connecting from home requires another approach, because it is impractical to register the IP addresses for authorized patrons' home computers. A solution is to use a proxy server, which authenticates users and makes them appear to the publishers' or vendors' systems to be coming from a registered IP address. IP address recognition and proxy server technology have become the most common means for librarians to provide their patrons access to subscribed databases. If a librarian finds a need to add a proxy server they should contact appropriate computer network support services, either locally or through a library consortium.

Linking Technologies

Providing convenient access to databases is just part of the battle. The issue remains of how to link patrons seamlessly to the content they seek. The purpose of link resolvers, OpenURL, and Digital Object Identifiers (DOI) is to provide links from any database to all subscribed full-text content.

A link resolver checks to see that a user trying to login is authorized, keeps track of what the library subscribes to, and links patrons to content in subscribed databases. The library providing a link resolver is responsible for maintaining the database of authorized users. The subscribed databases entered into the link resolver are called "sources." Information on each source will include the URL for accessing the source and relevant licensing terms. For example, if a license for a source allows on-campus access only, the link resolver will check the IP address and deny access to the database if the patron is off campus. Link resolvers work best when the sources also provide targets to individual pieces of information. A target is any resource identified at a level that can be queried by a link resolver. If targets are not available for individual articles in a database, the link resolver can only link the user to the database search interface. This is better than no link, but can be confusing to the user.

OpenURL and DOIs are means of providing targets to individual units of information, such as journal articles. OpenURL embeds citation data in the URL link, so the link resolver can match the citation in the database being searched with the article in a different source. The metadata about the information object encoded in the OpenURL includes the source containing the article. Elements contained in the metadata for the article may vary. Elements of the OpenURL can include the author's name, the title of the article, title of the journal, volume, number, date, and pages.

A DOI is an encoded unique identifier for a document such as a journal article. An example of a DOI for an article from the *Journal of Biological Chemistry* is doi:10.1074/jbc.M403697200. By analogy, one can think of a DOI as the functional equivalent of a call number, URL, or accession number. Each is a means of uniquely identifying an item in a collection. DOIs uniquely identify remote access serial articles. Theoretically they could work for other types of documents, but DOIs are intended by publishers to provide targets to serial articles.

DOIs are registered with CrossRef, a not-for-profit network built with publisher cooperation found at http://www.crossref.org. The CrossRef registry may be searched directly by a user, but searches are normally conducted by link resolvers. When a patron is viewing a citation and clicks on the link resolver icon, the DOI is sent by the link resolver to CrossRef at http://dx.doi.org/. CrossRef matches the DOI with the "handle," the URL for that particular item. That URL is returned to the link resolver. If the patron is an authorized user of the source, the link is made and the target article is sent to the patron's computer. A DOI is sufficient for identifying an article, but it contains no descriptive information about the article's content.

Link resolvers work well for articles that have OpenURL metadata or DOIs registered with CrossRef. Articles and other information objects without the metadata or DOI targets cannot be directly retrieved. The success of link resolvers is thus largely dependent on serial publishers' and database vendors' willingness to create OpenURL metadata or register DOIs with CrossRef. In practice, reliance on publisher compliance means that sometimes links to articles work, and sometimes they do not. The issue of inconsistent linking will persist for some time to come, especially for links to serials published by smaller publishers lacking the resources to implement the metadata.

Access versus Ownership

Many librarians have canceled print serials and have devoted more resources to packages of remote access serials. This shift has been largely due to economic necessity. An important consideration is that a subscription to a serial delivered online is typically a lease of the content for one year. Some libraries and consortia have negotiated contracts allowing them to own the published online serial content, and store the articles on their own servers. An example of ownership rather than leasing access is OhioLINK's Electronic Journal Collection (EJC). The majority of the published serial articles in the EJC are owned by OhioLINK. The content of a few journals is not owned outright since the publishers were not willing to agree to the needed contractual terms. However, the practice of contracting to own serial content is not standard practice. OhioLINK is an innovative leader in ownership of remote access serials.

In contrast to the terms of most licenses for remote access serials, subscriptions to print serials give ownership of issues to the subscriber, which can be kept as long as desired. The one-time payment for a subscription conveys the right to access the print volumes indefinitely. This advantage of owning serials rather than leasing access to them is partially offset by multiyear access to content with most online subscriptions. Publishers usually offer multiple years of content for the annual subscription price. For example, an annual subscription to an online package of American Chemical Society (ACS) journals gives the subscriber access to all volumes of the journal in the package, beginning with volume one. Immediate access to a run of journals is great for newly added titles, because patrons can access back issues right away, rather than having to wait years for a run of print volumes to accumulate on the shelves. For example, if a librarian begins a print subscription to *Biochemistry* in 2005, only the issues published in 2005 will be available to patrons. But if a librarian subscribes to ACS online package instead, all volumes of

Biochemistry are immediately available. The down side of online subscriptions is that when the library does not own the content, if the subscription has to be dropped in the future, all access to the content is lost. Some license agreements allow subscribers to keep backup copies for the subscribed years, but local electronic archiving requires time, effort, resources, and expertise.

Long-Term Access

The emphasis librarians place on reliable long-term access to serials varies by their collection development policies. Research librarians have a particular need for and commitment to long-term access. Libraries with collections designed for undergraduate study or use by the general public have less of an obligation to ensure that old volumes remain available. Many journals lose their current relevance within a decade or so, and are then only of historical interest. While it is difficult to predict which serials will be of interest to someone doing historical research, older volumes of serials in disciplines that emphasize the timeliness of information may not need to stay on the shelves. Relying on online subscriptions to leased serials content may be more appropriate in those cases.

A potential benefit of remote access serials is that saving back issues on servers can be cheaper than maintaining print volumes on library shelves; yet, challenges of digital storage remain to be resolved. The challenges include deciding who is responsible for saving files, who pays for and maintains servers, and who and how to ensure that content remains accessible in the long run. The cost of maintaining content on servers includes copying files and backup of files on a regular schedule and converting files when software is updated. It is likely that information embedded in documents requiring plug-ins to view or hear will be difficult or impossible to access years from now. Accounting for inevitable changes in hardware and software is a daunting task. In contrast, print serials require no special equipment to read, and serials on microfilm are readable with a light source and magnification. Current logic still calls for print or microform for true long-term preservation of serials. The question going into the future is whether the opportunity cost of maintaining print or microform is worth the benefit of ensuring long-term access to every serial.

A creative and promising partial solution is LOCKSS, "Lots of Copies to Keep Stuff Safe", ... described at http://lockss.stanford.edu/projectdescbrief.htm. The LOCKSS solution, created at Stanford University, is for participating libraries to cache copies of online serials at each local institution. The open-source LOCKSS software controls access to prevent unauthorized users from getting free copies of articles. The software is designed to keep permanent copies and to check for errors by validating files among LOCKSS servers. Research libraries employing the software have the responsibility for maintaining the servers and the content. Redundancy is the key to long-term preservation. If enough libraries use LOCKSS and maintain copies, the odds of content being permanently lost are very low. Libraries that implement LOCKSS do not use it as a substitute for functioning publishers' websites, but it can be used to provide back-up content when a publisher's or vendor's website is down. Since LOCKSS only works for HTML and image formats that work in HTML (e.g., JPG and GIF), it is not a total solution to long-term preservation of online journals. The software also does not address the need to migrate data from one format to another as software and hardware evolve.

COSTS TO LIBRARIES OF REMOTE ACCESS SERIALS

Libraries experience a variety of costs for providing and maintaining both print and remote access serials. While the most readily apparent cost of serials comes from subscriptions, libraries' other costs occur in the following areas:

- Collections development
- Negotiations and licensing
- Subscription processing, routine renewal, and termination
- Receipt and check-in
- Routing of issues and/or tables of contents
- Cataloging
- Linking services
- Physical processing
- Stacks maintenance (including current issues areas)
- Circulation
- Reference and research
- User instruction
- Preservation
- Other (Schonfeld et al. 2004).

The study by Schonfeld et al. (2004) found that of these, the only process requiring more staff time for remote access serials than for print was negotiations and licensing. Even linking services required less staff time, since catalog records for print serials are also maintained in link resolver databases. Costs of maintaining a print collection are particularly high for subscription processing, receipt and check-in, cataloging, physical processing (including binding), and stacks maintenance.

The authors reported annual nonsubscription costs of a current print subscription for 15 libraries. These costs range from $29.37 to $313.89 per serial. The median annual nonsubscription cost of a current print subscription is $63.77. In contrast, the median annual nonsubscription cost for a remote access serial for the same sample of libraries is $16.01. So aside from subscription costs, the cost of maintaining print subscriptions is roughly four times as much as the cost of maintaining online subscriptions. It must be noted that the authors chose to exclude the cost of electronic infrastructure, like computers, networks, and printers, on the logic that it is too difficult to separate out the portion of costs devoted to serials. Potential long-term costs to libraries and/or patrons of any loss of back issues due to incomplete archival coverage were also not predicted. They did investigate infrastructure costs for six of the fifteen libraries, though, and concluded that those costs do not significantly affect the ratio of print to electronic nonsubscription costs (Schonfeld et al. 2004).

In practice, electronic infrastructure costs on college campuses are typically not paid for out of libraries' budgets although public librarians have to include those costs in their overall budgets. For all libraries, there are hidden costs in what some call "technostress," the discomfort and stress caused by adapting to new technologies and new work flows. Dealing with new systems and constantly changing interfaces, experiencing added duties, and trying to fix troublesome machines can be difficult for librarians and library staff. It can be difficult for patrons, too. Sometimes new positions are added to help handle the changes, but more often the current workers are expected to adapt. The mantra "work smarter, not harder" sounds nice, but does not always translate into job place reality. The costs to librarians and patrons of these disruptions and stresses are difficult to quantify, but are nevertheless quite real.

The practices of managing and cataloging serials have had to evolve faster than new rules and standards have been developed. Serials librarians choose various interpretations of existing rules to adapt to their current situations. Cataloging rules are in the process of being revised to catch up with what is being practiced in the field. Since librarians address problems with various solutions, redefining standards relating to serials and relevant cataloging rules is a difficult and sometimes even contentious process.

A major change for serials librarians is that processes that once took place entirely within the serials department may now require working with systems librarians, administrators, or systems people working outside the library. For example, creating and maintaining correct links to remote access serials can require the expertise of programmers and network administrators. The job cannot simply be sent over to the Information Technology (IT) staff, because they are unlikely to fully understand what needs to be done. Collaboration between librarians and computer professionals is necessary to maintain working access to online periodicals. Remote access serials require frequent collaboration between serials librarians and library administrators. Licenses are often entered into through consortia. The terms of the licenses are agreed to after negotiations between the consortium and the publisher or vendor. Participation in consortial agreements is usually handled by the library director or other senior library administrator. Serials librarians have to communicate extensive information about the serials collection to their administrators for them to work effectively in any consortium.

LIBRARY CONSORTIA

A consortium is a partnership or association of organizations. Library consortia are created to establish and maintain cooperative agreements. Consortial agreements allow groups of libraries to enter into licenses with publishers and vendors as single entities. While each member library may have an individual contract, the terms of the contracts are worked out by the consortium. Any group of libraries can form a consortium. Consortia have been created which are local, state-wide, regional, and national. Libraries can be and often are members of more than one consortium. Consortia overlap geographically, and the only rules controlling membership are the consortia's own policies and the limits of what publishers and vendors will accept. The member list of the International Coalition of Library Consortia (ICOLC) at http://www.library.yale.edu/consortia/icolcmembers.html gives a good idea of the variety of library consortia. Most of the consortia listed at the ICOLC website have links to their websites with more information about their members and activities.

The most obvious benefit to libraries from licensing access to databases through consortia is that member libraries typically negotiate a lower subscription price than they could get acting alone. Since the total number of patrons is greater and the size of the negotiated contract is larger, publishers and vendors are more willing to negotiate with the consortium. Another factor favoring consortia over libraries acting alone is that the contract negotiator for a consortium probably has more expertise in the process than librarians at individual libraries. Knowledge of laws, practices, precedents, and what competitors are offering can all give the consortium's negotiator a stronger hand. Publishers and vendors benefit from dealing with consortia because working through consortia reduces the number of contracts that must be handled. Also, since lower prices can be offered on larger contracts, they are able to reach libraries that may otherwise choose not to subscribe.

The development of state-wide consortia has led to innovative licenses and systems that deserve close attention. OhioLINK's Electronic Journal Center is an example of a state's solution to its libraries' challenges of providing patrons access to scholarly periodicals. As mentioned previously, the OhioLINK consortium negotiated contracts with publishers to allow serial content to be loaded on consortium servers. Saving the serial content on consortial servers gives OhioLINK control over (and responsibility for) current and future access. The extent to which other states follow Ohio's lead will be interesting to observe in the coming years.

Contracting licenses through consortia is not without risk. The content provided through a state-wide consortium is vulnerable to cuts beyond the control of member institutions (http://www.ohiolink.edu/about/snapshot2004.pdf). The terms agreed to by a consortium may be more or less expensive, and provide more or fewer titles than an individual library would prefer. In general, the more the libraries in a consortium have in common, the more agreeable the terms will be to all members. If the terms are not agreeable, a library can always choose to subscribe to a vendor's product on its own instead.

The essential point regarding consortia for a librarian new to serials management is that one needs to become familiar with the consortia with which the library may participate. Since consortia are often able to negotiate better deals for packages of serials (as well as bibliographic databases and reference works), it is wise to investigate purchasing materials through a consortium rather than licensing them as an individual library.

COSTS TO PUBLISHERS OF PRODUCING SERIALS ONLINE

When applications of technologies are new, the attraction of solutions to old problems can lead some people to place too much emphasis on the potential benefits of the technology. They may tend to ignore challenges of integrating the new technology into the existing social and economic system. One of the early optimistic views of remote access serials was that online delivery would save publishers a great deal of money. It appeared that saving the costs of printing, mailing, and related costs could be translated into lower subscription rates. Unfortunately, the reality has been that offering online versions of serials has actually increased publishers' costs. The reasons are that the cost of publishing online is substantial, the cost of producing print issues is not the majority of total costs, and the transition from print to online can take several years.

To produce a journal online, the publisher must provide (directly or by contract) the servers, Internet connections, and programmers to load, maintain, and provide access to articles. Typesetting software does not create fully web-ready documents. Additional work is required to translate a document ready for printing into a document ready to post online. Even if articles are saved as PDF files, work must be done to load the content to a server and create metadata and links. Additional work is required if the serial includes any multimedia content.

Most of the cost of producing a serial is in producing the first copy. Estimates vary, but if a publisher produced no print issues of a serial, it would save them roughly 30 percent of total production costs. The transition from print to online publishing increases the total costs to publishers because they cannot flip a magic switch to go overnight from all print to online-only publishing. To satisfy subscribers' needs, most publishers continue to offer their serials in both formats. While some customers became comfortable early on with the online format, others continue to prefer print. Librarians want print serials to ensure reliable long-term access. As the market for online serials matures, comfort levels with online-only rise, solutions for long-term archiving are developed, and more publishers may stop producing print issues. But in 2005 most publishers still produce serials in both formats.

CONSOLIDATION AMONG PUBLISHERS

A time-honored method of growing a company is to acquire competitors. Serials publishing is no different. Large publishers regularly buy out small publishers, and commercial publishers frequently add titles by taking over periodicals formerly produced by scholarly societies. Acquisitions of smaller publishers' serials give the buyer more titles to offer to potential subscribers, and the sellers see their publications continue while making a financial gain. Scholarly societies are very tempted to sell the publishing rights for established journals because it gives them revenue and takes away the hassles of producing and marketing their journal. Editors are thus freed to focus on selecting the best content and managing the peer review process. Of course, then the society can no longer control the subscription price, and will probably have less control over the appearance and marketing of their journal.

The Big Deal refers to publisher packages of bundled full-text serials provided to libraries under license conditions determined by the publisher. Elsevier's Science Direct package has attracted much attention in the library community as an example of the Big Deal. Elsevier stipulated that a library or consortium of libraries could get access to all the journals in ScienceDirect for a fee based on their print subscriptions, plus an incremental fee. Members of consortia could pool their print subscriptions. Each member library got access to hundreds of titles even though some libraries started with only a handful of print subscriptions. Such a Big Deal offered enormous bang for the buck. The catch was that once committed, the library could not cancel subscriptions to individual titles. In essence, libraries subscribing to Elsevier's *ScienceDirect* gave up the freedom to cancel subscriptions in return for greatly expanded access to a package of content. Much of that content would not be directly relevant to the institution's educational mission, but the shear size and breadth of topic coverage made the tradeoff worthwhile. Or did it?

Kenneth Frazier (2001) argued that libraries should not enter into these Big Deal contractual arrangements. His argument was based on a game theory called the Prisoner's Dilemma, in which individuals acting in their own self interest make everyone involved worse off. Frazier's thesis was that the Big Deal can make the publisher's serials indispensable. Over time, being indispensable will cause packages to become more expensive and give the Big Deal publishers too much control over the terms and conditions of the use of scholarly literature.

Frazier's cogent statement of his opinion about the Big Deal opened a discussion among librarians, publishers, vendors, and others concerned with serials and scholarly publishing that continues to this day. Librarians continue to push for control over which titles they are paying for, while publishers continue to aggressively market bundled packages of journals. Librarians responsible for negotiating licenses are pushing hard for lower prices, and are insisting on putting the licenses' terms and conditions on the table during negotiations. The largest consortia (e.g., University of California system, OhioLINK) have been the most successful in negotiating contracts that retain libraries' control over payment for individual titles, rather than accepting an "all or nothing" package.

Consolidation of publishers is worrisome. Lack of competition among publishers for serials may lead to higher prices, a lack of diverse voices, and a general lack of choice. The free flow of information requires venues for authors to reach readers. Independent publishers of niche periodicals are an important means of linking authors to readers. If the independents fail, authors will have fewer outlets for their works, and readers will have fewer choices. The reduction in venues for expressing ideas may ultimately be the worst consequence of the serials crisis. Most scholarly journals depend on library subscriptions for survival. Publishers not able to make the transition to online and compete against Big Deals will likely fail. The web has made it much easier than ever for an individual to make information available to a wide audience. However, the costs of producing a quality scholarly journal remain high, even if print issues are not produced. The expense of making the transition to online may ironically lead to the death of many serials.

Providing patrons convenient access to online serials can be challenging and requires the application of new skills. Serials librarians need to understand the strengths and weaknesses of the available formats of online serials and the types of delivery of remote access serials. Librarians should be aware of the direct and indirect costs of online serials and carefully consider the consequences of replacing print subscriptions with online serial titles and full-text database packages. It is important to be aware of library consortia that offer opportunities to subscribe to remote access serials more economically. Serials librarians consider all these factors in the context of budgeting and selecting their library's entire serials collection.

SUGGESTIONS FOR FURTHER READING

A concise comparison of HTML and PDF with more depth than was explained in this chapter is Thom Lieb's "HTML, PDF and TXT: The format wars," *The Journal of Electronic Publishing*, 5(1), September 1999, http://www.press.umich .edu/jep/05-01/lieb0501.html. Examples of multimedia scholarly journals include the *Journal for Multimedia History* at http://www.albany.edu/jmmh/ and *Linguistic Discovery* at http://linguistic-discovery.dartmouth.edu/webobjbin/WebObjects/ Journals.woa/xmlpage/1/issue.

Jeanne Galvin provides an overview of issues surrounding journals online, including acceptance by stakeholders, various alternatives to traditional publishing models, and archiving concerns in "The next step in scholarly communication: Is the traditional journal dead?" *Electronic Journal of Academic and Special Librarianship*, 5(1), Spring 2004, http://southernlibrarianship.icaap.org/content/v05n01/ galvin_j01.htm. Librarians' experiences with shifting from print to online collections are reported in nine articles compiled by guest editors Cris Ferguson and Ajaye Bloomstone in "Cancellation of print journals for electronic versions: Issues and challenges," *Against the Grain*, 17(6), December 2005–January 2006.

For an overview of the types of delivery of remote access serials including an annotated list of publishers, platform providers, and index- and abstract-based aggregators, see Jeff Kosokoff, "Aggregators," in Cheryl LaGuardia, ed., *Magazines for Libraries*, 12th ed. (New Providence, NJ: R.R. Bowker, 2003). For insight into the relationships existing between database vendors and journal publishers, see Mary Beth Chambers and SooYoung So, "Full-text aggregator database vendors and journal publishers: A study of a complex relationship," *Serials Review*, 30(3), 2004, 183–193.

OpenURL is explained in Herbert Van de Sompel and Oren Beit-Arie, "Open linking in the Scholarly Information Environment using the OpenURL framework," *D-Lib Magazine*, 7(3), March 2001, http://www.dlib.org/dlib/march01/vandesompel/03vandesompel.html. Digital Object Identifier technology and the project to implement it is explained by Norman Paskin, "DOI: A 2003 progress report," *D-Lib Magazine*, 9(6), June 2003, http://www.dlib.org/dlib/june03/paskin/06paskin.html.

For an in-depth treatment of the need for trusted archival storage of remote access serials and the issues that must be addressed to attain a system for preservation, see the 2001 report by the Research Libraries Group (RLG)/OCLC, Attributes of a trusted digital repository: Meeting the needs of research resources, online at http://www.rlg.org/longterm/attributes01.pdf. Extensive information about LOCKSS and the issues surrounding its implementation and the need for archiving are at http://lockss.stanford.edu/. See especially the FAQ at http://lockss.stanford.edu/projectdescfaq.htm.

The research study by Roger C. Schonfeld, Donald W. King, Ann Okerson, and Eileen Gifford Fenton, *The Nonsubscription Side of Periodicals: Changes in Library Operations and Costs between Print And Electronic Formats* (Washington, DC: Council on Library and Information Resources, June 2004) http://www.clir.org/pubs/reports/pub127/pub127.pdf is an excellent treatment of the costs incurred by libraries. The survey used by the researchers listing the variety of activities in libraries' serials operations is included as an appendix.

The International Coalition of Library Consortia (ICOLC) website at http://www.library.yale.edu/consortia/ includes statements on the purpose and activities of the organization. Official statements of the ICOLC represent a consensus view of the issues addressed. The ICOLC has published several best practice guidelines, all linked from their website.

One of the few published studies of publishers' costs is Todd A. Carpenter, Heather Joseph, and Mary Waltham, "A survey of business trends at BioOne Publishing Partners and its implications for BioOne," *portal: Libraries and the Academy*, 4(4), 2004, 465–484. This article describes the sources of revenue for 12 journals at a level of detail not often seen in the literature. Keith Seitter of the American Meteorological Society presented the costs and revenue sources of AMS journals at the 19th Annual NASIG (June 17–20, 2004) in his presentation "The print/electronic tightrope: A case study in publication finances for a medium-sized nonprofit society."

Many responses were made to Ken Frazier's "The librarian's dilemma: contemplating the costs of the 'Big Deal,'" *D-Lib Magazine*, 7(3), March 2001, http://www.dlib.org/dlib/march01/frazier/03frazier.html. One of particular interest is Ellen Finnie Duranceau, "Cornell and the future of the Big Deal: An interview with Ross Atkinson," *Serials Review*, 30(2), 2004, 127–130. Atkinson, associate university librarian for collections at Cornell, describes the faculty resolution supporting opposition to accepting Elsevier's *ScienceDirect* "Big Deal" and Cornell's future plans. Cornell's actions in this regard have gotten considerable attention from libraries world wide.

REFERENCES

EBSCO Publishing. 2005. *Full Text Databases, Print Journals, and Electronic Journals . . . Distinctly Different Products*, http://www.epnet.com/academic/publishers.asp.

Frazier, Kenneth. March 2001. The librarian's dilemma: Contemplating the costs of the "Big Deal." *D-Lib Magazine* 7(3), http://www.dlib.org/dlib/march01/frazier/03frazier.html.

Schonfeld, Roger C., King, Donald W., Okerson, Ann, and Fenton, Eileen Gifford. June 2004. *The Nonsubscription Side of Periodicals: Changes in Library Operations and Costs between Print and Electronic Formats*. Washington, DC: Council on Library and Information Resources, http://www.clir.org/pubs/reports/pub127/pub127.pdf.

Sprague, Nancy, and Chambers, Mary Beth. 2000. Full text databases and the journal cancellation process: A case study. *Serials Review* 26: 19–31.

Chapter 3

Budgeting, Selection, and Deselection

Since, as previously discussed, libraries' serials budgets seldom increase fast enough to cover annual inflation of subscription rates and patrons' demand for new titles, budgeting, selection, and deselection will be treated together in this chapter. Deselection is defined here as the process of choosing those titles that will not be renewed for the coming year. Print volumes of serials already received might be weeded from the collection, but whether volumes will be removed of titles not renewed is a separate issue from this definition of deselection.

The inflation rate for journal subscriptions since about 1980 has been approximately 9 percent per year. According to *Library Journal's* (*LJ's*) 2004 periodicals price survey, the average price of a scholarly journal indexed in the Institute for Scientific Information (ISI) databases was $915 (Van Orsdel and Born 2004). *LJ's* projection for 2007 is yet another 7–9 percent increase in the price of periodicals (Van Orsdel and Born 2006). New journals are launched every year to meet the needs of researchers in new fields of endeavor. In addition to budgetary pressures caused by inflation and proliferation, library patrons are expecting more serial content to be available online. Adding access to online serials often increases a library's expenses in the short term. Online access to bundled packages and index- and abstract-based aggregations, discussed in the previous chapter, typically costs more than the library can save from canceling print subscriptions. Further, the packages and aggregations are not reliable substitutes for individual subscriptions.

Rising subscription prices, online alternatives to traditional print subscriptions, and budgets insufficient to continue all of the current year's subscriptions are spurring many libraries to cancel many subscriptions. In one sense, "cancel" means to halt a subscription before it is complete. Since many publishers charge substantial penalties or may give no refund for subscriptions halted early, it is seldom worthwhile to cancel a title in mid-subscription. Serials librarians typically use the terms "cancel" and "cancellation project" as synonyms for "nonrenewal" and "nonrenewal project." "Cancellation project" is the most commonly used term for the process of choosing serials to not renew for the coming year. This begins with the discussion of budget.

BUDGETING

Before describing best practices for choosing which journals to add, retain, or cut from a library's subscriptions, some general description of serials budgeting practices is in order. The portion of the materials budget devoted to serials varies widely among libraries depending on the patron population served, the topic areas collected, and the funds available. Another factor in the apportionment of the serials budget is how a library chooses to allocate expenditures for full-text database subscriptions. Databases may be considered as sources of serials and budgeted as such, or they may be allocated to a separate online resources line, or some other budget line.

When deciding details of how series, serials, and full-text databases will be allocated in their budgets, librarians work within available materials funds to select the books and serials that best meet patrons' needs. Purchasing a book is a one-time decision. Serials are different because they present a long-term commitment. They have no predetermined end date and forthcoming volumes are likely to remain of interest to patrons. Patrons will come to expect the subscription to continue even as the price of the serial probably increases every year. The portion of overall materials budget devoted to serials must be carefully monitored to ensure that money remains for other materials. It is especially important to give close scrutiny to the long-term impact on the budget of initiating new subscriptions to journals. This includes a discussion of the methods of budget allocation, including variation in subscribed titles and variations in patrons and ends with a discussion of reporting concerning budget issues.

Methods of Budget Allocation

The subscription costs of serials desired by patrons practically always exceed the funds available. The first step in serials budgeting is to put a cap on how much will be spent. Without a limit, within a few years the periodical subscriptions will consume or exceed the entire materials budget. Caps can be placed on the serials budget as a whole, or on separate allocations within that budget. Librarians can take two basic approaches to allocation. One is to have one fund for all serials. Series can be part of that single budget allocation, be grouped on their own, or allocated with books. The other basic approach is to break the serials budget into discipline or topic areas. If a grant or other special funding source is available, a separate allocation can be maintained for that pool of money.

Having one general serials fund usually gives librarians more control over what is subscribed to because they have discretion to move funds into areas as they see fit. This level of control can create more efficient allocations if librarians objectively consider all patrons' needs, and this differs between public and special and academic librarians. Public and special librarians must understand their patron needs to effectively allocate funds by potential patron use. Academic librarians may allocate by enrollment or by discipline to efficiently match the serials budget to academic programs.

Allocation by Discipline. In academic libraries, allocating funds for subscriptions often means balancing the expressed needs of faculty with the needs of students. However, the one serials fund approach runs the risk of alienating faculty who may believe "those librarians" do not understand their needs. Allocating the serials budget among disciplinary funds facilitates greater involvement by faculty. When discipline-based fund categories are budgeted, academic departments can be given some control over which serials to subscribe to. This allows the librarians to draw on the faculty's expertise and fosters an atmosphere of partnership between the departments and the library. When the faculty feel a sense of ownership in the collection, they tend to better understand budgetary pressures and be more deliberative when requesting new serials. A potential drawback to giving faculty more say in subscription decisions is that faculty interests in specific disciplines and sub-disciplines may cause fewer general interest and interdisciplinary titles to be subscribed to than students need. Whether that represents a problem depends largely on the library's serials collection development policy. If the policy emphasizes supporting faculty research, then it makes sense to give faculty responsibility for choosing titles. When the policy states that the collection is for the academic and recreational reading needs of students, the serials librarian should take a proactive role to ensure those needs are met, even if it means disappointing some faculty.

When a serials budget is allocated among disciplines, expenditures will vary widely among departments. Variation by discipline is due to the balance of books and periodicals purchased (or licensed), the number of reputable journals published in the discipline, and the costs of the journals. Disciplines such as psychology, medicine, and most of the sciences place very high value on the currency of information. Faculty and other professionals doing library research in those disciplines will prefer that a very high percentage of the materials budget be allocated to periodicals. Other disciplines, including those in the humanities, tend to place greater emphasis on long-term access to information, and may desire more monographs in the budget allocation. These preferences are reflected in the publications in each discipline and expectations for academic advancement in rank and gaining tenure. Because preferences by faculty in each institution vary, assumptions should not be made about the proper allocation of funds without consulting with them first.

The option to have some serials available online in full text complicates matters. Many faculty and other professionals still prefer to have both online and print versions. If they have a say in budget allocations, it is important for faculty and researchers to understand the budgetary ramifications of subscribing to both formats. The ramifications vary, as some print subscriptions come with free online, while others charge more to get both versions. The availability and reliability of access to online serials, including the ability to print articles, are important factors in the choice to pay for online to supplement or replace print serials. Reliability depends partly on vendors' services and partly on the quality of the local network and technical support staff. Also important is the level of need for remote access to serials outside of the library. For example, it may be a high priority to supply online serials to distance learners. Finally, the expense of binding and shelving should be considered as a part of the overall budget ramifications of subscribing to print, online, or both formats.

Allocation by Number of Patrons Served. A factor to be considered in budget allocation is the percentage of patrons likely to be interested in materials in a topic area. While an academic librarian has access to enrollment, a public librarian would not have exact numbers of patrons interested in topic areas. The public librarian must have knowledge of the community to be able to suggest how many patrons might be interested in periodicals on certain topics. In a special library, the number of employees or clients served in various topic areas could be the guide for the portion of patrons interested in a topic. Once the percentage is determined, it can be factored into budget allocations in concert with the library's collection development policy and the institution's mission.

When the percentage of patrons likely to be interested in materials in a topic area is determined, it is probable that some topics will be of interest to a small number of patrons. Two possible approaches address the situation of having relatively few patrons interested in periodicals on a certain topic. One approach is to judge the importance in the budget of the titles based on per-patron rates of use. The per-patron rate is determined by dividing measured uses by the number of patrons expected to use the serial. For example, suppose there are ten majors in a discipline at a college and a $2,000 journal allocated to that discipline is used 50 times a year. The per-patron rate of use is five, while the cost per use is $40. Another discipline at the same college may have 250 majors who use a $100 journal 500 times. The per-patron rate of use is two, and the cost per use is just 20 cents. The journal serving more majors is a much better value in terms of cost per use. But the ten majors each using a journal an average of five times suggests that those few patrons highly value the collection. The librarian can choose to retain titles because they are especially valuable to those few patrons, even though the subscription cost per use may be relatively high. The philosophy behind this approach is that it is worthwhile to support relatively costly journals that are appreciated by the patrons who use them.

The alternative approach is to concentrate spending on areas that interest the most patrons. A choice to build on the collection's strengths is a policy decision to be made by the institution the library serves. The institution may decide it is important to support a diverse range of disciplines or interests, even if some have low enrollment. In practice, this often means subscribing to just a few prominent journals in disciplines with low enrollment. A broader range of titles are subscribed to in disciplines with higher enrollment. How many titles are subscribed to in each discipline is decided at each library in the context of the institution's mission, strategic plan, and priorities. Precisely which titles are subscribed to within each allocation is affected by variation in subscribed titles and the patrons served.

Impact of Variation on Budgeting

A library's list of subscribed serials may tend to be continued from one year to the next, but subscribed titles will vary for reasons other than the librarian's choice. One source of variation is the serials publishers offer for sale. Some titles cease publication, some merge with other titles, and some split into new titles. Quite a few can be expected to be delayed in publication and therefore not due for renewal. In the author's experience, roughly 8 percent of a library's subscriptions are delayed in publication at any one time. Tracking the delayed titles and when payment is due again for them is one of the services offered by subscription agencies. Sometimes titles are "suspended," meaning that they are not being published, but the publisher has not decided to officially end the periodical. Suspended titles often end up ceasing, but some do come back to life.

Another major source of variation in the titles a library subscribes to is the rate of increases in subscription prices from one year to the next. Many titles will remain at the same price or almost so, while others will increase dramatically. Price increases of two or three times the prior year's price are not uncommon, especially when a different publisher takes over a serial. Dramatic price increases may force a librarian not to renew some subscriptions. For example, a librarian may have the good fortune to have an eight to 10 percent increase in the serials budget, roughly matching the average annual inflation rate for serials. To maintain the average increase for all subscribed serials, the titles that are increasing by 50, 100, or even 300 percent may need to not be renewed. This is especially true of more expensive titles, since a 300 percent increase in a $300 title affects the total budget more than a 300 percent increase in a $20 title. As careful as a librarian might be in adjusting for increases, variations in the community served can affect selection of serials.

The community of patrons the library serves is another source of variation affecting the list of titles. In academic libraries, the addition or deletion of a major program of study, or of a concentration within a program, will cause demand for serial titles to change. It is very important for the serials librarian to keep track of dropped majors or programs. New programs and majors have advocates who should communicate their needs for serials with the library, but a ceased program will probably have no one to tell the librarian which titles are no longer needed. Titles of little or no interest to remaining programs should not be continued. In public libraries, demographic changes in the community can change the demand for particular serials. Changes in the activities conducted by organizations or businesses can change demand for serials in special libraries. In all types of libraries, patrons' needs must be monitored to maintain an appropriate serials collection. Under all circumstances, the serials librarian must be prepared to report the funding needed to those who prepare budgets.

REPORTING

Serials librarians have several ways to collect and report data and a variety of persons to whom they report. Librarians in academic institutions need to report not only to administrators but also to faculty committees. Data may be collected from several sources, and, even under the best circumstances, the serials librarian must deal with uncertainty. The first step is to determine to whom reports are made.

An important duty of serials librarians in academic institutions is reporting information about the serials collection to administrators and interested groups such as library committees. Serials librarians in academic libraries report to departments about the titles allocated to their budget lines. These reports may be sent as part of a cancellation project.

Public librarians must monitor the cost of serials subscriptions and monitor patron interest in them. Familiarity with cost and use is needed for reporting to funding sources, whether a library board or the city council. Sharp increases in the prices of scholarly journals do not affect public libraries' magazine collections, but price increases still need to be monitored. Reports of serials expenditures and predictions of price increases inform the overall budget process.

Special libraries often exist as cost centers within a larger organization. Special librarians working to support research and development, or doctors in a hospital, or lawyers in a law firm, or another enterprise typically report to superiors on the cost effectiveness of their library's collection and services. Serials may represent a large portion of special library expenditures, whether as subscriptions, database licenses, or individual articles purchased from a document delivery service. Reports on the effectiveness of the library need to include details on the use of serials and their costs and benefits to the organization. In organizations that bill a client or charge a particular project for subscriptions and articles, special librarians may have to make very detailed reports of serial costs and use.

Data Collection

Several ways are possible to collect data to report. If the academic librarian has to report on proposed cuts, introductory material explaining why cuts are necessary will accompany data on serials titles. Data reported for each title will vary depending on the purpose of the report, but typical data elements include the list of current titles, subscription price, price trends (cost in recent years and/or percentage increases), and counts of use. The reports may also include rankings of titles, lists of titles cancelled in recent years, indexing coverage, and online availability in full-text databases. Tracking all this data on the title level and keeping it up-to-date are quite time-consuming tasks.

Another way to create reports is from data recorded in a library's integrated library system (ILS). The acquisitions module in an ILS can record each serial issue checked in and record prices, and if serials circulate, the circulation module can track use. The catalog module can record data on serial titles and the library's serial holdings. Reports created from data stored in an ILS may meet a serials librarian's reporting needs in academic, public, and special libraries. But an ILS may not be the most efficient means for tracking the data needed for regular reporting. Because ILS acquisitions modules are typically designed to keep track of current information only, they do not conveniently track prices over time, and it may not be possible to add into the ILS desired data on use counts or availability online. These limitations on using an ILS to keep all the data needed to create reports are the reason many serials librarians choose to keep a separate database or a spreadsheet to allow greater reporting flexibility than their library's ILS can provide. A database may include information not typically recorded in an ILS, such as which research project should be charged for serials in a special library. Many ILSs easily export data to database programs, so the separate database need not be created from scratch.

Data in a database can be easily converted into a spreadsheet, and vice versa. The relative ease of transferring data from a database to a spreadsheet and back again means the selection of one over another will not prevent a librarian from manipulating the data as needed. The advantage of using a spreadsheet is that it is somewhat easier to perform mathematical calculations on the data. An advantage of using a database is that there are more sorting and filtering functions that can facilitate the creation of custom reports.

While the details of reporting the costs, benefits, and use of serials will vary from one type of library to another, serials librarians can expect report creation as part of their job description. Effective reports require knowledge of the serials budget and collection as well as familiarity with patron needs. Unfortunately, creating reports is complicated by unavoidable uncertainties and ambiguities in serials management.

Dealing with Uncertainty

Creating accurate reports can be far more difficult than someone not familiar with serials management might think because titles, prices, publishers, and subscription status of titles constantly change. It is very helpful if the director (or whoever the serials librarian reports to) understands that some degree of uncertainty is inherent in serials management. A little tolerance for ambiguity goes a long way towards making manageable the job of reporting serials data. For example, a straightforward question that a library director is likely to ask is "How much more money will we be spending on serials in this fiscal year?" The report to answer this question would need to include separate figures for each department or discipline in an academic library if the budget is allocated that way, or by any other means of distribution of funds.

At first glance, this would seem to be an easy question to answer, just look at the unpaid subscriptions for the year, and total them. Five things impede this simple process: knowing the price, different subscription cycles, different budget cycles, delayed publications, and serials that cease publication.

It is impossible to know for certain how much the price for unpaid subscriptions will change from the previous year. Also, it would be nice if all the subscriptions began on January 1, but publishers have many different subscription cycles. These subscription cycles do not all match libraries' fiscal years or budget cycles. Many academic libraries have budgets that start in the summer. Public libraries' budgets may match state or local government budget cycles, which can suffer delays. But even if a library's budget reliably begins on January 1, some subscribed serial titles may begin a volume in another month.

Subscription agents smooth the payment process out considerably by charging an estimated price for each title. They work hard at getting an accurate price from the publisher at the time of billing, which is typically around October; however, the subscription agent cannot stop a publisher from changing the price of the next year's subscription. Subscription agents intermittently send supplemental invoices notifying the librarian of publishers' increases in rates. These mid-cycle increases can be estimated from experience in prior years, but exact prediction is not possible. Another challenge comes with standing orders.

A few serials are by standing order only, meaning the library commits to buying them without knowing in advance the price or exactly when it will be received. Since standing orders are billed when shipped, their prices defy precise prediction.

The majority of prices remain the same as reported in the subscription agent's October bill, and the changes that occur typically represent only a few percent of the total bill for subscriptions. So it is fairly easy to report the approximate amount left outstanding for standing orders, and past trends allow predictions of how much will be added from supplemental invoices. But predicting exactly what the standing orders and supplements will be, and for which departmental allocation, is impossible.

Another source of uncertainty that complicates reporting is delays in publication. If a periodical is running behind schedule, payment expected to be made at one time is deferred and then may become due at a later, unexpected date. For instance, a library might pay their subscription agent in October 2004 for the 2005 volume of the *Journal of Fish Choreography*. Imagine that the editorial board suffers from a freak grizzly bear encounter that causes no issues to be published in 2005. The October 2005 renewal from the subscription agent would state "delayed publication," and the library would not pay for issues expected in 2006. The editors might then get things back in order, catch up on their work, and publish all the expected issues for 2005 and the first issue for 2006 in February 2006. The subscribing library will then be hit unexpectedly with the bills for both 2005 and 2006. This hypothetical example is mirrored by real instances. When a periodical has "delayed publication" status, it is not possible to predict when, if ever, the expected issues will arrive or when payment for them will be due.

Serials budgets are also disrupted when titles cease. Some publishers have the good grace to cease publication at the end of a volume, so subscribers get the issues they paid for. But sometimes periodicals cease in the midst of a volume. Honorable publishers refund subscription fees for the issues that were not published. Cash is best, but it is not uncommon for publishers to fulfill a subscription with issues of another title. Sometimes no refund is made at all. Subscription agents can be very helpful in this regard, as they have the clout and staff time to press the publisher for refunds. One can never predict which titles will cease, or when, or how much of a credit will be added to the budget. It is not only the marginally important titles that cease. Well-regarded publications cease to the surprise of subscribers. Recent examples include *Lingua Franca*, *The Sciences*, and *World Press Review*.

Having allocated budget funds for selection, the next task of the serials librarian is the selection process. Unfortunately, the current budget situation makes this often a less than pleasant task.

SELECTION

In theory, the first step of serials work flow in a library is the selection of which titles the library will subscribe to. Only rarely will a librarian have the task of selecting a list of titles from scratch. In practice, a librarian hired to manage, or help manage, serials will inherit a list of subscriptions that tends to be continued from one year to the next. If the budget allows, newly hired librarians can simply choose to continue subscribing to the same titles, but they may have to decide whether to subscribe to print, online, or both formats for some titles. They may be faced with very difficult decisions concerning reduction of titles.

For many serials librarians, serials collection development is an exercise in selecting which titles to not renew. With subscription inflation rates of 8–10 percent per year and new journals being launched every year, a newly hired serials librarian can expect to inherit a wish list of serials that have been requested by patrons, but not added to the collection. Lists of requested serials may also exist from interlibrary loan (ILL) requests that were denied because more than five requests had been placed in a year. Requests for journals are not equally worthy, and the librarian is responsible for subscribing to titles that best fulfill the library's mission within existing budget constraints and the guidelines of a good collection development policy.

Collection Development Policies

The selection of serials needs to be rooted in a good collection development policy. It is essential to define the purpose of the collection, outline its scope, and define the population served. The policy should give a consistent rationale for why titles should and should not be part of the collection. A clear policy is especially needed when the library denies requests for subscriptions or offers of gifts. The serials librarian does not want to be in the position of saying, "no," to a request, with no more rationale than "because I said so."

Serials collection development policies are created in relationship to the institution's mission. The desired comprehensiveness of a serials collection is central to policy development. A library serving Ph.D. programs should have a policy much different from a library serving only undergraduates. College library collection development goals will be different from the policies of a corporate library or a public library. What policies should have in common is a clear statement of the scope and purpose of the serials collection. Here is an example of a collection development policy from a liberal arts college serving undergraduate and masters' degree students where the author works:

> The purpose of serials collection development is to provide a balanced, carefully chosen collection of periodical literature that supports the educational mission of the College. A secondary goal is to provide journals of general and cultural value for students to enrich personal growth. The Library carries out this function in accord with the Library Bill of Rights, which proscribes censorship and ideological favoritism.
>
> The addition and cancellation of periodical subscriptions in the collection will be determined by the Serials Librarian working in close consultation with the faculty, and with the approval of the Library Director. For a new journal to be added to the collection, a journal (or journals) of approximately equal cost may need to be cancelled. Budget and space limits necessitate a general policy of zero net growth. Exceptions will be made for new programs or programs that are demonstrably underrepresented in the current collection.

Some points are worth emphasizing because they address issues faced by most academic libraries. Note that the policy has the college's educational mission at its heart but leaves room for titles desired for recreational reading. The proscription of censorship or favoritism strongly implies that titles from widely ranging points of view will be included in the collection. The ultimate responsibility for title selection in this policy statement lies with the serials librarian. This is not always true, as some policies place final responsibility with an administrator, a committee, or others.

Some institutions of higher learning give final say to the faculty in the affected discipline(s), but that may create unbalanced collections. Some faculty may give too little emphasis to important titles outside their own areas of expertise and fail to work toward a well-balanced collection. A policy giving final say to the librarian, "working in close consultation," helps strike the right balance between individual needs and the long-term balance of the collection. An explicitly stated policy of zero net growth reflects economic necessity, and helps clarify why so many requests for new titles must be turned down, noting that growth is allowed when needed.

Policies vary, based on the comprehensiveness desired, the population served, budgetary constraints, organizational culture, and the relative importance of serials in the overall collection development policy. Serials collection development policies draw from a common set of selection criteria, but emphasize them differently. The practice of selection also varies among libraries because others besides the serials librarian may be involved. In small libraries, the director may make the choices, and indeed there may not be a librarian solely responsible for serials. In large libraries, public and academic, subject bibliographers or collection managers may have primary responsibility for selection within their disciplines, including serials. In special libraries, the clients (e.g., research scientists, doctors, attorneys) may choose the serials. Regardless of who is ultimately responsibility for selection, collaboration and communication among users and librarians is necessary to provide a serials collection that best meets patron's needs within the available budget.

Selection Tools

Some of the information needed to apply selection criteria is local, such as the institution's mission and patron interests. For further help, bibliographic and contact information can be found by looking titles up in the venerable reference sources, *The Serials Directory* and *Ulrich's Periodicals Directory,* or databases provided by subscription agencies to their customers.

Directories and Databases. Both reference sources are now available online as well as in print, *The Serials Directory* as an EBSCOhost database and *Ulrich's Periodicals Directory* as Bowker's http://ulrichsweb.com. The entries for each serial in both directories include the title, ISSN, a brief description, the indexes that cover the title, and the publisher's name and contact information. The two publications are equally capable of providing this basic information; yet differences exist, particularly in the online versions.

In addition to the basic information, entries in ulrichsweb.com contain reviews from *LJ* and *Magazines for Libraries*. This nice feature is not surprising, since all three are published by Bowker. The entries in the database include many searchable fields, and the advanced search engine is powerful and precise. Searches can be limited in many ways, including by publisher, price range, and whether the title is peer reviewed. The records for serials in ulrichsweb.com include retrospective bibliographic details such as title history and ISSN history. ulrichsweb.com allows one to view all of the preceding and succeeding titles in one record.

This provides an advantage over using the bibliographic records in OCLC or WorldCat, which follow successive entry cataloging—only one preceding or succeeding title is listed in a record. The company also touts its OpenURL compliance, which facilitates linking of records from ulrichsweb to records in integrated library systems (ILSs) and online databases.

Each record in EBSCO's *Serials Directory* is indexed with many useful searchable fields, just like Ulrich's *Periodicals Directory*. Data include whether the serial is peer reviewed and Library of Congress (LC) and Dewey Decimal classifications. Either publication is a fine source for basic information about serials. The online versions of both are powerful, effective tools for finding current bibliographic, pricing, and publisher information. Subscription agents also provide databases with similar information.

The databases made available by subscription agents to their customers also serve the same function. For example, customers of Harrassowitz have access to their *OttoSerials* database (http://www.harrassowitz.de/ottoserials.html), and customers of Swets Information Services may use *SwetsWise* (www.swetswise.com). As mentioned in connection with ulrichsweb, reviews of serials can be useful.

Reviews of Serials. The reviews section in every other issue of *LJ* includes reviews of newly published popular magazines. *LJ* also publishes an annual Best Magazines feature in the May 1 issue. In typical *LJ* style, the reviews include the price, publisher, intended audience, and are about 200 words long. These can be helpful for the new publications that are reviewed, but many new serials are never reviewed, and titles that have been around for a long time do not appear in the *LJ* Best Magazines feature.

The primary source for reviews of serials is *Magazines for Libraries*. Bill Katz edited the first edition in 1969, and it has been published by Bowker since that time. Now in its 12th edition and edited by Cheryl LaGuardia, *Magazines for Libraries* selectively lists, describes, and evaluates periodicals. The latest edition contains entries written by 179 subject expert librarians for 6,856 titles. For each subject category, the reviewers write an introduction, list the basic or core periodicals and indexes for the subject, and provide reviews of the titles deemed by them to be most important for a library to acquire. The narrative evaluations are very useful, as they describe content and features only possible with long familiarity with the titles. Both scholarly and popular periodicals are listed and reviewed, with clear indications of the intended audiences. *Magazines for Libraries* is thus equally useful in collection development for both public and academic librarians.

As with any edited reference work written by many authors, the entries in *Magazines for Libraries* can be somewhat uneven. Variation can be found among topic areas in the number of titles selected as basic, number of titles reviewed, length of reviews, and the balance of descriptive and evaluative critiques of the titles. For example, the Chemistry section lists only eight basic titles, while the category Women: Feminist and Special Interest lists more than 30 basic titles.

While nothing is inherently wrong with this, the reader needs to be aware that the selection of core titles is a subjective choice made by the subject experts. The variation among subject entries is certainly no worse than what one would find in any other edited reference work. *Magazines for Libraries* is an excellent source of information, and is a positively essential tool for the serials librarian selecting titles. It is a good reference source for patrons, as well, since it can answer questions like "What are some good gardening magazines?"

Knowing sources of reviews, and holding the requests in mind, selection begins. Despite very low odds of having money to spend on serials beyond existing requests, selection development criteria that one might use for starting a collection from scratch still apply to any new subscriptions.

Selection Criteria

The most commonly used criteria for the selection of serials are:

1. *Content supportive of mission of institution.* How does the title support the goals of the library? For academic libraries, what course work or research programs will be supported by the serial? For public libraries, how do the serials fit into the overall collection? For special libraries, do the serials meet the research and information needs of the clientele?

2. *Content relevant to patron interest.* Since public libraries typically do not strive to support particular academic programs, they use patron interest as a primary selection criterion. Most academic libraries subscribe to some popular titles of general interest that do not fall under any particular discipline. Academic journals with interdisciplinary content may also be selected with patron interest as a primary criterion. This is a somewhat subjective criterion based on patron requests, feedback, and observed use of similar titles.

3. *Content indexed or available in a database.* Patrons typically enjoy browsing current issues of popular magazines and newspapers; but for all other periodicals, index or bibliographic database coverage is an important consideration to be heavily weighted in the selection process. Researchers often begin their search for periodical literature by looking in indexes or by searching in databases. If a serial is not covered in an index or database held by the library, it will probably get very little use.

4. *Content peer reviewed.* For journals intended to serve an academic mission, an important consideration is whether the articles in the serial have undergone peer review, the process of experts critiquing the content of articles before publication.

5. *Price.* Considering the cost of a serial is unavoidable. Some titles with very similar coverage have very different prices. *Library Administration and Management* (published quarterly by the American Library Association) is $65 per year. *Library Management* (published nine times a year by Emerald) is $10,784 per year. The average library science journal costs about $350 per

year. Obviously, a librarian would have to weigh very carefully paying 30 times the average for a single subscription. Most cases are not so extreme, but the relative prices of similar titles are important to consider.

6. *Level of use.* For selection, educated guesses can be made about how much the serial is likely to be used, based on use patterns in the topic area and the number of patrons likely to be interested in the topic. For cancellation, actual use data can be used. Cancellation decisions are typically based in part on cost per use data. A serial can be expensive, but if it is heavily used, it can represent a better value than a less used, less expensive title.

7. *Publisher reputation.* Prices tend to correlate strongly with publishers, so most have reputations of being affordable, expensive, or somewhere in be- tween. Other important publisher-related factors to consider include the following: Does the publisher get most issues out on schedule, and do the published issues arrive regularly? If not, do they respond promptly to claims for missed issues? Do they accurately handle payments? Are their titles stable? That is, do the titles last for a reasonable length of time before changing or ceasing?

8. *Citation rates and impact factor.* The *Journal Citation Reports* (*JCR*) pro- duced by ISI rank journals by how frequently they are cited. Impact factor is a measure of how often articles in a journal are cited, taking into account how many articles are published each year. The rankings can be used as a measure of quality, and thus as a selection criterion. Unfortunately, many journals are not included in the *JCR*. A few other rankings of journals based on citations have been published, but the *JCR* is the primary tool used for measuring citation rates.

9. *Physical quality.* Are the quality of the paper, the resolution of text and images, and durability of the binding appropriate for the audience and in line with the cost of the serial? Most serials are of acceptable quality. A few have poor quality paper and printing, but still have worthwhile content. Others are exceptionally well done, and thus represent better value for their price. Although rarely a deciding factor, these physical characteristics are worth considering.

10. *Comparable titles in the library.* This criterion is a question of balance. Since each article in a serial is unique, one title is never a true substitute for another. So there is no intrinsic harm to having subscriptions to many titles covering the same topic. However, to meet the interests of patrons and the needs of scholars, the serials librarian needs to balance the mix of titles to fairly represent the literature in various topic areas, matching the local patrons' needs. A new gardening magazine might be nice to add, but if the library already has six gardening magazines, the funds might best go to a topic area with no current subscriptions.

11. *Type and frequency of requests.* Requests for serials are not created equal. Some are made pretty much on a whim, while others have been very carefully considered by the requestor. It can help to have a request form that

must be filled out, asking questions matching the serials collection development policy. For instance, if the policy specifies that the collection is intended to fulfill an educational mission, the form may ask: "Why is this journal worth adding to the collection?" or "For which courses will this journal be used?" or "Which patrons have requested information that is available in this periodical?" Forcing the requestor to write answers to questions clarifies why the title is desired, and provides a record for future reference.

12. *Longevity.* A title with a track record may be more likely to last, since it usually takes three to five years for a new periodical to break even (if it ever does). But one can never really predict whether a serial will cease publication. The flip side of this is that it is good to have full runs of journals, so starting with volume one has its appeal. Longevity is a consideration when looking at whether to cancel a title. How long has the library subscribed? If the answer is from volume one, maintaining the full run of the title may have some value. Patrons prefer a straightforward answer to the simple question, "Do you have this journal?" If the library owns the full run, the answer is a simple "Yes," not, "Well, it depends on which volume and issue you need." Continuing runs and avoiding frequent changes in subscriptions also saves work. Plenty of changes happen outside of the librarians' control, so there is no sense in creating more changes than necessary.

13. *Availability elsewhere.* If a serial being considered is available at several other libraries within a reasonable driving distance, it can be a lower priority than another serial that is not available in the area. Some library systems have cooperative collection development, where they carefully, purposely avoid duplicating subscriptions, especially of titles that get relatively little use. These systems often use couriers to transport materials quickly from one library to the next. Interlibrary loan (ILL) can be used to meet the needs of patrons willing to wait a few days.

14. *Reviews.* Many serials are never critiqued in a published review. But if a review is available, it can help the librarian determine whether the title is appropriate for the collection. The brief but authoritative reviews published in *Magazines for Libraries* factor strongly in many libraries' selection processes.

The precise mix of serials selection criteria, and the emphasis given to each, must be determined in the context of the library and the needs of its patrons. The process of selection and deselection is more an art than a science. Rigid, precise formulas, with numerical values for selected criteria do not work well in practice. The relative values of criteria change from discipline to discipline, from one budget year to the next, and from changes in curricula and patron populations. Citation rates may not correlate with use by students and other patrons, and the reviewers in *Magazines for Libraries* may emphasize characteristics that do not matter much in a certain library. However, using criteria and data are still very helpful in selection, budgeting, and deselection of serials, and may be most important for managing gift subscriptions.

Gift Subscriptions

At first glance, gifts of serials to libraries appear to be a great deal. The library does not have to pay for the subscription, the patrons get to use the serial, and the donor has the satisfaction of helping others. But gifts can be more trouble than they are worth. The reasons for this are all rooted in the library not being the subscriber in the publisher's records. Renewal notices bypass the library, future payments are up to the donor and claims cannot be made for missed issues. If a gift subscription to a desired title is accepted, the librarian may have to unexpectedly pick up the cost in the future in order to meet patrons' expectations. At times when budgets are very tight, the renewal of the gift subscription may place a strain on the budget.

But accepting gift subscriptions can be tempting because the difference in individual and institutional subscription rates can be quite significant. Scholarly journals are often included in society membership fees, and most commercially published scholarly journals cost much more for libraries than for individuals. For example, a 2004 subscription to the *Journal of the American Chemical Society* cost $333 for individual members, but for a library the price is $2,939. So it is tempting for an institution to have the individual faculty member pay for the subscription and send the issues to the library; however, this should not be done because it is unethical. Gifts should not be accepted for the purpose of subverting publishers' pricing policies. It is wrong to misrepresent oneself when subscribing even if the librarian disagrees with the publisher's pricing policies. When pricing is not the reason for the gift, there are still practical reasons to accept gift subscriptions only sparingly for titles deemed not essential to the collection. When the library is not the subscriber the serials librarian cannot control renewals, payment, or claims for missed issues, and the gift may not match the collection development policy.

An offer of a gift subscription may also be problematic when the offered title has a strong ideological point of view, for example, a gift subscription to an evangelical religious publication. Refusing the gift may seem to the patron like censorship, but the collection development policy may state that subscriptions must either be of general interest or specifically match curricular needs. Based on the policy, the gift may be declined. Accepting one subscription for a serial of interest to a minority of patrons may be harmless; but the collection development policy may have a goal of a balanced collection that does not advance any specific ideology. Accepting one special interest serial implies that the library must also subscribe to serials representing opposing points of view. So accepting one gift could lead to purchasing many other publications at the library's expense. Obviously, having a clear collection development policy in place is quite helpful in these situations.

Selecting serials for a library requires a clear policy, knowledge of patron needs and interests, awareness of available funds, and familiarity with the serials currently published. The serials librarian has the challenging but interesting task of combining policy, patron needs, funds, and serial publications to create a collection.

When the act of creation focuses on adding titles to the collection, the challenge can be quite enjoyable. When economic necessity forces removal of titles, the challenge is less pleasant.

DESELECTION

Selecting which titles to not renew for the coming year is a difficult, even agonizing, process. The "fat" of periodicals that were nice to have but not really needed to fulfill libraries' goals was cut long ago. After all, the "serials crisis" of too few dollars for too many periodicals that cost too much has been going on for over 20 years. Now the cuts are noticed, and usually cause complaints. The best the serials librarian can do is track costs and use, draw on expert opinion, and keep communication open with those affected by the cuts. Several tools can help in this process.

Tools for Deselection

Tools for deselection include price trend data, cost per use, rankings, and local recommendations. The tools discussed in the previous section on selection are combined with information gathered about the use of serials in the library's collection. Information about the collection and its use come from both published sources and locally gathered data.

Price Trend Data. Price trend data are helpful for showing decision makers and affected patrons the big picture, giving them the broad context of circumstances that are driving subscription cuts. Price trend data is available from an annual feature in *Library Journal* (*LJ*), from subscription agents (for their customers), and from local data tracked by the librarian. *LJ*'s Annual Periodicals Price Survey is published in each April 15 issue. The Survey provides a thorough, concise, and highly informed narrative account of factors influencing serial subscription prices alongside a series of tables. The tables show average prices and price increases for titles grouped by LC subject, average prices by country of origin, and price trend data covering five years.

One of three samples of journals represented in the Annual Periodicals Price Survey includes titles covered in the three Institute for Scientific Information (ISI) citation databases: *Arts & Humanities Citation Index, Social Sciences Citation Index*, and *Science Citation Index*. These indexes provide international coverage of scholarly publications that reflect the holdings of research libraries.

The second sample of journals in the annual price survey is titles indexed in the EBSCOhost Academic Search Elite database, a database covering mostly English-language serials and relatively few highly specialized STM journals. Since many smaller academic libraries collect mostly English-language publications and relatively few STM journals, this sample provides a cost history tailored to smaller academic libraries.

The third sample of journals is the serials indexed in EBSCO's Magazine Article Summaries. This sample is intended to reflect the collections of school and small public libraries. The 2005 price survey predicted price increases of 7.5–9.3 percent for research libraries, 9.3 percent for smaller academic libraries, and 5–7 percent for school and public libraries (Van Orsdel and Born 2005).

The Library Materials Price Index Subcommittee of the ALA/ALCTS Publications Committee publishes an annual U.S. Periodical Price Index in *Library Resources and Technical Services*. Compared to the price survey published in *LJ*, this index breaks price trends down into more detailed LC classifications and lists trends for more years. The introductory material has more detail of the methods used to collect the data and avoids interpretive analysis of the serials marketplace. The strengths of the *LJ* and ALA/ALCTS Publication Committee reports complement one another, and both are useful sources of information.

Price trend data may also be obtained by libraries from their serials subscription agents. Subscription agents' price trend reports are focused on a single library's collection, and can thus be more directly applicable than published price trend data. But unfortunately for ease of obtaining accurate data, most libraries do not place all subscription orders through one agent. The library may work with more than one agent, some publishers will not work through agents, and some subscription packages cost substantially less if ordered directly from the publisher.

As helpful as the *LJ* feature and subscription agent reports are, it is almost always necessary to keep local price data. This data is especially valuable when combined with counts of periodical use. A spreadsheet or database containing the subscription price of every serial for every year, with use counts for as many years as data can be collected, is a highly valuable collection development tool. It contains data only on the titles actually in the library. Additional data on online journal use, department allocations, and notes can be added as needed. While time-consuming to create and maintain, such a database allows a variety of reports to be created, and it becomes more valuable with each year it is maintained. More about how to gather, record, and report on the use of serials will be discussed in the chapter on journal use.

Cost per Use. The cost per use of a serial is probably the single most useful bit of information for deciding whether or not to continue subscribing to the title, but it is not the only important factor. The cost per use is calculated by dividing the annual subscription price by the measured number of uses. For example, if a periodical costs $300 per year, and it is counted as used 30 times, the cost per use is $10. If cost and use data are available for multiple years, averages can be calculated for each title, and trends can be tracked. Cost per use provides better information for decision-making than cost alone. Some expensive journals are heavily used, and represent better value than less expensive, seldom used titles. If a $1,000 is cut from the budget, it can be tempting to simply cut one journal that costs $1,000. But that expensive periodical may actually be heavily used and, therefore, cost effective.

Average subscription prices vary widely among academic disciplines, as do rates of journal use. In academic libraries, it is important to consider cost per use relative to the serials within the disciplines. Cost per use comparisons across disciplines often place topic areas with higher prices and fewer users at a disadvantage. A benefit of allocating the serials budget among disciplines is that it allows comparison of cost per use within topic areas, helping to avoid bias against disciplines with relatively high costs per use. As discussed previously, whether a librarian chooses to continue subscriptions for disciplines with high average costs per use is a policy decision, rooted in the institution's mission and priorities.

Enrollment data typically kept by the college registrar may be used to assess the rates of use of titles within disciplines. This is done by dividing the measured uses of the titles in a discipline by the number of students enrolled in that discipline. The result suggests how many times, on average, students majoring in each discipline use the journals allocated to the discipline. Enrollment divided by uses is only an approximate measure because people other than students majoring in the discipline may use the allocated titles. Rates of journal use within disciplines may also be measured based on the number of courses offered or on the number of professors in the departments. Data on courses and professors may be easier to gather, but do not account for variation of enrollment in courses. Regardless of the method used, adjusting for the number of users can be more informative for collection development than relying on serials use counts alone, particularly when the institution expressly supports disciplines with relatively low enrollments.

Rankings and Recommended Lists.   Another source of information for helping to decide which journals may not be renewed is journal rankings. Among published sources, the most commonly used rankings are *Journal Citation Reports* (*JCR*) and Katz's *Magazines for Libraries*. These were discussed in detail in the section on selection tools. *Magazines for Libraries* is not really a source of rankings, but the lists of core journals for each topic area provide "best of " lists. The benefit of including rankings with cost and use data is that rankings add a measure of what *should* be used. Professors lament that students tend to use sources that are not sufficiently scholarly, and cite magazines like *Newsweek* when they should have cited something like *Political Science Quarterly*. Since *JCR* measures the frequency of citation in scholarly journals, and *Magazines for Libraries'* core lists are based on expert opinion, these two sources suggest which titles would be used by students in a perfect world.

The *JCR* and *Magazines for Libraries* are helpful, but locally produced rankings are a valuable supplement to those published sources of journal rankings. The most common method for creating a ranked list of serials locally is to create a survey and administer it to the faculty. Serial titles allocated to each academic department are listed and individual faculty are asked to mark each title on a scale. The criteria for ranking must be clearly explained on the survey and should be firmly based on the library's collection development policy. For example, if the collection development policy states that serials are for students' academic advancement, the scale could be based on, "How important is this title to your students' academic success in your courses?" The rating scale could be labeled "essential," "very important," "important," "optional," "not necessary." The labels can be quantified in typical Likert-scale fashion, where "essential" would be scored as 5 points, "very important" as 4 points, and so on. Assuming that all faculty members complete the survey, total scores for each title will give a good indication of how important the department as a whole deems each title. Serials with lower scores would be top candidates to not renew. The chief disadvantage in employing such a survey is that the return rate may be low. The results will thus be skewed in favor of the interests of faculty who bothered to fill out the survey.

One could reasonably argue that such skewing is acceptable because the faculty who cooperate with the library's efforts deserve to have their opinions count more; however, students could end up being inconvenienced through no fault of their own, and their interests should be duly considered. It is also important to remember that faculty come and go and curricula are revised, so rankings derived in one survey can be expected to change over time. Public and special libraries can create rankings with the same method, by having patrons complete the surveys.

Polling users of the serials collection on their opinion of subscribed titles has several benefits. First, the survey shows them that the library values their input and thus fosters collaboration. Second, it provides a means for averaging the opinions of individuals and presenting them back to the group objectively. Third, it raises the awareness among those polled of just which serials are in the collection. Finally, if cuts are necessary, those involved know that they have had input. In short, polling users is a politically astute move.

Subscription prices, rates of use, number of patrons likely to use serials, and rankings are quantifiable criteria. The other criteria discussed in the section on selection of serials in the chapter on work flows are important, but more difficult to quantify. Those factors worth considering include quality of printing and binding, reputation of the publisher, indexing, whether peer reviewed, and availability online. Since the quality of online copies and assurances of stability of content varies among full-text databases, the characteristics of the sources of online content must be carefully considered before canceling print in lieu of online access.

Cancellation Projects

Adding new serials to a library's collection makes patrons happy. Canceling subscriptions may go unnoticed, but that is unlikely. Serial cancellations are usually only grudgingly accepted, and often only after a fight. Faculty and other patrons can become quite angry when their favorite titles no longer arrive in the library. A cancellation project must be done with care, attention to detail, good communication, and political sensitivity.

Paul Metz (1992) has described steps that should be taken to successfully implement a cancellation or nonrenewal project. Paraphrasing Metz, the steps to be taken are:

Step 1:   Measure Use, to help identify titles that are seldom used and provide objective data that can be shared with others.

Step 2:   Do It, since subscription inflation will most assuredly exceed increases in the library's budget, and procrastination will only make the problem worse.

Step 3:   Put One Person in Charge, so there is one contact person, and one person who can devote their energy to the process.

Step 4:   Start Early, at least six months before decisions must be made.

Step 5:   Automate, and integrate into one database the available information on titles, prices, and use.

Step 6:   Control the Momentum by Nominating Titles. Do not leave it up to patrons to start from scratch. Suggest more cuts than are needed to allow for some proposed cut subscriptions to be continued when compromise is necessary.

Step 7:   Think in Terms of Dollars and Prioritize, since the ultimate goal is to make the subscriptions fit within a certain budget. Get everyone to think in terms of cost-benefit analysis. Acknowledge that all the titles are nice to have, but force people to ask if they are worth the tradeoffs imposed by the subscription prices.

Step 8:   Solicit feedback so that affected patrons know their concerns are being heard even if they do not get all they want.

Step 9:   Be Flexible, willing to find creative ways to meet needs within the budget.

Step 10:   Honesty is the Best Policy. Be completely open about the process, the budget, and the data. Be prepared to share information in a timely fashion to anyone affected by the process. In Metz's words, "There aren't that many people out there who care anyway, and those who do probably expect your budget to be more irrational than it really is. Daylight is the best antidote to the shadows of paranoia" (Metz 1992, p. 80). People who actually care about the serials budget are rare indeed, and should always be considered allies. If they disagree about an allocation, take them seriously, and respect and value their input.

Step 11:   Use a Variety of Criteria in Making Decisions, including cost per use, faculty input, indexing coverage, and librarian input.

Step 12:   Scale Down to a Future List so data collection for the next cancellation project does not have to start from scratch.

Step 13:   Publicize What You Have Done so patrons, administrators, and colleagues at other libraries understand the process and its results (Metz 1992).

The gist of best practice in serials cancellation projects is to obtain good data, organize it into one database, plan ahead, be fair, be open, be firm, be reasonable, and welcome input. If the process is fully described and everyone affected is treated equitably, the project will succeed. The librarian charged with the unpleasant and difficult duty of canceling serials must plan on communicating frequently and spending the effort required to collaborate effectively with whomever is involved in the project.

This chapter has provided an overview of the process of budgeting for, selecting, and deselecting serials. The variety of tools used to support decision-making combine published information with locally gathered data. Every time a serial is added or removed from a library's subscriptions, the change impacts workflows. The next chapter presents issues and practices in the day-to-day work of managing a serials collection.

SUGGESTIONS FOR FURTHER READING

For a recently published general treatment of collection development, see Peggy Johnson, *Fundamentals of Collection Development & Management* (Chicago: American Library Association, 2004). Johnson's work includes treatments of electronic resources and collaborative collection development. A slightly less recent but well-regarded work on collection development is G. Edward Evans and Margaret R. Zarnosky, *Developing Library and Information Center Collections* (Englewood, CO: Libraries Unlimited, 2000). Also valuable is F. Wilfred Lancaster's *If You Want to Evaluate Your Library* (Champaign: University of Illinois, Graduate School of Library and Information Science, 1988), which addresses advantages and disadvantages of various methods of evaluating collections in various situations, and cites studies using the methods.

Discussion of collection development policies with references to helpful materials may be found in Richard J. Wood and Frank W. Hoffmann, *Library Collection Development Policies: A Reference and Writers' Handbook* (Lanham, MD: Scarecrow Press, 2002).

The user's guides in *Ulrich's International Periodicals Directory* and EBSCO's *The Serials Directory: An International Reference Book* contain clear explanations of the elements of the entries, including abbreviations used. Familiarity with the abbreviations and codes is necessary to use the directories to help assess the usefulness of a title to a library collection. *Magazines for Libraries*, edited by Cheryl LaGuardia, is published by R.R. Bowker each December. As mentioned in the chapter, http://ulrichsweb.com incorporates the reviews published in *Magazines for Libraries*.

Paul Metz's "Thirteen steps to avoiding bad luck in a serials cancellation project," *Journal of Academic Librarianship*, 18(2), May 1992, 76–82, contains tips for a successful serials cancellation project. Although somewhat dated, the article is still accurate and relevant. Metz does not emphasize employing cost per use, but he does highlight the need to gather and consider use data.

REFERENCES

Metz, Paul. 1992. Thirteen steps to avoiding bad luck in a serials cancellation project. *Journal of Academic Librarianship* 18(2): 76–82.

Van Orsdel, Lee, and Born, Kathleen. 2004. Closing in on Open Access *Library Journal* 129(7): 45–50.

Van Orsdel, Lee, and Born, Kathleen. 2005. Choosing sides. *Library Journal* 130(7): 43–48.

Van Orsdel, Lee and Born, Kathleen. 2006. Journals in the time of Google. *Library Journal* 131(7): 39–44.

Chapter 4

Serials Workflow in Libraries

The life cycle of serials from initial selection through receipt and processing to life on the library's shelves usually extends far beyond any one serials librarian's tenure. A newly hired serials librarian will probably inherit a collection, a list of subscribed titles, and established processes. It is important to respect the value of the existing system while being willing to question established practices and look for improved ways of managing the serials work flow.

Magazines, journals, and series have a life cycle in the library, from acquisition, to useful life on the shelves, to possible shifting to storage or perhaps removal from the collection. A serials collection steadily develops as the printed issues arrive day by day, slowly growing and changing in response to what publishers sell and what the library buys. Developing a print serials collection is a long-term process requiring attention to both day-to-day detail and the long-term value of the collection to patrons.

This chapter focuses almost entirely on the work processes involved in managing print serial subscriptions. Management of subscriptions to online journals and full-text databases requires very different processes. These are addressed in Chapter 2, "Remote Access Serials." The details of managing the work flow vary from one library to another, but certain goals and tasks are common among libraries. The goals and tasks are organized here as: ordering, receiving, claiming, shelving and access, and maintenance. The chapter closes with a discussion of binding and weeding.

ORDERING

The defining characteristic of serials "intended to be continued indefinitely" makes ordering them somewhat different from ordering books, videos, and most other materials acquired by libraries. The most common method of ordering serials is by subscription, whereby publishers are paid in advance for issues scheduled to arrive over a specific period. Publishers may offer subscriptions for two or three years, but librarians usually order one-year subscriptions because the accountants may not allow payments for something received over multiple years. Another way of ordering serials is by a standing order, which is more common with series but the method used by some publishers of periodicals. With a standing order, a library commits to buying volumes without knowing the price ahead of time. The obvious drawback to standing orders is the inability to precisely budget for them. If inflation from one volume to the next is reasonable, the increase is not a problem; but if the price doubles, the commitment can be difficult to cover. The advantage to standing orders for serials is that all volumes will be received without having to place orders for each one. Placing a standing order is convenient when a library is confident that every volume in a series will be desired for the collection.

Serials Subscription Agents

Orders placed by subscription or by standing order can be made directly with publishers or through a subscription agent. Direct orders to publishers save the roughly 3 percent fee charged by the serials subscription agent, but require the librarian to make the contact and prepare the invoice. Someone in the library or accounts payable office has to process payments. If issues do not arrive on time, the librarian must contact the publisher. All of these steps take time that is probably worth more than 3 percent of the subscription price.

Serials subscription agents, or serials vendors, subscription services, or serials jobbers, offer a range of services to save libraries time and money in the serials ordering process. The essential functions of serials subscription agents are to centralize and manage the process of placing orders, making payments to publishers, and claiming missing issues. Serials subscription agents also create, upon a customer's request, a variety of reports on the serials a librarian has (or has not) ordered. A great advantage to the serials librarian in using a serials subscription agent is consolidating ordering, payment, and claims. Savings are realized whether one or more serials subscription agents are used. Orders are consolidated and tracked together, both U.S. and foreign. Payments can be made with one big check in one currency, rather than scores of checks to many addresses denominated in various currencies. Claims go through a unified process, and the serials subscription agent tracks information about known delays in publication, cessations, and title changes. The serials subscription agent's database of information about publishers, prices, and titles brings together data that would be very time-consuming for librarians to gather on their own.

Because so much of any library's budget may be taken up with subscriptions to serials, great care must be taken in the choice of serials subscription agent. Even an established company can have problems as happened with divine/Rowecom/Faxon. One of the biggest news stories in the library world in 2003 was the bankruptcy of the serials subscription agent divine/Rowecom/Faxon. The Faxon Company was the first subscription agent to operate in the United States. It had been in business since 1918 and had a long-standing reputation for excellent service. Beginning in 1994, a series of legal moves and mergers resulted in a company known as divine/RoweCom/Faxon Library Services. The company declared Chapter 11 bankruptcy in late 2002 after cash generated by the traditional subscription agency services wasdiverted into nonprofitable company activities. The immediate consequence of the bankruptcy to library customers of divine/Rowecom/Faxon was that the subscription money they paid never reached the publishers. An especially disturbing part of the bankruptcy was the complete lack of communication with customers. In a message to the SERIALST discussion group on December 17, 2002, Amanda Zeigler wrote:

> I . . . have just heard disturbing rumors that Faxon/Rowecom/divine may be filing for Chapter 11. They have yet to place and pay for over 150 periodical titles that we have ordered from them, and we paid them in June. Has anyone on the list heard the same rumors? If you have found yourself in the same situation, have you had a chance to develop a plan of dealing with this? Any and all information is welcome at this point. Please feel free to reply to the list as I'm sure the information will be applicable to anyone in the same situation.

The replies on SERIALST to this message made clear that many others had been given no information by the company of either the impending bankruptcy or that publishers had not been paid. The bankruptcy created major headaches for all serials librarians who used Faxon as a subscription agent and shook confidence in agents in general. Astute librarians took the fiasco as a reinforcing lesson that it is good practice to be aware of the financial health of the companies they rely on for materials and services. Since acquisitions librarians are charged with responsible stewardship of the library's budget, monitoring the viability of vendors is wise.

In the wake of the Faxon/Rowecom/divine bankruptcy, many publishers graced subscriptions and absorbed the losses. EBSCO Subscription Services acquired the subscription services portion of divine/RoweCom/Faxon and worked with publishers to fulfill as many library subscriptions as possible. This acquisition made EBSCO Subscription Services an even larger agency. EBSCO worked very hard to help libraries and publishers through the difficult time, and deserves recognition for their efforts. One must hope that they remain good corporate citizens now that they have less competition, although other serials subscription agents vendors are available.

Competent and reliable subscription agencies remaining in business besides EBSCO include Karger Libri Subscription Agency, Swets Information Services, Harrassowitz Periodicals Acquisitions Services, Wolper Subscripton Services, and W.T. Cox Subscriptions; yet regrettably few companies are left that are capable of handling the number and variety of serials required by large academic libraries. The lack of choice and competition among serials subscription agencies is a concern. The choice of vendors currently available may be found in the list of members of the Association of Subscription Agents and Intermediaries (http://www.subscription-agents.org/). This lack of many choices may make the task of choosing a serials subscription agent even more difficult.

Choosing a Serials Subscription Agent

As mentioned earlier, ordering serials directly from each publisher is feasible; but most librarians find the services of a serials subscription agent to be well worth their fees or handling charges. The quality of service that librarians should expect from a serials vendor encompasses timely renewal of subscriptions, accurate invoices, prompt responses to claims, and rapid placement of orders. The country the agent is based in may be important, as agencies located in the same country or region as publishers may be better able to promptly handle orders and claims. As the Faxon fiasco demonstrated, the financial health of the agent is also an important consideration. Librarians may choose to contract with more than one subscription agent, to take advantage of regional expertise and avoid relying exclusively on any one vendor.

The Serials Section Acquisitions Committee of the Association for Library Collections & Technical Services (ALCTS) published a slim but highly informative *Guide to Performance Evaluation of Serials Vendors* (1997). The goals of vendor performance evaluation are to judge the vendor's adherence to the terms of the business relationship, and to assess the library's accountability in serving patrons and spending funds (ALCTS 1997, p. 4). Library staff, vendors, and publishers all benefit by raising awareness of their own and each other's practices. Effective evaluation of vendor performance addresses each stage of the life cycle of a serial. The *Guide* lists questions to address concerning the vendor's performance on these points:

- Accurate ordering of newly added titles
- Frequency and success rate of claims
- Information about and billing for titles with delayed publication
- Renewals without gaps or overlaps
- Timely ordering of standing order volumes
- Information about and cross-references for changes of title, frequency, or publisher

- Timely notification of substantial increases in subscription rates
- Accurate and timely processing of cancellations
- Success in obtaining credit for ceased titles (ALCTS 1997, pp.10–11).

The relationship between library and serials subscription agent is, in many ways, a partnership. Just as a vendor is expected to provide accurate and timely service, library staff is responsible for ordering, renewing, and canceling accurately and on schedule. Problems must be communicated with the vendor in a timely fashion, and should be handled in a spirit of mutual cooperation to resolve the issue. Serials ordered by whatever means begin arriving in the library, and the next task involves records of the reception of serials.

RECEIVING

When the ordering process goes smoothly, issues are received continuously from one year to the next. Gaps in expected issues will not occur except for titles that the librarian has cancelled, or that the publisher has ceased publishing, or that have changed title. Before librarians implemented computers to record the receipt of serials, the standard practice was to keep a Kardex file, a steel cabinet with shallow drawers holding cards for each subscribed title, to record receipt of issues. When each issue of a serial arrived, the date of receipt was written in the appropriate box on the card. To check if an expected issue was missing, a staff member either had to notice the previous issue was not received, or manually flip through the Kardex to look for boxes that should not be blank.

Integrated Library Systems

The Integrated library systems (ILSs) have replaced Kardex files in most libraries. Once initial data has been entered into an ILS, receipt of periodical issues is more efficient than keeping a Kardex. Some time is saved in the check-in process, but the real benefit comes with claiming. The ILS can create reports of missing issues that greatly speed the process of making claims. The procedure for creating serials records varies among library systems, but it typically involves entering information separate from the bibliographic record in an acquisitions or serials module. Information to be entered typically includes publication patterns, budget allocations, claiming cycles (how long after the issue is expected the system reports it missing), and special processing notes.

If records are created in the acquisitions or serials module of an ILS, some one has to link a bibliographic record to the record in the separate ILS module. If the ILS is used to check in serials, the expected publication pattern, the expected interval at which a serial is expected to be published as based on the caption, must be entered for each title. The caption is the word, phrase, or abbreviation in the serial that indicates how each issue will be designated. Examples include volume, issue, part, year, season, or month. The publication pattern also includes the relationship of the numbering systems, for example, whether issues start with one with each new volume, or whether the issue numbers continue consecutively. Systems vary in how familiar one needs to be with MARC Format for Holdings Data (MFHD) to correctly enter publication patterns, a process addressed in Chapter 5, "Bibliographic Control of Serials." An ILS typically provides a list of the most common patterns to choose from and a calendar-based template to allow editing of the common patterns. Familiarity with MARC format holdings data is helpful for understanding why the system will easily handle some variations in patterns, but others are intractable. Unfortunately, publication patterns usually cannot be migrated from one ILS to another. When a library migrates systems, the serials staff can count on having to enter publication patterns for every serial currently received.

Publication Patterns Initiative

In order to avoid unnecessary duplication of effort, Cooperative Online Serials (CONSER) created a Task Force on Publication Patterns and Holdings in the 1990s to investigate the feasibility of sharing publication pattern data. This grew into the Publications Pattern Initiative, which is now in full operation. The initiative got off to a strong start with the loading of the Harvard libraries' holdings data in 2001. At the heart of the initiative is implementation by all libraries of MFHD. The publication patterns to be shared are standardized in MARC format. Since libraries have had to convert from descriptions of holdings that had no standard format, the conversion of holdings into MFHD is a major undertaking.

Now that the CONSER Publication Patterns Initiative is in place, new records include the publication pattern in MARC format in field 891. A serials cataloger can cut and paste the publication pattern into the holdings record. If the pattern must be entered into an ILS's acquisitions module, the information in the 891 can be used for reference. This is helpful because many serials do not describe their publication patterns in the issue in hand. For instance, the first issue of a serial received might be captioned Vol. 10, no. 1, January, 2004. One cannot tell from the single issue if the serial is published monthly or quarterly. Other librarians who have cataloged and received the periodical over time have determined the pattern. The CONSER Publication Pattern Initiative facilitates the sharing of this experience.

Routing

Check-in procedures vary depending on the ILS used, staffing, and the needs of the patrons. An example of a practice that varies is routing. Some libraries route serials soon after they arrive to a list of patrons known to be interested in the serial. The purpose of routing is to ensure that the patrons most interested in the title see it in a timely manner. In a public library, some serials may be routed among the library staff. In a special library, titles may be routed to a researcher particularly interested in the most recently published articles on a topic. The disadvantages of routing are that issues are out of the library as they make the rounds, and some readers may not send the issues along in a timely manner. An advantage of online journals is that patrons can be alerted by e-mail when a new issue is available, and no print issue need be routed.

Receiving Process Choices

Checking issues in the ILS has several benefits. The library can display in the catalog the most recent issue that has arrived. Seeing the receipt history on screen, as each issue is checked in, alerts the librarian to changes in publication patterns, title changes, mergers, and splits. The check-in records also provide the data needed for claiming missing issues and automating the binding schedule.

Checking in serials is often done by staff other than the serials librarian at academic, public, and special libraries. Staff and/or student workers are trained to bring up the check-in record in the ILS, carefully check that the title and caption match the record on screen, and click a "check-in" box. If something does not match or seems unusual, the issue is given to a supervisor responsible for serials. The supervisor determines if there has been a change in publication pattern or title, or if the title is new to the library. Adjustments to the publication pattern and expected issues of a title can be made in the ILS at this point when needed. After checking the issue into the ILS, other, more clerical tasks are necessary.

Any "property of" stamping, call number labeling, and security stripping is done before issues are shelved. Exactly what is done to mark the issue as owned by the library varies, but it is typical to put some kind of ownership stamp on the issues. If periodicals are classified, call number labels will be attached, either at check in or after issues are bound. In cases where a cover title is different from the serial title, a label may be added to the cover to indicate the correct title. This is important in collections arranged alphabetically. Security strips, narrow adhesive metallic tapes, are placed in an inconspicuous place in the issues to prevent their being taken through the library's security system. Strips can be put in every issue or can be embedded in the binding of bound volumes. Creating item records for issues or volumes is another choice.

A major decision to be made by a librarian is whether to create item records for each serial issue or volume. Item records and barcodes can be created at check in or when volumes are bound. A separate item with one barcode corresponding to one item is usually created in the ILS for anything that will circulate. The advantage of creating item records is that issues or volumes are individually identified for circulation and for tracking use.

Rick Anderson of the University of Nevada, Reno, caused a great deal of discussion among serials librarians with his choice to do away with most checking in of periodicals. He and his library administrators decided that the costs in time and energy needed to check in issues were greater than the benefit to patrons. Since most issues arrive on time, and there is never any guarantee that issues stay in the library after arrival, it seemed worth the risk to skip the check-in procedure. However, his library had a high proportion of electronic periodicals relative to print (Anderson and Zink 2003). Whether librarians choose to check in periodicals or not, holdings records are needed.

Holdings Records Maintenance

Holdings records indicate which volumes and issues of a serial are in the library collection. Holdings records are distinct from the bibliographic records to which they are linked. Before integrated library systems, periodical holdings were recorded manually as notations on cards in the catalog or as a separate list. The time required to manually update holdings limited the currency of holdings records. In the days before integrated library systems, the librarian in charge of the Kardex would be responsible for answering questions about specific current issues, for instance "Did the September issue of the *Journal of Confusion Studies* arrive yet?" Such questions could come from patrons, reference librarians, or interlibrary loan staff. By the 1970s, lists could be generated from a database maintained by the librarians and printed from a mainframe computer. Printouts on paper and/or microform would be run only once a year or so. Once librarians had access to personal computers, lists could be maintained and printed off within the library.

Keeping a holdings list separate from the records in the ILS still has some advantages. A holdings list can be created in HTML, a word processing program, spreadsheet, or database. When a spreadsheet or database is kept for tracking the budget and use, relatively little effort is required to generate a title list from it. Some patrons and reference librarians still like to refer to a printed list. It can be difficult to get an ILS to report data just as one would like, so using a word processing or database program on a PC to maintain a title list can give greater control over its appearance and make it easier to print. Another benefit of keeping a separate list is that it provides a means for error checking by comparing the holdings recorded in the ILS and the separately maintained list. A printed list is also handy for shelf reading and shifting volumes. Because title lists can be reported from integrated library systems, many libraries choose to rely on the ILS alone for maintaining holdings records. The next step, claiming, comes with a missing issue.

CLAIMING

To claim an issue means to send the publisher notice that an expected issue has not arrived on schedule. An issue may be late for many possible reasons. It may have been lost in the mail, not yet published, the title may have changed, or the publisher may no longer have the library on record as a current subscriber. Claims can also be for issues that arrived but were damaged in the mail or contain production errors such as blank pages or missing pages.

As discussed earlier, one of the major advantages of ordering periodicals through a serials subscription agent is that the agent tracks delays in publication, title changes, and subscription payments. If the library uses an agent, claims are made through the agent rather than directly with the publisher. Whether or not an agent is used, the serials librarian establishes a routine schedule for designated staff to run claims reports. An ILS can automatically send claims to the agent using the EDI X12 standard for communicating claims data. However, accuracy of claims is improved when staff check the initial claims list against what is actually on the shelf to make certain the claimed issue did not arrive, or arrived but was not recorded as having arrived.

Unfortunately, claiming is not always successful. Publishers can give a variety of reasons for not sending a replacement copy. Dogged persistence can help, but it is likely that some issues will never be obtained, and gaps will remain in the collection. While some libraries do not receive expected issues, other libraries receive duplicate issues. Serials subscription agents supplement claims to publishers with alternative means of obtaining missing issues. For example, EBSCO Subscription Services has a Missing Copy Bank and W.T. Cox has a Replacement Issue Library for their customers to donate duplicates and request missing issues. Another alternative to claiming is to offer or request issues on the Backmed (http://nalist1.swets.com/mailman/listinfo/backmed) or Backserv (http://nalist1.swets.com/mailman/listinfo/backserv) e-mail discussion groups hosted by Swets Information Services. Issues of serials subscribed to online present a special problem for claiming.

For journals in aggregated full-text packages, it makes little sense to attempt to track whether titles are up-to-date. Librarians subscribe to the packages as wholes, and the titles in them do not substitute for individual subscriptions. It is best to leave it to the vendor to maintain the issues in the database. Of course, it is still important to report any missing articles when one runs across them, but the report goes to the database vendor, not the publisher.

Librarians may also subscribe to individual titles online. With print subscriptions, the presumption when claiming is that the issue was published, and the other subscribers got theirs, but the expected issue did not arrive. With online subscriptions, there is no reason to think that one library is getting an issue before another. The question is whether the online connection to the most recently published issue is working. The exception would be when content is loaded on the subscriber's servers, as in the case of OhioLINK's Electronic Journal Collection (EJC). For the typical contract for access to serial content, the online equivalent to claiming is verifying that patrons have online access to the title. Failure of access may be caused by problems with the publisher's server, network problems, or patron authentication problems. Re-establishing the connection requires determining the source of the problem, which usually involves at least the systems librarian and possibly also the institution's technical support staff. While online subscriptions do not require shelf storage, print titles do.

SHELVING AND ACCESS

Decisions on where to shelve serials and whether to classify them will most likely be made long before a new serials librarian begins work at a library. Since changing shelving arrangements is a major undertaking, a newly hired serials librarian will probably inherit a system and be forced to live with it. When new library buildings and additions are constructed, choosing how serials will be shelved may fall on a serials librarian's shoulders. Shelving arrangements may vary by type, monographic series, conference and annuals, or periodicals.

Shelving Arrangement

Monographic series are typically cataloged and classified as individual titles and shelved with other circulating books. Other serials like conference proceedings and annuals may also be treated as books. In fact, any serial can be classified and shelved with books in a unified collection, which facilitates browsing the stacks for all print materials held on a topic. The drawback to shelving serials with monographs is that a large amount of empty shelf space must be reserved for future issues. Estimating how much shelf space will be needed is more difficult with serials since they cease and change titles, but estimating how many new monographs will be added is also difficult. Ample room for growth must be allowed to avoid frequent shifting of volumes, which is very time-consuming and annoys some patrons. This is one of the reasons periodicals are often shelved in a separate area.

It is common practice in libraries to shelve periodicals separately from monographs and monographic series. Three basic considerations with a separate periodicals area are whether stacks will be open or closed, whether current issues will be shelved with older volumes, and whether serials will be classified or shelved alphabetically by title. Closed stacks are accessible only by the library staff who retrieve items on request. Closed stacks have the advantages of helping protect the collection from damage, controlling use, making it easier to measure use. Also the space saving advantages of storage facilities described next can be realized with closed stacks. Closed stacks have the disadvantages of requiring additional staffing and preventing patrons from browsing the collection at their leisure.

Current issues of periodicals are shelved separately from older issues for two reasons. Patrons like browsing through the most recent issues without combing through the stacks, and a separate area for current issues can facilitate a smooth work flow for binding. Serials staff can go through and easily gather all the completed volumes of loose issues and send them to the bindery. The bound issues are then shelved in the separate stacks of bound volumes. The loose current issues may be arranged alphabetically, even if the bound volumes are classified.

No standard exists for whether serials are classified or arranged alphabetically by title. The general trend is for libraries with smaller periodical collections (less than 1,000 titles) to alphabetize, and libraries with larger collections to classify, but many smaller libraries classify their periodicals and some larger libraries shelve periodicals alphabetically. An advantage of alphabetizing is that once a patron knows a title, they do not have to look up its call number. The advantages of classifying are that periodicals on the same topic are shelved together, and succeeding and preceding titles are kept together, as long as the subject area remains the same. Either method works, but classifying can make browsing easier for patrons. The caveat to this advantage is that since many serials can be classified in more than one classification, patrons may still have to look in several areas to find the journals covering a topic area.

Shelf Space Requirements

Serials fill a great deal of shelving, and providing shelf space is expensive. New library space costs roughly $100 a square foot to build. A reasonable rule of thumb is that ten volumes can be housed per square foot, taking into account aisles, reading areas, staircases, and so on. Therefore, it costs roughly $10 to provide the building space for one volume. Once built, the space has to be lit, heated, cooled, and kept secure. These high costs cause librarians to seek more affordable ways to house serials. The basic approaches to saving shelf space are to use compact shelving, to create separate storage facilities, to acquire serials on microform, and to digitize serials.

Compact shelving comes in many varieties. A common one for public areas is movable shelving that slides along tracks, allowing stacks to be right against one another with no aisles in between. When needed, the stacks are moved by hand cranks or electric motors. Compact shelving allows about double the amount of shelf space for the square footage. Since it can be inconvenient for patrons if they have to wait for one person to finish before they can move the shelves, compact shelving is less appropriate for collections receiving constant use. They may also discourage browsing because considerate patrons may wish to avoid delaying others. Some patrons in the aisles of moving compact shelves may be concerned that they will be squashed. However, safety features make the risk very low of anyone being hurt in movable compact shelving.

Separate storage areas are an option for saving space within the library. A storage facility separate from the public area of the library is typically accessible only to library staff. Periodicals in a storage area can be shelved with narrower aisles, taller shelving, and no regard for the aesthetic appearance of the stacks. Some large libraries, led by the example set by Harvard, have created high-density storage in special warehouses that use techniques to maximize the volumes stored per square foot. Warehousing serials in this way can save money. But the "Harvard model" makes volumes less accessible to patrons because it takes time for their requested materials to be retrieved. On the other hand, the volumes are more accessible than if they had been weeded! If serials are put into a storage area, the use of titles should be tracked. Items in storage tend to get relatively little use, so a checklist of titles retrieved is relatively easy to maintain. The storage checklist allows the librarian to see which titles get enough use to justify moving them back to the public area, if possible. The checklist can also indicate those titles that have gotten no use over the years and are thus prime candidates for weeding.

Acquiring serials on microfiche or microfilm saves a great deal of space, even though the savings are somewhat offset by the space needed for the microform cabinets and readers. A policy of acquiring periodicals in microform can mean paying for titles twice, once for the current issues in print, and again for the microform version. Patrons tend to dislike using microforms, and the machines to read and print from them are expensive to buy and to maintain. Nevertheless, microforms are an excellent medium for preserving information for long periods of time in relatively little space. Since microforms exist in a physical form that can be read with a light source and magnification, it is unlikely that the information on them will have to be converted in the future to a different medium to be read. This gives microform a significant long-range advantage over digitization. Future availability of microform reader/printers could be a problem, but enough micro-film is in libraries to ensure a market for the machines for some time to come. Microform readers that easily integrate with desktop computers and networked printers are already available.

The last method, digitizing serials, has been assisted by the creation of JSTOR, a project intended to provide high-quality, online, archival access to journals commonly held by research libraries. In their words,

> JSTOR began as an effort to ease the increasing problems faced by libraries seeking to provide adequate stack space for the long runs of backfiles of scholarly journals The basic idea was to convert the back issues of paper journals into electronic formats that would allow savings in space (and in capital costs associated with that space) while simultaneously improving access to the journal content. It was also hoped that the project might offer a solution to preservation problems associated with storing paper volumes. http://www.jstor.org/about/background.html

The creation of JSTOR required working closely with publishers since it would be a violation of copyright for a librarian to scan in periodicals and make their content available online. Other digitization projects use publications that are in the public domain. The Library of Congress' American Memory Project http:// memory.loc.gov/ammem/ includes content from some serials. Several vendors are creating collections of digitized periodicals to which librarians can subscribe. The vendors pay fees to copyright holders, which are covered by the cost of subscriptions to the packages of digitized serials. Even if copyright management can be arranged, the cost of scanning, storing, and providing access to serials online is prohibitive for most libraries. Cooperative efforts such as JSTOR will probably be the means whereby serials are digitally archived. Digitally archived remote access serials are available at patrons' computers. Patrons accustomed to reading at their desktops may want to use print volumes of serials outside the library.

Access: Circulating Serials

Some librarians choose policies that allow periodicals to be checked out of the library, but many do not. Some librarians allow faculty to check journals out, but not students. The primary reason to limit circulation of periodicals is the same reason reference books are not circulated; both need to be available at all times for patrons to use. Aside from the concern with an issue being out when one needs it, circulating periodicals may increase the risk of creating gaps in runs of titles when items are not returned. Gaps also occur with collections which do not circulate when volumes and issues are stolen from libraries. Circulation records indicate the patron who checked a volume out, while no such record exists for a stolen volume. But when a security system is in place to reduce theft, the overall risk of losing volumes may be greater for a circulating serials collection.

For those periodicals which get used only a handful of times per year patrons can take journals home with low risk of inconveniencing other patrons. The risk of two patrons wanting the same volume at once is further reduced if the print issue is also available online. As mentioned previously, when periodicals circulate, item records and bar codes should be created for each volume or issue. Preserving and keeping track of circulated serials is made easier when volumes are durably bound.

BINDING

A T-shirt for serials librarians reads "Free the Bound Periodicals." Behind the joke lies a real question, "why bind them in the first place?" Despite the advantages of binding periodical issues into bound volumes, it is not absolutely essential to do so. Several options are available for issues that are not bound. One option is to discard the issues after a period of time. Retaining issues for a limited time makes sense when issues are replaced by microfilm, are deemed to have little long-term appeal to patrons, or they are simply too bulky and unwieldy to keep. Another option is to simply shelve the issues as they are. They will be more difficult to keep in order, and they may suffer more physical damage in use, but avoiding binding saves money. Not binding does not work well with tall, thin issues. Issues that will not stand on their bottom edge without support will tend to sag, slide, and then fall off the shelves, especially if their covers are printed on glossy paper. A third option is to put the issues on the shelves in cases popularly known as Princeton files. These plastic, steel, or cardboard boxes are designed to neatly hold a year's worth of magazines. At about $2–$8 a piece, Princeton files help keep loose issues organized at a lower cost than professional binding.

Serials collections unfortunately experience disorganization and lost items, particularly in open stacks. Inconsiderate patrons will shelve items in the wrong place, remove pages from bound periodicals, take entire issues outside the library, and not return them. Since bound volumes can be more difficult to surreptitiously remove from the library than individual issues, not binding may increase the need to replace a missing issue. Replacement of older issues can be expensive if the issue is available at all. Binding issues helps prevent the loss of individual issues of a volume in the years after they have been received and shelved. Binding helps protect the issues during handling and photocopying, it keeps them conveniently grouped together, and helps keep them neat on the shelves. The bindings can also provide a clearer label of the title, volume, and year on the spine than would be found on the individual issues. Notes on the spines of bound volumes can indicate if there are any missing issues. Any serial may or may not be bound by the library, and the librarian may choose in house or commercial binding processes for periodicals and other serials.

Periodicals may be bound "in-house" meaning in the library, or binding may be outsourced to commercial binding services that specialize in binding materials for libraries. Several methods exist for binding in-house. Basically, they involve some combination of sewing, gluing, and taping. Various machines exist to facilitate binding; each use materials suited to the particular method. In house binding is adequate, but most methods are not as durable or attractive as professional binding. The cost of binding in house can be substantially less than professional binding, but it depends on the costs of labor and materials. Binding is a time-consuming process requiring significant hours of labor. When labor and materials costs are compared to the quality of the finished bound volumes, many librarians choose to have serials professionally bound.

The Library Binding Institute (1986) has published a *Standard for Library Binding*, and ANSI/NISO/LBI Z39.78-2000 describes the standard for binding materials for use in libraries, including periodicals. The front matter of the NISO Library Binding standard at http://www.niso.org/standards/resources/Z39-78.pdf includes a list of certified library binders. The gist of the standard is that the binding should be strong so the binding does not tear or lose issues or pages. Also, the binding should allow the pages to be opened That is, a patron should be able to press the bound volume onto a photocopier to get a whole page to copy without damaging the binding. Because this type of binding requires special machinery to bind according to the standard, there is a market for certified library binders. The going rate in 2005 is about $8–$10 per volume to have issues bound professionally. When issues are sent out for binding, the librarian invests staff time in gathering the issues, putting them in order, providing any special instructions, and monitoring timely receipt of the bound volumes.

Serials that are bound in-house or sent to a bindery should be processed on a regular schedule. Unless the collection is very small, there are too many items to process in a short time. It is best to divide the number of volumes to be bound by the months when workers are available, and plan to do that many each month. It is important to account for the fact that many titles will be bound in more than one volume per year. ILS reports can be set up to periodically list titles scheduled to be bound.

Patrons will be inconvenienced when the issues they are looking for are out being bound. A list should be kept for reference to check if a missing issue is being bound. A lost issue can be requested on interlibrary loan (ILL), but an issue at the bindery is forbidden by ILL rules to be requested via ILL. For patrons, it is important to minimize the turnaround time in binding. Volumes are unavailable to patrons from the time issues are pulled from the shelves until newly bound volumes are reshelved, whether issues are bound in-house or sent to a bindery. In academic libraries, it is preferable to concentrate binding activities during breaks; although the student workers typically needed to help gather issues and prepare them for binding are away at those times.

Missing issues present a special problem for binding. Ideally, the missing issue will be replaced before a volume is bound. If a title comes up on the schedule for binding when a missing issue has been claimed, binding should be delayed until the claim has been resolved. Similarly, if current periodicals circulate, issues may be out of the library when the serial is scheduled to be bound. It is much easier and cheaper to delay binding than to redo a binding. If the missing issue was received but is missing from the shelf, some time should be allowed for it to be found. The issue may have been stolen, but it may also simply be misplaced somewhere within the library.

The cost of binding periodicals is a normal part of a library's budget. How many volumes are sent to commercial binders, how many are bound in-house, and how many are left unbound are determined largely by the funds available. To budget for binding, the serials librarian must have a good estimate of how many volumes need to be bound in a year and how much it will cost for each volume. A silver lining to journal cancellation projects is that the total cost of binding can be reduced as the number of volumes received goes down. But it takes three years from the cancellations until the savings are realized, one year to make the cancellation decisions and not renew the subscriptions, the year for the issues to not arrive, and the year when they would have been bound. Another decision for preservation of serials is which to store over time and which to weed.

WEEDING

Weeding is the removal from the collection of items deemed of less value to patrons than the value to the library of the shelf space taken. Since shelf space runs out if new building space is not added, weeding serials is often necessary. Weeding is difficult because the selection of volumes to discard can never be based on more than educated guesses; however, low-use titles are very expensive to keep on the shelves. Journal use studies have consistently shown that some titles get very little use, and some are not used at all. Rates of use of some titles drops with the passage of time, as their content becomes less timely. How quickly rates of use drop after serials are published varies from discipline to discipline, but it is a first consideration in weeding.

Records of use help, because patterns of use tend to carry into the future. Fussler and Simon (1969) concluded that measuring a five-year pattern of use can give a valid prediction of future use of volumes in research libraries. However, past patterns of use do not always accurately predict future use. Changes in patron populations, degrees and programs offered, and availability of serials online impact the demand for each serial. In the author's experience with weeding serials, as one finds when cleaning out a closet or attic, the item will not be needed until shortly after it was thrown away. Librarians prone to agonizing over the odds of a discarded item being requested later will find weeding to be quite stressful. To weed without undue stress, one must remember that any issue discarded is not totally lost; the patron will be able to request the missing item through ILL. A serials librarian should cultivate an attitude like the author's predecessor at The College of Saint Rose in Albany, New York, Sister Katherine McPeak. She was affectionately known among colleagues as "Sister Pitch" because her philosophy was "When in doubt, throw it out." When shelf space is gone and the periodicals keep coming in, serials librarians may see the wisdom of "Sister Pitch's" approach.

The best practice for weeding is to remove volumes from the serials collection on a regular basis. Doing a little weeding every year is less work and is less disruptive than waiting until a shelf space crisis looms. When deciding what to weed, the following criteria can be used:

- *Measured use.* Low-use titles are candidates for weeding, particularly those with zero measured uses.
- *Currency.* Depending on the discipline, older materials may be of little interest to patrons.
- *Physical condition.* Sometimes damaged volumes should be discarded rather than repaired. Water damage from leaks are especially destructive, as they make pages stick together and foster the growth of molds and fungi.
- *Binding.* Unbound issues may be better candidates for weeding than bound volumes because of the investment in bindings and the added durability of bound volumes.
- *Completeness of runs.* Short, broken runs of periodicals are usually deemed more expendable.
- *Shelf space taken.* Some titles are shelf hogs, taking far more space than justified by their use.
- *Support of curriculum and/or local interests.* If a subject is no longer taught, or a special interest group is no longer represented, the items may not be needed.
- *Duplication in other formats, either microfilm or online* (e.g., in JSTOR). If a reliable alternative source is available, the print volumes can be candidates for weeding.
- *Availability in and stability of online databases.* If the title is included in an acceptably complete and legible format in a database one trusts to retain the content, the print may be expendable. This is risky, because content in many full-text databases is not guaranteed, and the price of the database may become unaffordable at a future date. Titles deemed most important to patrons should not be weeded just because they are currently in a full-text database.

- *Availability in another library easily accessible to patrons.* If a half dozen other libraries hold a serial, it is easier to choose to weed the title. Conversely, if only one library in a region has it, the serial probably should not be weeded.
- *Indexing.* Coverage by indexes subscribed to by the library correlates with use. Titles not indexed can be expected to get little use. The dates of coverage of bibliographic indexes are important. If coverage does not go back to the dates of the issues, the older issues are better candidates for weeding.
- *ILL requests.* Cooperation among libraries is central to our missions. If a title is requested regularly, it should not be weeded. Care must be taken that a weeded serial is not the only copy available.
- *Faculty/researcher input.* It is always smart to run lists of titles that may be weeded by affected faculty and researchers. They may have particular insight into why a title should be kept. If not, it still keeps them involved in collection development and raises awareness of the library's space issues.
- *Bibliographer input.* If the library has a subject bibliographer, they should review the lists of titles proposed for weeding. Sometimes, low-use titles have special value and have not received levels of use commensurate with their intrinsic value. Similarly, titles positively reviewed in Katz's *Magazines for Libraries* may need to stay off the chopping block.
- *Historical value.* Some older items become valuable simply because they provide a record of activity in a discipline or topic area. The value of the content for historical research should be considered.

No formula exists for weighing these criteria. Weeding is far more an art than a science. At minimum, the librarian in charge of discarding volumes should take into account availability of serials elsewhere or in other formats and the opinions of the faculty, researchers, and bibliographers most familiar with the titles.

As discussed earlier, discarding volumes can be stressful. Librarians dedicated to the preservation of knowledge may have fleeting visions, if they toss volumes into the dumpster, of crowding around a bonfire in Germany in 1933. Fortunately, a few alternatives to the landfill exist for weeded serials. Companies buy runs of journals and resell them to new libraries, to librarians expanding into new subject areas, and to librarians whose collections are recovering from floods, fires, or other calamities. Many of these companies monitor messages on the Backserv listserv discussion group dedicated to the exchange of periodicals, including back volumes. Information on how Backserv works and instructions on how to participate may be found at http://lists.swetsblackwell.com/mailman/listinfo/backserv. It will be interesting to see if the demand for runs of journals will decrease as more becomes available online.

Librarians establish policies and have ultimate responsibility for the acquisition of and access to serials in their libraries. Staff and students working under the supervision of a librarian perform many of the day-to-day processes necessary to maintain a serials collection. Receiving and shelving serials accurately and on time is essential work, but it can be delegated to employees who have had some basic training. Claiming and binding require more training, and are often performed by paraprofessionals. Ordering and weeding usually require the guidance of a professional librarian, as those processes require thorough knowledge of patron needs and the serials environment. Another process requiring the knowledge and expertise of a professional librarian is the bibliographic control of serials, the topic of Chapter 5.

SUGGESTIONS FOR FURTHER READING

Since workflows vary a great deal from library to library, and the various integrated library systems each lend themselves to particular work flows, relatively little has been published precisely detailing the entire serials work flow process. One dated source containing several case studies of workflows is Peter Gellatly, ed., *The Good Serials Department* (New York: Haworth Press, 1990). Chiou-sen Dora Chen's *Serials Management: A Practical Guide* (Chicago: American Library Association, 1995) addresses the various aspects of work flow in greater detail than was provided in this chapter. The overview of serials control processes in Chapter 8, "Serials processing in libraries" in Thomas Nisonger's *Management of Serials in Libraries* (Englewood, CO: Libraries Unlimited, 1998) includes extensive bibliographic notes and further readings for each major process.

Libraries are still adapting to managing online journals, so establishing best practice is a work in progress. A succinct overview of problems introduced into workflows by remote access serials is Ellen Finnie Duranceau and Cindy Hepfer, "Staffing for electronic resource management: The results of a survey," *Serials Review*, 28(4), 2002, 316–320. In an earlier article, Ellen Finnie Duranceau describes the differences between workflows for print- and web-based serials in "Beyond print: Revisioning serials acquisitions for the digital age," *Serials Librarian,* 33(1/2), 1998, 83–106. A report of serials procurement and management processes at 11 libraries may be found in Primary Research Group, *Prevailing and Best Practices in Electronic & Print Serials Management* (New York: Author, 2006).

For treatments of how integrated library systems affect work flow, see Eleanor I. Cook's "Taking the good with the bad: How migration to an integrated library system can affect serials work flow," *Serials Librarian*, 32(1/2), 1997, 107–121, and Steve Oberg, Laura ill, Pamela Nicholas, and Lisa Stienbarger, "Serials workflow adaptation and the new ILS: A case for continuous process improvement," *Serials Review,* 28(4), 2002, 298–315.

The *Guide to Performance Evaluation of Serials Vendors* (Chicago: American Library Association, 1997) does an excellent job of defining terms and addressing the aspects of workflow involving a subscription agent. It includes a bibliography of works addressing how subscription agencies function and how to select and evaluate a vendor. The Association of Subscription Agents and Intermediaries at http://www.subscription-agents.org/ has more information about the benefits of using a serials subscription agency. The member directory on their website provides a list of reputable serials subscription agents.

The best source of information about the divine/Faxon/RoweCom bankruptcy is a group of six articles in *Serials Review* (29(4), Winter 2003, 271–275). The articles by Connie Foster, Dan Tonkery, Julia A. Gammon, David R. Fritsch, Susan Davis, and Amira Aaron describe the causes of the bankruptcy, provide reminiscences of Faxon and its many contributions to serials, and the unfortunate impacts of the demise of the company.

The CONSER Publication Patterns Initiative is fully explained at http://www .loc.gov/acq/conser/patthold.html. This website includes lists of participants, some history of the initiative, and background information on its purpose and why the initiative is worthwhile.

An overview of high-density off site storage may be found in Ron Chepesiuk, "Reaching critical mass: Off-site storage in the digital age," *American Libraries*, 30(4), April 1999, 40–43. A useful example of how to make best use of shelf space is Gregg Sapp and George Suttle, "A method for measuring collection expansion rates and shelf space capacities," *Journal of Academic Librarianship*, 20(4), 1994, 145–161. A detailed method for calculating the cost of shelf space may be found in Bruce Kingma, *The Economics of Access vs. Ownership: The Costs and Benefits of Access to Scholarly Articles via Interlibrary Loan and Journal Subscriptions* (Binghamton, NY: Haworth Press, 1996). Kingma concluded that shelf space in 1996 cost 56 cents per volume on average. For a thorough treatment of the origins and development of JSTOR, see Roger C. Scholfeld's *JSTOR: A History* (Princeton, NJ: Princeton University Press, 2003).

The ANSI/NISO/LBI Z39.78-2000 standard for library binding online at http:// www.niso.org/standards/resources/Z39-78.pdf describes the vocabulary and techniques of professional binding.

Weeding is best seen in the context of broader collection development goals. For a thorough and authoritative introduction to weeding processes, see Dennis K. Lambert's *A Guide to Review of Library Collections: Preservation, Storage, and Withdrawal*, 2nd ed. (Chicago, Lanham, MD: Association for Library Collections & Technical Services; published in cooperation with Scarecrow Press, 2002).

The participants in the SERIALST e-mail discussion group are an excellent resource for information about workflow issues. Information about SERIALST, including how to subscribe and how to search the archive of messages, is at http:// www.uvm.edu/~bmaclenn/serialst.html.

REFERENCES

Association for Library Collections and Technical Services. 1997. *Guide to Performance Evaluation of Serials Vendors*. Chicago: American Library Association.

Anderson, Rick, and Zink, Steven D. 2003. Implementing the unthinkable: The demise of periodical check-in at the University of Nevada. *Library Collections, Acquisitions, & Technical Services* 27(1): 61–71.

Fussler, Herman H., and Simon, Julian L. 1969. *Patterns in the Use of Books in Large Research Libraries*. Chicago: University of Chicago Press.

Library Binding Institute. 1986. *Standard for Library Binding*, 8th ed. Rochester, NY: Author.‘

Chapter 5

Bibliographic Control of Serials

This chapter will introduce issues of bibliographic control of serials. Bibliographic control is "the process of creating, organizing, and maintaining standardized bibliographic records that describe library materials, and providing access to those records so that library patrons might find, identify, select, and obtain access to those materials" (Fritz and Fritz 2003, p. 172). For serials, this process of identifying, organizing, and retrieving information includes not only creating and maintaining catalog records, but also managing access to full-text serials in databases. The phrase "nailing Jell-O to the wall" is often used by serials librarians to describe the challenge of describing and providing access to serials. The metaphor implies that something precise and permanent needs to be done to an inherently wiggly and slippery thing.

Information will be provided to help the serials librarian understand how to describe and provide access to serials addressing how serials are organized, searched, and displayed in online catalogs and other databases. The intent of this chapter is not to teach the reader all the steps required to catalog a serial because the Anglo-American Cataloguing Rules, 2nd ed. (AACR2) and resources provided

by the LC's Cooperative Online Serials Program (CONSER) are the appropriate sources of information to learn how to create bibliographic records for serials. Rather, issues and challenges involved in the bibliographic control of serials will be introduced so the reader may gain a sense of the relevant issues and practices.

Although cataloging is designed to precisely describe items in bibliographic records, serials challenge catalogers because serials are published in successive parts and are intended to be continued indefinitely. A serials cataloger works from one part or perhaps a few parts of a publication that will eventually have many parts. The future parts may change in many details, causing the bibliographic record to become outdated unless it is edited. Other means of bibliographic access to items, such as web lists of titles and link resolvers, are subject to change and inaccuracy when URLs and database coverage change. These and other issues are a part of cataloging serials.

CATALOGING SERIALS

Descriptions in bibliographic records lay the foundation for access and control of serials. The first step in cataloging a serial is to determine whether the item to be described is in fact a serial. As described in Chapter 1, a serial is a continuing resource issued in a succession of discrete parts.

The term "continuing resource" was introduced into the 2002 revision of the AACR2. "Continuing resource" is an umbrella term encompassing both serials and other resources that are continued indefinitely, but do not otherwise meet the definition of a serial (Reynolds 2005, p. 8). Databases and websites that integrate new content into the existing resource are continuing resources, but not serials, as the new content is not designated in discrete parts. An integrating resource is added to or changed by means of updates that do not remain discrete and are integrated into the whole (AACR2, 2nd ed., 2002 Revision). An integrating resource can be finite (e.g., a website for a conference that becomes static once the event is complete) or continuing (e.g., an updating database). Cataloging rules and practices differ for serials and integrating resources. To be cataloged as a serial, the bibliographic resource must be issued in successive parts.

CONSER and AACR2

Rules for cataloging serials in the United States are described in publications of LC's CONSER Program (CONSER), which are based on AACR2. CONSER, designed to facilitate the sharing of the serials cataloging workload while maintaining the high quality of the serials master records, is a component of the Program for Cooperative Cataloging (PCC). The *CONSER Cataloging Manual* is an essential training and reference tool that describes AACR2 and LC Rule Interpretations (LCRIs) as they apply to serials. Since bibliographic records for serials often need to be updated, the *CONSER Editing Guide* is also an essential

resource. The *CONSER Editing Guide* describes in detail correct ways to input and edit bibliographic records in MARC 21. The CONSER manuals cover all continuing resources, including serials and ongoing integrating resources (e.g., updating loose leaf publications and websites).

The Serials Cataloging Cooperative Training Program (SCCTP) provides authoritative training materials and trained workshop leaders who have experience in creating and maintaining records for continuing resources. SCCTP workshops are held in locations around the country several times a year. A librarian finding herself in the position of cataloging serials or websites would benefit greatly from attending a SCCTP workshop. The brief introduction to serials cataloging presented here is no substitute for CONSER publications and SCCTP workshops.

The Role of MARC

The cataloging standards for bibliographic records described in the CONSER publications and AACR2 are expressed in online catalogs through the MARC standard. MARC encodes bibliographic descriptions in a standard format designed to communicate and display records with computers. The process of cataloging a bibliographic resource requires entering data in accordance with both cataloging rules and the MARC format. For example, the CONSER Cataloging Manual describes how to describe the title of a serial, including where in the publication the title is to be found, what qualifies as an alternative title, how to handle parallel titles, and how to handle punctuation. The MARC format specifies that the title statement is to be entered in field 245, with the title proper in subfield code a, and alternate title in subfield code b. MARC format for field 245 includes two one-digit indicators to instruct the computer how to file and/or display the information. The cataloging standards describe what information is to be provided, and MARC determines how the information is to be entered in the bibliographic record. The CONSER materials and SCCTP workshops do a fine job of explaining the interrelationship of cataloging rules and MARC format.

Process of Cataloging a Serial

The process of cataloging a serial begins by examining the issue(s) of the bibliographic resource, and determining that it meets the definition of a serial. Rules for cataloging a serial say that the first issue is consulted for title and other identifying information, but the issue(s) of the serial available to the cataloger may not include the first issue published. After examining the issue(s), the next step is to search OCLC, union catalogs, and perhaps other catalogs for any existing bibliographic record for the serial. In practice, the bibliographic record for the serial is often already in OCLC. This is particularly true for serials librarians who are not working at a CONSER member library. Beginning with a copy of an OCLC record contributed by a CONSER member saves the librarian work and helps maintain consistent records. The origin of the record can be determined from the library's OCLC symbol in field 040 (cataloging source) in the OCLC record. The

list of CONSER member libraries is at http://www.loc.gov/acq/conser/conmembs
.html. While records for serials can often be copied from OCLC, any serials
librarian may need to occasionally create original bibliographic records for local
publications (e.g., student newspaper or library newsletter). Even if no original
serials cataloging is necessary, records often need editing after they are copied.
Therefore, it is important for even those librarians who rarely or never perform
original serials cataloging to understand correct practices.

Librarians who create original catalog records will describe the serial, determine
the name and title access points, and may assign subject headings and class numbers. CONSER has defined three levels of catalog records for serials: full, core,
and minimal (*CONSER Editing Guide*, Section B6).

Full records include description, name/series headings, and all appropriate subject headings. Classification with appropriate LC, Dewey, or other class number is
encouraged but not required in full records. All elements corresponding with an
authority file must match an authority record in full records. Authority files are
used to ensure consistency of names, titles, and subjects. Each record in an authority file contains an established heading verified by a qualified librarian. Authority records have their own MARC format, and are maintained in OCLC. If a
new authority record is needed, creating it is part of the cataloging process.

Core records also include authoritative description and name/series headings,
but only the most essential subject headings are required, and classification is
optional. Minimal records are defined by CONSER as those without authority
work on names and subjects, but are otherwise the same as core records. Minimal
records will contain the most essential subject headings, and classification is
optional. The extent of serials cataloging work needed for a title is thus partly
dependent on the level of the existing records, and partly dependent on local needs
and policies. Librarians responsible for a library's catalog will choose whether to
create full, core, or minimal records for serials in their library. More decisions are
made once the level of records is chosen.

Local cataloging decisions for serials records include choosing a classification
number (if any) and subject headings for each serial title. If the serials are shelved
alphabetically by title or otherwise unclassified, the library will not assign a class
number. If a LC or Dewey class number is used, it may be changed from the
classification in the OCLC record to suit local needs. Subject headings may be
added to those in existing OCLC records to make records more useful to local
patrons. Various other changes may be made to records, but, if the records are
shared, rules governing the relevant union catalog must be followed. This particularly applies to major changes to serial records. Major changes include title
changes, but by definition include other changes as well.

Major Changes to Serials Records

The CONSER Cataloging Manual, 2002, states "Serial records often need to be
modified because serial publications exhibit changes.... Record modifications

have consistently represented over one-half of the transactions on the CONSER database in recent years" (Module 21, p. 3). Serial records in WorldCat include an entry date when the record was input into the OCLC database, and the date when the record was last updated. It is uncommon to see records that do not have an update date different from the entry date, since serials by their nature are prone to change.

Changes that require that a new record be created in accordance with correct successive cataloging practice are called major changes. Changes that do not require a new bibliographic record are called minor changes. Precise rules have been created (and perennially discussed, and occasionally modified) that define what constitutes a major change or a minor change (Hirons and Hawkins 2002). A change to the words in a serials' title may or may not constitute a major change.

Rules for what constitute a major title change that requires a new record were revised in 2002. The intent of the rule change was to require fewer new records and fewer new ISSNs. The revised rules were also intended to resolve some discrepancies between cataloging rules and the practice of assigning new ISSNs. In general, the new rules allow more changes in title wording before the change is deemed major. Major changes in these fields require a new record: title proper, corporate body, main entry corporate body in uniform title, uniform title for translations, physical format, and edition statement. For titles, the basic rule states that if any of the first five words of a title change, or if the title change results in a change of the meaning or subject, the change is major. Exceptions exist though, and posts to the SERIALST discussion group indicate that there remains some confusion about the rules for title changes. The need for discussion and clarification is to be expected, as no set of rules can precisely cover every creative modification to titles the publishers dream up.

Major changes, including titles that cease all together, create significant work for serials staff. Revising bibliographic records for serial titles typically includes these edits to MARC fields, which are listed to exemplify the work involved:

1. Edit field 008 in the bibliographic record of the old title to indicate that it has ceased.
2. Edit field 362 in the bib record of the old title to show its ending date.
3. Add field 785 (successive title) to the record for the old title, thereby creating a link to the title and ISSN of the new title.
4. Check the other fields for any necessary edits, which may vary due to the level of detail in the record and local policies and procedures.
5. Check field 780 (preceeding title) in the record for the new title to ensure it correctly links to the old title.

Major changes also entail updating holdings and records for physical processing, which are described in the next section on holdings. What makes serials cataloging distinct from cataloging finite resources is the changing nature of the bibliographic resources being cataloged. The challenge of "nailing the Jell-O to the wall" is an ongoing process as the discussion of issues regarding the practice of cataloging serials will confirm.

ISSUES REGARDING THE PRACTICE
OF CATALOGING SERIALS

Cataloging rules and standards are not static, and the issues to be resolved are not solved by a single person. Many individuals are involved in a number of groups devoted to improving cataloging practice, including for serials. These groups include the Continuing Resources Cataloging Committee http://www.ala .org/ala/alctscontent/serialssection/serialscomm/contresourcecata/contresourcescat .htm, the Committee on Cataloging: Description and Access http://www.libraries .psu.edu/tas/jca/ccda/, the Machine-Readable Bibliographic Information (MARBI) Committee http://www.ala.org/ala/alcts/divisiongroups/marbi/marbi.htm, and the Library of Congress (LC) http://loc.gov/library/. These groups would not exist if there were no outstanding issues surrounding the practice of cataloging. Development and maintenance of cataloging rules is coordinated and ultimately decided by the Joint Steering Committee for Revision of AACR2 (JSC) http://www .collectionscanada.ca/jsc/index.html. The development of cataloging rules for integrating resources distinct from rules for cataloging serials is one example of an issue resolved by JSC working with the constituent groups. Another issue that has been resolved for the present is the serials cataloging rules for successive entry versus latest entry cataloging.

Successive Entry versus Latest Entry Cataloging

The rules for successive entry cataloging of serials are accepted practice, but debate over the relative merits of successive versus latest entry cataloging has remained alive for decades. In successive entry cataloging, one bibliographic record is produced for each major change in a serial. When the title of a serial undergoes a major change, the record for that title is closed and a new bibliographic record is created for the new title. The cataloger adds to the existing serial record a field 785 (succeeding entry) that links to the new record's title, ISSN, and OCLC number. If the title splits, there may be multiple successive entry fields. The record for the new title includes field 780 (preceding entry) containing the preceding title, ISSN, and OCLC number. If the title is a merger, there will be multiple preceding entry fields. Integrated library systems (ILSs) are programmed to link fields 780 (preceding entry) and 785 (succeeding entry). When a patron searches for a title that has changed, the system will also retrieve the records for the preceding and/or succeeding titles. However, even if the title changed its name multiple times, the system will only retrieve the most recent preceding and succeeding titles. Bibliographic records do not have the full history of the title. Successive entry catalog records only contain the history of one title change before and/or after the title in the bibliographic record.

Of historical note, before 1908, the year the ALA rules were published, serials were often cataloged using earliest entry cataloging. With earliest entry, the bibliographic record represented the first title of the serial, and successive titles were indicated by notes. This method had the distinct disadvantage of requiring the patron to identify the earliest title in order to find the catalog card for the title being sought. Aspects of earliest entry cataloging can be found in the current treatment of minor changes, which are treated as notes in existing bibliographic records. Charles Cutter's rules for cataloging periodicals allowed for either earliest or latest entry cataloging, but latest entry cataloging was specified in the ALA red book rules (Rule 5C1) based on the American 1908 rules (Smith 1978). The British continued earliest entry cataloging until 1967. Anglo-American cataloging code abandoned both earliest and latest entry systems and codified successive entry cataloging for periodicals, and successive entry was adopted by LC in 1971 (Osborn 1973, p. 208).

Prior to the adoption of AACR in 1967, latest entry cataloging was applied to serials in the United States. The practice of latest entry cataloging integrated the records for all titles representing the same serial no matter how many times the title changed. The bibliographic record for a serial in the latest entry had the current title as the form of citation, and the preceding titles would be indicated in notes. Latest entry cataloging allowed one bibliographic record to express the complete title history of a serial, including titles, corporate entities, and publication patterns. For some serials, the notes were extensive, complicated, and seemed cluttered, especially when typed on a catalog card. The narrative descriptions were also difficult to convert into MARC format, and thus difficult to share among systems. For these and other reasons, successive entry cataloging replaced latest entry cataloging as accepted practice when AACR were adopted. Latest entry cataloging retains some appeal.

Latest entry catalog is appealing because it allows the patron to view the complete history of a serial in one record. Since an online catalog can provide as many links within a record as needed, there is no technical reason why every title for a serial (even one that has undergone many changes) cannot be linked from one record. The patron could search for any title within the serial's history and find the master record with all the titles along with each title's link to a holdings record. The capabilities of online catalogs mean it is possible that latest entry cataloging will become the standard for serials again at some future time. Latest entry cataloging is currently used for integrating resources under the name "integrating entry;" but for now, successive entry cataloging is accepted practice for serials.

Uniform Titles for Serials

Uniform titles are used for two separate reasons. For most bibliographic resources except serials, the most common use of uniform titles is collocation. Uniform titles are used to bring together in the catalog all the variations on a title representing the same work. For serials, collocation with uniform titles is used for translations, legal serials, and multiple formats. The second use of uniform titles for serials is to differentiate publications with the same title. Differentiation is an important use of uniform titles for serials. One might think that publishers of serials would check first to see if their creative title (e.g., *Bulletin* or *Update*) was already in use. Alas, duplicate titles abound. The serials cataloger enters a uniform title in field 130 (title as the main entry) or field 240 (corporate or conference name as the main entry) to distinguish it from other publications with exactly the same title. Qualifiers which may be chosen to distinguish a title include place of publication, corporate body, and dates of publication. Choosing the corporate body responsible for the publication is the most informative for the patron, but if it changes, a new record is required. Thus, the place of publication is more often used because a change in place of publication does not require a new bibliographic record.

Public Display of Records

Catalogers have good reasons for creating serials records with rich and detailed information. Unfortunately, some patrons may have difficulty interpreting public displays of these records because some fields can be misleading or confusing. Modern integrated library systems can be customized; so certain MARC fields do not display in an online catalog. When fields are set to not display, it is not necessary to edit unwanted fields out of the MARC records. However, repressing a MARC field in serials records so they do not display usually requires repressing the field for all bibliographic records. Some fields not wanted for serial records may be desirable for the records for monographs, sound recordings, visual materials, and so on. Even though the information may not be very helpful in serials records, librarians may choose to display the MARC field because it is helpful elsewhere. This section will discuss common concerns librarians have with the public display of four elements in MARC format bibliographic records: physical description, numbering, "description based on," and subject headings.

Physical Description. The physical description of a book is naturally a very important part of a bibliographic record for a monograph. The physical description of a serial is required by AACR2 to be recorded in MARC field 300. However, since the physical description of a serial is not very informative, field 300 is optional in CONSER core records. The rule is to use "v." as the extent of the item, regardless of the caption and numbering scheme of the serial. As with monographs, illustrations are indicated with "ill.", and the height of the issue is given in centimeters. Unlike a book, a serial's issues may inconsistently contain illustrations, and the height may change over time. Thus, some librarians are of the opinion that displaying field 300 in a serials record is of little use to patrons.

Numbering. According to AACR2, every serial record must include the numbering of the serial in either field 362 (dates of publication/sequential designation) or field 500 ("Description based on" note). The purpose of the 362 is to show the start date and numbering system of the first issue of a serial. This makes sense, as it informs the patron reading the record of when the title began publication. If the title ceases publication or changes its name, the 362 is edited also to show the end date. It can also be very helpful for determining that a requested title is the one desired among a set of similarly named serials. One can project the numeric and chronological designation and compare it to the volumes and dates of the requested item.

The problem with field 362 is that patrons may have difficulty distinguishing it from the local holdings. It depends on how the ILS is configured to display fields in the online catalog, but the records patrons view typically display two date ranges. One is the date range of local holdings, and the other is the dates of publication displayed from field 362. Many patrons will not know which date range represents what is available to them in the library. In other words, they do not know or discern the difference between holdings and dates of publication. Showing the start date of a serial makes sense, as one might well want to know when the title began publication. It is also helpful for shared records, as this is the only date in the record that describes the serial rather than individual libraries' holdings. But reference librarians often see the confusion patrons experience because of two date ranges appearing in the records, and may question whether the benefits of displaying field 362 outweigh the confusion is causes.

Whether to keep or delete field 362 from serials bibliographic records is a local call, but it cannot be removed if the record is shared in a union catalog requiring it. A workable solution might be for online catalogs to suppress field 362 for serials records only, but display them for other types of bibliographic resources.

"Description Based On". Patrons may also be confused by the field 500 "Description based on" statement that is required when the serial is cataloged from anything other than the first issue in hand. The note describing where information for cataloging was drawn is important for accurate records, especially if the first issue is different from the issue in hand. A "description based on" note may be essential for a cataloger to determine whether an item in hand is described by that record. Yet, the note can confuse patrons. It is very difficult to imagine a patron caring much about whether the record was created from the first or second issue of the serial. Patrons usually approach serials by finding citations in databases or the works cited in books and articles. Since they typically only want to know whether the serial is in the library and where it is shelved, the title and holdings statement usually suffice and there is little reason to display the note. Repressing field 500 would be unwise because it would also hide all notes in that field, and field 500 notes contain a wealth of information that is useful to patrons. Subject headings are also intended to help patrons identify the serials that meet their information needs.

Subject Headings. Subject headings for journals (but not all serials) end with "—Periodicals." If a patron wishes to browse for journals on a topic, a search can be done combining their topic with the subject "periodicals." However, the level of specificity of subject headings is too precise to use them to answer the question, "May I have a list of all your periodicals that cover this topic?" In most cases, this seemingly simple question is actually very difficult to answer. Librarians may choose to add subject headings appropriate to help provide lists of periodicals on topics. In academic libraries, it is fairly common for faculty to want a list of the journals in their discipline, and adding subject headings not in the copied catalog record may help.

Serials librarians can expect to be involved in decisions regarding the public display of MARC records in public catalogs. As described earlier, information that is important for bibliographic control may be unnecessary to patrons or even confuse them. Library systems can be customized to some degree, but tradeoffs between completeness and clarity still arise. Awareness of both the reasons for the details in the MARC records and the needs of patrons is necessary to make good decisions on editing and displaying serials records.

HOLDINGS

Holdings records describe which issues of serials are available in a library or consortium of libraries. Library serials holdings are recorded in records that are separate from but linked to bibliographic records. The holdings and bibliographic records are typically integrated into one screen in the online catalog. Since an ILS can be configured to show holdings pretty much anywhere within the display for a serial, patrons do not know, and have no reason to know, that holdings records are distinct from bibliographic records.

Prior to the adoption of online catalogs, librarians typically maintained holdings information as notes on catalog cards and/or lists of the serials in their collections. The goal was to inform patrons of the library which issues of which serials were available. Consistent wording gave the catalog or list integrity, but there was no pressing need to have a consistent format for holdings across libraries. The wording and format librarians felt was appropriate for their patrons was chosen. Union catalogs and shared bibliographic utilities created a need for a consistent format for holdings.

MARC 21 Format for Holdings Data

Efforts to standardize holding information began in the 1980s. The standard Z39.42 (1980) described the proper format for summary holdings, which record the first and last parts of the range at the highest level of designation (e.g., volume and year). Standard Z39.44 (1986) allowed for more detailed holdings. Most recently, standard Z39.71 (1999) details MARC 21 Format for Holdings Data (MFHD) (Moeller and Lu 2005). In a study of the acceptance and use of MFHD, Moeller and Lu (2005) found that only 44 percent of the libraries surveyed provide holding information in the MFHD. Despite its limited adoption by libraries so far, and the challenge of converting holdings to the new format, the MFHD standard offers significant potential benefits to libraries (Alan 2003).

In official terms, "MARC 21 Format for Holdings Data [MFHD] contains format specifications for encoding data elements pertinent to holdings and location data for all forms of material" (MARBI 1996). Distinct from the bibliographic format describing the information resource, the holdings format describes what the library owns. For example, bibliographic format field 008 (fixed-length data elements) includes coded information about whether the item is still published, the dates of publication, frequency of publication, and language used. In contrast, MFHD field 008 codes information about whether the serial is currently received in the library, how long the library retains it in the collection, whether the library has the complete run, and so forth. So field 008 in MARC bibliographic format describes the publication, while MFHD describes what the library owns.

MFHD includes a pair of fields used to encode the successive parts of serials held by a library. Field 853 contains the caption and publication pattern, and field 863 contains enumeration and chronology. The caption and pattern field 853 encodes the schedule on which the serial is published. For instance, for a monthly journal published in one volume per year, codes are entered for volume, issue, year, and month. Field 863 encodes the enumeration and chronology of issues checked in, and field 863 data is paired with the captions from the 853 to create a public display of local holdings. For example, these MFHD fields

> 853 $a v. $b no. $i (year) $j (month)
> 863 $a 1–14 $b 1–12 $i 1991–2004 $j 01–12

can be automatically translated by the library system to display in the online catalog as:

> v. 1, no. 1 (1991:Jan.)—v. 14, no. 12 (2004:Dec.)

A librarian may choose to display holdings in the textual holdings field 866 instead of in the coded fields 853/863. However, using MFHD fields 853/863 allows more consistent display of holdings in union catalogs than can be obtained with notes in field 866.

Process for Modifying Serials Holdings

Changes in serials holdings require careful, detailed corrections to the catalog record and any other lists, databases, or spreadsheets kept by the serials librarian. Taking care of them is a primary reason why serials work requires true "attention to detail." Work on records is required with any major change to a serial, when a librarian chooses to add a new subscription, and when a subscription is canceled. In this section, the process of modifying holdings is interpreted in a broad sense, in order to convey the extent of work involved when titles are added or canceled.

When a new serial is added to the collection, the following steps will typically need to be taken:

1. Record that the title has been ordered. This may be done by adding the bibliographic record to the catalog, or by keeping a record in some type of log. Include the date the first issue is expected.
2. Add the title and its price to the budget records, however they are kept.
3. Add the bibliographic record to the catalog.
4. Create a check-in record, including the expected publication pattern. Add binding information, if appropriate.
5. Create shelf labels and/or spine labels, and make sure there is space on the shelf for the title.
6. Check in the first issue. Verify that information in the issue matches information in the bibliographic record, and that the caption and enumeration match that entered into the check-in record.
7. Add the title to any other holdings lists used beyond the catalog, both locally and in union catalogs.

When a serial is canceled, the basic steps for handling the title no longer received by the library are:

1. Record that the title has not been renewed. Include the anticipated arrival date of the last issue.
2. Indicate in the budget records that the title is canceled.
3. Once the last issue has arrived, make changes in ILS as needed to end expected issues for the title, to avoid claiming issues that are not published.
4. Edit the holdings record in the catalog. This includes editing field 008 to show the title is not currently received. Collapse all received issues, and edit the holdings record in field 863 or 866 (depending on which is used) to correctly display the holdings. If the record included a link to online that is no longer available, delete field 856.
5. Decide what is to be done with the volumes on the shelves. They may simply stay put, or be moved to storage, or discarded.
6. Make changes in holdings statements locally and in any union catalogs.

If a current subscription undergoes a major change, the library staff will need to perform most of the processes for a title change, an added title, and a ceased title. Depending on the change, new classification may not be necessary, but otherwise the three processes are quite similar whether the library chooses to make the change, or it is forced on them by the publisher.

Recording and Displaying Holdings in an ILS

MFHD provides functions beyond displaying holdings data in an online catalog. It is also used in ILS to predict the receipt of issues and to generate claims for missing issues. A publication pattern for a serial is determined and entered into the ILS when the first issue of a newly subscribed serial arrives in the library. Fortunately, the publication pattern in MFHD is typically entered in work forms built into the serials or acquisitions module of the ILS, and it is not necessary to learn the codes for patterns entered into field 853. However, learning the codes allows one to interpret the holdings record as displayed in MFHD, and one needs to know the codes to edit holdings encoded in fields 853/863.

An important issue with current systems is how holdings are collapsed. To collapse a holding means to convert a display of individual issues into a display of volumes. Some integrated library systems automatically collapse holdings, and others do not. For example, an online catalog displays holdings for a journal as v. 1, no. 1 (1991:Jan.)—v. 14, no. 12 (2004:Dec.). Assume that v. 15, no. 1, Jan. 2005 of the journal is checked in. Some systems will automatically collapse the holdings into the summary statement v. 1, no. 1 (1991:Jan.)—v. 15, no. 1 (2005:Jan). Other ILSs do not collapse the holdings, and instead create a separate line for the recently checked-in issue. To display holdings in one statement, library staff must edit holdings to collapse them into a single line. This is a very important factor to consider when choosing an ILS, as the level of automation in holdings displays significantly impacts the workload of serials staff. In fact, display and workload issues are a major reason for many librarians to choose to display holdings as textual information in field 866 instead of coding holdings in fields 853/863. Hopefully, demand by librarians will lead all the major ILS vendors to allow the option of automatic collapse of holdings into future versions of their products.

When holdings are displayed as text, standards Z39.42 and Z39.44 describe how data should be displayed. When there is a gap in holdings, the gap should be indicated with either a comma or a semicolon. A comma is used if the issue was published but the library is missing the issue. A semicolon is used if the expected issue was never published. Gaps can create very messy holdings statements. Holdings can be edited to remove information about gaps and thus create cleaner, more readable displays. But, it may be better to keep information on gaps so patrons and reference staff can tell if an issue is known to be missing before fruitlessly hunting for it.

It is also proper practice to have separate holdings lines for each publication pattern used by the serial. This can create very messy holdings data page if the title experiences many changes in pattern (e.g., quarterly, then bimonthly, then monthly, then bimonthly again). So some librarians choose to collapse the holdings into one line, even though the title may have been published in several patterns. Union catalogs may also allow only one line of holdings data per title. Losing information on changes in pattern is less critical than knowing that published issues are missing, since the citation the patron is working from should match whatever caption and enumeration the title used for that volume. The challenge is how to strike the best balance of providing detailed information in an easy-to-interpret display.

Holdings data are inevitably an issue when librarians choose to create a union catalog. As stated, less than half of the libraries currently use MFHD. Moeller and Lu (2005) also found that 39 percent of libraries used nonstandard holdings. Translating nonstandard holdings into data capable of being shared is a major challenge. Real examples of holdings statements that do not conform to standard include:

May 2004–present
Current & previous years
Bound: 1999–Sept. 2001
Sep 2001–(Jun–Aug not published)
Win 2003–04.

Compounding the problem of holdings conforming to no standard, some systems have had no separately defined field place for holdings data. Holdings recorded in the system being migrated from may be in the call number field, field 866 of the bibliographic record, or note fields in the bibliographic record. Migrating from one system to another is thus not simply a matter of copying field X to field Y, but is rather a complicated process requiring significant intervention by library staff.

REMOTE ACCESS ELECTRONIC SERIALS

According to the *CONSER Cataloging Manual*, the full, correct term for serials accessed online is Remote Access Electronic Serials (Module 31, p. 5). Electronic serials delivered in a physical medium such as a CD-ROM or DVD are known as Direct Access Electronic Serials. These became uncommon by 2005, as most electronic serials are now delivered via the web, that is, remote access.

Serial or Integrating Resource?

To be cataloged as serials, online resources must comprise successive parts bearing numerical or chronological designations. Continuing online resources without successive parts are cataloged as integrating resources, not as serials. According to AACR2 Revision 2002, an integrating resource is "a bibliographic resource that is added to or changed by means of updates that do not remain discrete and are integrated into the whole. Integrating resources can be finite or continuing" (Joint Steering Committee for Revision of AACR 2002) The AACR2 calls for an integrating entry approach to handling resources that are changed by means of updates that are integrated into the existing work. All major changes to the integrating resource are handled within one record. The current title of the resource is recorded in field 245 (title proper) and former titles are in field 247 (former title or title variations).

The practice of cataloging integrating resources is relevant to serials because some works published as serials in print can be integrating resources in their online manifestations. As the AACR2 definition states, integrating resources are unlike serials because updated content is not designated in successive parts. So a remotely accessed bibliographic database regularly updated with new citations is an integrating resource, while the corresponding print index issued in successive parts is a serial. For example, the PsycINFO database used to be published as *Psychological Abstracts*, a serial issued monthly in enumerated, successive parts. The PsycINFO database is updated weekly, but not in successive parts. While citations have an accession number and a load date, they are not grouped into issues or volumes. *Psychological Abstracts* was cataloged as a serial; PsycINFO is cataloged as an integrating resource. Therefore, the first step when cataloging a remote access continuing resource is to determine whether it is a serial or an integrating resource.

Catalog Records for Remote Access Serials

Librarians with remote access electronic serials must choose whether to have catalog records for them, or to provide access through a non cataloging approach. It is possible to have a mix of serials with records in the catalog and serials accessed through links outside the catalog. Which approach is chosen may depend on the means of access to the online serials. Remote access serials can be delivered as individual subscriptions from publishers, individual subscriptions via platform providers, packages of titles from publishers, and aggregations of titles from vendors based on an index or abstract. These modes of access were described in some detail in Chapter 2. Of the categories of access to online serials, the easiest to catalog are serials subscribed to individually and serials subscribed to through platform providers. These titles have distinct URLs and discrete library subscriptions that can be tracked the same as print subscriptions. Since individually subscribed online serials are similar to traditional serials, the catalog record will be quite similar to that of a print journal. The format coded in field 008 will be "electronic" rather than "print," and a field 856 containing the URL will be added. While there are other differences, for the most part periodicals subscribed to in this way may be handled in the catalog similar to the way serials always have.

Packages created by publishers or other organizations that provide some assurance of stability of the titles and dates of coverage may need to be handled a little differently. Examples of this type of package are JSTOR and the Sage Full-Text Collections. Since titles in these packages are reasonably stable, a catalog record following the rules for continuing resources may be created for each title in the package. As with individual subscriptions, a field 856 in each title's record will link to the title in the online package. For this to work, each serial in the package must have its own URL. The publishers and vendors have recognized that need and provided the title-specific URLs. If a librarian wants to have a record in the online catalog for the package as a whole, the package may be cataloged as an integrating resource.

Bibliographic Control of Serials in Aggregated Databases

Aggregated database packages of serials provide no guarantee of the stability of content or dates of coverage. Examples include the databases EBSCOhost Academic Search, InfoTrac OneFile, and Lexis-Nexis Academic Universe. While it is theoretically feasible to create catalog records for the titles in these aggregated databases, it is not practical for the staff of one library to do so. The serial content in the aggregated databases comes from thousands of titles with varying degrees of completeness. Since serial content in aggregated databases is volatile, it is very difficult to maintain even basic records for the titles in them. In response to demand for bibliographic records for serials in aggregated databases, at least one company, Serials Solutions, can provide MARC records to librarians for a price. The records are not inexpensive, but the cost is less than it would cost to create their own catalog records. When records are purchased, the serials librarian and/or others must write a profile describing where the data will go in the ILS. This requires detailed knowledge of the data being purchased, the capabilities of the ILS, and how the data should be displayed. Since the content of aggregated databases changes, batch loads of records are done on a periodic basis. Someone in the library, perhaps a serials librarian, must be responsible for ensuring that periodic updates are done correctly.

A-to-Z Lists

The downside to adding records to the catalog is that when titles are dropped from aggregated databases, the catalog records need to be removed or edited. An alternative approach is to maintain a list of serials separate from the catalog. Recognizing a need for records to link patrons to serials in aggregated full-text databases, several companies have created database products that list the titles available to patrons through their library's subscribed full-text databases. Such services include Serials Solutions, TDNet, and EBSCO AtoZ. As a group, these linking services are commonly known as "A-to-Z" services, since they generate alphabetical lists of titles that may be searched by patrons. These companies track the titles available in full text in dozens of commonly subscribed databases, and stay on top of any changes in coverage. Librarians subscribing to a service indicate which databases are available to their patrons, and may also add local records for their online subscriptions to titles not in the full-text databases.

If a separate A-to-Z list is used, patrons must learn to look at the list instead of the catalog to see if a title is available online. The lists can typically be searched by title or broad subject areas. The primary benefit to the library is that a reasonably accurate list of titles is made available to patrons with little intervention by librarians. The vendor is responsible for maintaining the records for titles in aggregated databases. The librarian only has to be involved with maintenance when there are changes to their subscriptions.

Aggregator-Neutral Records

When aggregated full-text databases were new products, CONSER librarians created separate records for the titles in various aggregated databases. Each presence of a title in an aggregated database got its own catalog record. So if *Time* magazine was in six aggregated databases, six records were created for it. CONSER librarians now use one "aggregator-neutral" record. When serials were first published online, there were usually only one or two online versions of each title. At that time, CONSER described an optional single-record cataloging standard, which allowed libraries to note the online version on the record for the print serial. This option became very popular because most libraries wanted to show multiple formats on one record instead of having separate catalog records for each format.

However, when librarians began to license access to aggregated full-text databases, they soon realized drawbacks in the single-record approach. Databases licensed by a library changed from year to year, and titles contained in full text in the databases changed. In the face of these changes, maintaining notes in the print serial records proved too labor-intensive. CONSER librarians decided that a set of separate records could more easily be added, deleted, or changed. CONSER defined the "aggregator-neutral" record to serve that purpose. Librarians can use a basic aggregator-neutral record for the remote access serial to cover all online versions of the serial. If they prefer more specific records, librarians retain the option of producing multiple records from the one aggregator-neutral record. In either case, the aggregator-neutral record is separate from the record for the print format, so that changes in the online version do not require changes to the record for the print version.

Issues of workload and patron convenience surrounding aggregator-neutral records are not entirely new. Cataloging rules have long specified that the microform of a serial must have a separate record from the print serial, but for years many librarians have fudged the rules and indicated microfilm holdings as notes or as holdings records on the same record with the print serial. This form of "cheating" avoided having a separate bibliographic record for the microfilm format, allowing patrons to see holdings for both formats on one record. It is not unusual for workload issues and concerns for patrons' access to spur local variance from cataloging standards. Sometimes, variance from a standard is subsequently incorporated into revised rules.

The process of deciding which type of record to use and managing the maintenance of the records has impacted the daily work of serials librarians. Serials work now typically includes tracking changes in databases, being responsible for changing records as needed when databases change, and ensuring integrity between the online catalog and other serials records. All these tasks typically involve cooperation among librarians responsible for serials, systems, and public services. The new duties and the need for cooperative problem solving have added new challenge to serials librarianship.

Special Concern about the Titles of Electronic Serials

As described previously, cataloging a serial requires that the first issue be consulted for title and other identifying information, and changes to the serial are accounted for in the bibliographic records with notes and added entries. When the title of a serial changes, a new record is created and links are made between the new title and the former title. This method of adding notes for minor changes and creating successive entry catalog records for major changes works because each printed issue's title and statement of responsibility is fixed.

Online serials may have no fixed title. Each article may be essentially an item in a database. What CONSER Coordinator Les Hawkins calls the "wrapping paper" of the publisher's home page and journal information page can change (Hawkins and Shadle 2004). So a patron may have a citation for the online *Journal of Blah*, which is now titled *Blah-Blah Quarterly*. Older print issues on the stacks in a library would still have *Journal of Blah* on their spines. But, nothing prevents the publisher of the online version from retroactively renaming the old issues *Blah-Blah Quarterly*. How widespread retroactive changes will become remains to be seen.

As discussed in the previous section on issues surrounding the display of information about serials in online catalogs, full MARC records may contain more data than patrons need. A possible simplified alternative to using MARC format and AACR2 to catalog online resources is the Dublin Core metadata element set.

Dublin Core Metadata

The Dublin Core describes any remotely accessed information resource, including continuing and integrating resources. The goal of the Dublin Core is to provide a standard that is simple enough for creators of information to adequately create their own metadata. That is, the author or publisher does their own "cataloging." If done according to the standard, the metadata can serve as a simple but effective catalog-like record for websites.

For online serials, Dublin Core can be used to describe online journals, individual articles online, or both. The idea is to include basic descriptive information in metadata embedded in files, usually in XML or HTML. The standard metadata elements closely resemble fields in MARC format, including: title, creator, subject, publisher, date, and language. Other Dublin Core elements include description (can be an abstract, table of contents, or free-text account of the information resource), identifier (e.g., URL, DOI, ISSN, ISBN), and rights management. For a full description of the Dublin Core Metadata Elements, see http://dublincore.org/documents/dces/.

If Dublin Core Metadata catches on, it may enhance the usability of online information and facilitate finding self-archived scholarly articles. Two large hurdles must be leaped for Dublin Core to really work, though. The first is for a critical mass of sites to implement it and describe their resources using Dublin Core metadata. The second is for Internet search engines to be programmed to search the metadata. That would require Internet search interfaces to allow controlled searching for the metadata elements, and for the engines themselves to search the elements.

The simplicity of Dublin Core means that it cannot encode the level of detail capable in MARC records. Even if the hurdles are jumped, records may lack enough specificity to be usefully searched.

Cataloging standards for serials will continue to develop as online delivery of serials becomes even more common and as methods of packaging and delivery continue to develop. Librarians and vendors will continue to experiment with noncataloging approaches to providing access to serials, and innovations may then influence cataloging standards. This chapter has described rules and standards that apply to serials in all libraries, and has addressed issues and practices for individual librarians applying the rules and standards to their local needs. The next chapter addresses another realm where broad forces impact individual libraries, namely how economic forces impact serials management.

SUGGESTIONS FOR FURTHER READING

Essential reading for cataloging is Jean L. Hirons, ed., *CONSER Cataloging Manual* (Washington, DC: Library of Congress, Cataloging Distribution Service, 2002). The manual is updated on an ongoing but irregular basis, depending on when rule changes are approved. Order information for the *CONSER Cataloging Manual* may be found at http://www.loc.gov/cds/. See also Carol Liheng and Winnie S. Chan, *Serials Cataloging Handbook: An Illustrative Guide to the Use of AACR2R and LC Rule Interpretations*, 2nd ed. (Chicago: American Library Association, 1998). The best resource for current, frequently updated information about serials cataloging practices is the CONSER website at http://www.loc.gov/acq/conser/homepage.html. The site is kept up-to-date with meeting summaries, updated documentation, and reports on current cataloging issues.

Extensive information about the Serials Cataloging Cooperative Training Program (SCCTP) may be found at http://www.loc.gov/acq/conser/scctp/home.html, which includes a schedule of workshops and a bibliography of SCCTP-related articles and resources.

An account of the methods OCLC uses to control the quality of records may be found at http://www.oclc.org/bibformats/en/quality/, which comes from Chapter 5 of the *OCLC Bibliographic Formats and Standards*.

For an overview of the changes in rules for what constitutes a major title change, see Jean Hirons and Les Hawkins, "Transforming AACR2" cited previously. Examples of major and minor changes are available online at the Yale University Library website for cataloging documentation at http://www.library.yale.edu/cataloging/Orbis2Manual/majorminorexamples.htm. More information on the process of rule changes and the role of the Joint Steering Committee is available at http://www.aacr2.org.

Les Hawkins, "Reflections on wrapping paper: random thoughts on AACR2 and electronic serials" cited previously in the References provides a concise, cogent overview of issues with cataloging online journals. Les Hawkins is CONSER Coordinator. His brief article discusses the need for stable citation information, the range of problems catalogers encounter with online journals, and hints for coping with the problems.

Extensive information about the Dublin Core Metadata Initiative may be found at http://dublincore.org/, including detailed descriptions of the standard, training materials, schedule of meetings, and tools and software.

REFERENCES

Alan, Robert. 2003. MARC holdings implementation: A long-term process with long-term advantages. *Library Collections, Acquisitions, and Technical Services* 27: 107–120.

Fritz, Deborah H., and Fritz, Richard J. 2003. *MARC21 for Everyone: A Practical Guide*. Chicago: American Library Association, p. 172.

Joint Steering Committee for Revision of AACR, American Library Association. 2002. *Anglo-American Cataloguing Rules,* 2nd ed., 2002 Revision: Ottawa; Canadian Library Association; Chicago: American Library Association, Appendix D, p. 4.

Hawkins, Les, and Shadle, Steve. 2004. Reflections on wrapping paper: Random thoughts on AACR2 and electronic serials. *Serials Review* 30: 51–55.

Hirons, Jean, and Hawkins, Les. 2002. Transforming AACR2: Using the revised rules in Chapters 9 and 12, Part 2, Workshop presented at the 17th annual conference of NASIG, published in Susan L. Scheiberg and Shelley Neville, *Transforming Serials: The Revolution Continues*. Binghamton, NY: Haworth Press, pp. 243–253.

MARBI [Machine-Readable Bibliographic Information Committee]. 1996. *The MARC 21 Formats: Background and Principles*. Washington, DC: Library of Congress, http://www.loc.gov/marc/96principl.html.

Moeller, Paul, and Lu, Wen-ying. 2005. MARC 21 format for serials holdings: A survey on the acceptance and use of standards. *Serials Review* 31: 90–102.

Osborn, Andrew D. 1973. *Serial Publications: Their Place and Treatment in Libraries,* 2nd ed., rev. Chicago: American Library Association.

Reynolds, Regina Romano. 2005. Continuing Resources: FAQ and Fiction, Present and Future. *International Cataloguing and Bibliographic Control: Quarterly Bulletin of the IFLA UBCIM Programme* 34(1): 8–13.

Smith, Lynn S. 1978. *A Practical Approach to Serials Cataloging*. Greenwich, CT: JAI Press.

Chapter 6

Economics and the Market for Serials

This chapter will describe in some detail the costs of serials borne by publishers, libraries, and patrons. Another purpose is to present economic principles that help explain how and why the serials crisis occurred. Following the overview of costs in time and money borne by stakeholders and economic principles is a discussion of how the existing system of serials production and use might function more efficiently.

Librarians operate "gift economies." Since libraries pay for subscriptions to serials made available to patrons, the serials are a gift from the library to the patrons. Of course the patrons have indirectly paid for the serials through some combination of taxes, tuition, or labor; but the librarian decides which titles to buy for patrons' use. Individual patrons do not decide whether each subscription is worth its price.

Patrons enjoying this gift economy are not required to think about the costs of receiving, binding, or shelving the serials and are insulated from the tradeoffs that all economic decisions require. Individuals would be aware that their $25 personal subscription to *Scientific American* cost what they could have spent toward a meal in a nice restaurant. But when they are in the library reading the *Journal of Personality and Social Psychology*, they have not had to give up the opportunity to own an expensive stereo system. Since the cost of subscriptions does not come directly from their pockets, patrons are not required to think about what is being given up in exchange for these expensive items in their libraries.

COSTS OF SERIALS

The production, acquisition, and use of serials entail direct and indirect costs of time and money. Most, but not all, of these costs are assigned monetary values and factored into publishers' subscription prices and libraries' budgets. A broad view of the costs of serials will consider costs of time and money to authors, editors, peer reviewers, librarians, and anyone who reads serials. The costs will be considered here in categories of libraries, patrons, and publishers.

Costs to Libraries

The portion of budgets in different types of libraries devoted to serials, average costs of serials, and financial pressures from subscription inflation have been detailed in other chapters. Even though the most obvious cost of collecting serials to libraries is subscriptions, librarians face significant direct and indirect costs beyond subscriptions. For example, a direct cost comes when a serials subscription agency is used and the percentage fee charged by the agent is reflected in the serials budget. Other direct costs include the staff needed to handle all phases in the workflow of acquiring and maintaining a serials collection. Binding requires payment to commercial binders and/or purchase of binding supplies, including labels, tape, Princeton files, binders, and similar items. These supplies are not a huge expense, but they add up, and must be included in the budget.

Indirect expenses include the library building, shelving, office space and equipment for serials staff, heating and cooling, lighting, and building maintenance. The serials librarian is not usually responsible for tracking these expenses. In fact, the library director may not be directly responsible for them, either. Town councils, college administrators, or company financial officers may oversee some or all of the building and maintenance expenses. Nevertheless, they are real costs of maintaining a serials collection.

Serials delivered online represent some savings over print periodicals, but also introduce new costs. One might think at first glance that subscribing to serials online saves all the valuable shelf space and square footage required by print journals; however, providing access to online journals requires an Internet connection, a network, electricity, computer work stations, and printers. Remote access serials eliminate the need for stacks, but support costs are expensive and require library space. Space savings will be realized since workstation space is much less than the shelf space needed to house the print equivalent of thousands of titles accessed online.

The space savings are somewhat offset by the costs of purchasing, installing, and maintaining computers and printers. Not only does the equipment have to be replaced every three to five years, well-trained people are needed to maintain the system. Employees qualified to maintain computers and networks cost more than employees qualified to shelve issues and put labels on volumes. These costs of computers, networks and their maintenance are usually not included in a serials budget; however, when the overall cost of providing serials is calculated, some portion of their costs should be included in the equation.

Costs to Patrons

Serials are published and subscribed to so they can be read, and librarians maintain collections so they can be used by patrons. Libraries provide many, many more serials to patrons than they would ever want to subscribe to individually. While serials collections provide a significant social benefit, using them is not free to patrons. The most obvious cost to patrons of public and academic library expenses is the mix of taxes, fees, or tuition patrons pay to support libraries. Patrons may also encounter out-of-pocket expenses when they choose to print articles or make photocopies. The cost to special library users will depend upon whether or not charges for these services are charged back to the user's department or absorbed by the corporation. In any case, these obvious expenses are assigned monetary values.

The category of costs to patrons not assigned a monetary value is patrons' time and effort spent using serials collections. People must make choices among options of how to allocate the scarce resource of their time. Traveling to a library, seeking citations in catalogs and databases, finding items on shelves, and reading, taking notes, or making copies all take time. The time could be spent working, with family, relaxing, sleeping, doing laundry, or tending the roses. The value of patron's time is never figured into publishers' or libraries' budgets, but it is a real cost in the overall serials economy that should be accounted for. Librarians can consider the value of patrons' time in decisions regarding services and collections, even if patrons' time is not assigned a monetary value. This is particularly salient when considering adding remote access serials.

Patrons often want a hard copy of an article, whether printed from a computer or photocopied from the print collection. A substantial portion of library photocopying continues to be for patrons' reproduction of articles in print serials; and a substantial portion of printing in the library is attributable to patrons printing full-text articles from remote access serials. A librarian can choose to pay for the costs of copying and printing out of the library budget, but most academic and public libraries cover printing and copying costs by charging patrons.

Three options are available to charge patrons for copies and printouts. One is to charge cash for each copy, a common practice in the use of photocopiers. A coin box can be attached to the printer or copier. Be aware that coin boxes cost several hundred dollars to purchase and install, and they have an ongoing maintenance expense. Some librarians have used honor systems to charge cash for copies, which saves the transaction costs incurred by coin boxes. A second way to charge patrons is with cards or tags that register value on a magnetic strip. Readers attached to printers and copiers deduct value for each page.

A combination of the first and second and a frequently used method is to install machines attached to printers or copiers that accept either cash or magnetic strip cards. Many academic institutions are now using one card that serves as an ID, copy card, and meal card. Public libraries can sell copy cards, too, and may offer a discount for using a card instead of cash. As with coin boxes, copy cards create transaction costs. The readers on the machines and a method to sell the cards are an expense for the library. Responsibility for the cards and readers can be, and often is, outsourced to a vendor.

A third way to charge patrons is by using software to track use. With the software method, patrons log on to computers with their personal ID and password. The software counts the number of prints made, and deducts the appropriate amount from the individual's account. This can work well on an academic campus where the patrons are all registered users. An advantage of the software approach is that it saves the expense of installing and maintaining coin boxes or magnetic readers. It also enables the institution to allot each registered patron a certain number of prints for "free" and charge for prints over that limit. The transaction costs with a software system lie in network and database maintenance and administration of individual accounts.

When deciding which method to employ, the librarian or the parent institution should look carefully at the transaction costs involved and the impact of the decision on the library's mission and policies. Systems to collect money can cost more to implement than the paper, toner, and maintenance would cost. Systems that rely on restricting printing to registered users may adversely impact a general user population that is welcome to use the library. While these decisions are unlikely to be made by a serials librarian alone, the serials librarian's perspective can help inform those who are responsible for choosing how to cover the costs of copying and printing. Choosing how to cover costs is a central concern for publishers.

Costs to Publishers

Publishers of serials incur costs with creating content, producing and distributing issues in a fixed medium, marketing, accounting, and administrative expenses. The costs of creating the content of serials are part of the first copy costs. First copy costs are those incurred to create an issue ready to produce in print or online, including content such as articles, book reviews, and letters to the editor. Magazines and newspapers pay for content by having writers on staff or by paying writers for individual pieces. Readers may also contribute content such as letters to the editor without receiving any payment from the publisher.

Ownership of copyright affects publishers' costs. The copyright for material written by staff writers is held by the publisher under "work for hire" rules. Since the writer's salary is paid for by the publisher, the publisher owns the work created for them by that writer. When a publisher buys an individual work, the contract usually stipulates that the author gives the copyright to the publisher. The *New York Times Co. v. Tasini* Supreme Court decision in 2001 stated that authors' copyright to print and online versions of their works are separate. Contract agreements between authors and publishers now address rights to online publication, but contracts made before publishers anticipated online publishing were silent on the right to publish authors' works online.

The costs of producing a scholarly journal are different from magazine publishing, in part because authors of scholarly research articles are usually not paid. In fact, in the sciences, authors often have to pay page charges to have their work published. Publication in some medical journals is an exception, as authors of articles, case studies, and other works may receive payment for their writing. But in most disciplines, no payment is made to authors. Since publication is expected of professors for them to gain tenure and achieve rank, the financial incentive to write and publish is in the salary paid by their institution.

Other first copy costs beyond paying authors include editing, the production of graphics, and page layout. Substantial time and effort is required to convert an author's draft into content that matches the standards and style of the serial. Publishers of scholarly journals have substantial first copy costs even though authors are not paid for articles. Expenses include editing for content, copy editing, graphics production, page layout, and the peer review process. The process of having experts review manuscripts for accuracy and quality requires paying for an editor, office expenses, and postage. Since many editors of scholarly journals do the task part-time for a modest stipend, the editing portion of first copy costs may be kept relatively low for scholarly journals. The expenses of graphics and page layout vary greatly according to the requirements and production standards of the serial.

Producing issues of serials and distributing them in a fixed medium creates additional variable costs beyond the first copy costs. Print issues must be printed and mailed. The cost of printing varies by the size of the print run, the type of paper and binding used, and the print quality, including resolution and whether color is used. The quality of paper and printing do affect the prices of serials, and publishers have used the prices of supplies and improvements in quality as reasons for rising subscription prices. Interestingly, though, art journals have relatively low prices even though most have very high-quality printing and paper. The average cost in 2005 of art and architecture journals was $135, an average lower than any LC subject area except general works and music (Van Orsdel and Born 2005, p. 44).

Shipping issues is a cost that varies by the size and number of issues mailed. The United States Postal Service has periodicals rates formerly known as Second Class mail. Regulations for qualifying for the relatively low periodicals rates require that the title be clearly displayed, an ISSN or postal service code be printed on each issue, and that a publication pattern must be established and maintained. (Unfortunately for serials librarians, these rules leave publishers great leeway in where on the issues the title, ISSN, and publication pattern information is printed.) The Postal Service's Periodicals rates vary based on several factors. For example, serials presorted and packaged by the publisher for subscribers in one ZIP code qualify for the lowest rates.

Claims for missing or damaged issues create additional costs for the publishers. Usually, extra copies will be created during the print run to provide issues to cover claims and for sample copies. On top of the cost of printing extra issues, the publisher's staff must spend time responding to the claim and must pay the postage for the replacement issue.

Publishing Online. Publishing serials online saves the costs of printing and mailing issues and handling claims for missing issues. But added costs of online publishing offset those savings. When journal articles were first beginning to be posted online, some observers of the serials marketplace speculated that publishers could save 10–40 percent of their costs by publishing online, and should pass those savings onto subscribers. These savings never really materialized because publishing online incurs new costs in addition to the continuing costs of print production. Servers, databases, and Internet connections must be installed and maintained to publish online. The online content needs to be kept available over time, and maintaining articles on a server requires time and effort. (How long publishers will keep articles on their servers, and whether it is their responsibility or the responsibility of libraries, remains an open question.) Fixing technical problems requires the expertise of highly trained, well-paid professionals.

Many subscribers still desire print subscriptions, so publishers still have to pay for the print runs, postage, and claims for print issues. Posting and maintaining serials content online thus represents an additional expense to publishers rather than a way to save expenses. If there were a magical way for a publisher to throw a switch and immediately convert from print publishing to online only publishing, they might save about 30 percent of their costs. But as long as they have to publish in two media, no savings are realized, and overall costs may well go up.

Whether published in print or online, publishers have administrative costs inherent in the business of creating and selling periodicals. It costs money to attract and keep subscribers, keep accurate records of current subscribers, and collect subscription fees. Expenses found in any business, like office space, computers, phones, files, and so forth, must also be covered.

Methods Used to Cover Costs. How publishers cover their expenses for first copies, variable costs, and online publishing vary by the type of serial. Magazines and newspapers typically receive a substantial proportion of their income from advertising and the balance from subscriptions. Advertising rates are based on the number of issues circulated, and on the demographics of subscribers and other readers. Publishers that rely on advertising revenue emphasize maximizing circulation to the people advertisers wish to reach. Subscription and cover prices of magazines are usually kept low to maximize circulation.

Most scholarly journals receive the majority of their revenue from subscriptions and relatively little revenue from advertising, but there are exceptions. Medical journals in particular receive substantial revenue from advertisers. The publishers' costs not covered by advertising are covered in a variety of ways. Commercial, for-profit publishers rely primarily or exclusively on subscription revenue. But they may also charge author's fees known as page charges for their articles to be published. Page charges paid by authors to publishers help cover the costs of producing published articles. Whether page charges are used to raise revenue from authors varies by discipline. For instance, page charges are standard practice in chemistry, but they are unheard of in the humanities.

Nonprofit societies mostly use a combination of subscriptions, author page charges, and membership dues to cover publication costs. Society publishers often produce more than one periodical, and use the same office space and administrative staff to conduct the organization's other activities. The costs of producing a journal thus get mixed up with other costs of society business. Some societies price their journals to generate enough subscription revenue to subsidize other activities. Other societies subsidize the costs of producing journals from membership dues and/or conference fees. No standard exists, and practices vary widely among societies.

Additional possible sources of revenue for publishers include selling back issues and reprints, acquiring sponsors, and receiving royalties from full-text databases. As of 2005, royalties from full-text databases comprise only a small portion of total revenue for publishers of scholarly serials. It will be interesting to see if that remains the case going into the future.

Publishers' Profits. When publishers choose to derive a profit from the sale of their periodicals, it is figured into the price of subscriptions. Profits made by some publishers are controversial because many librarians deem the profit margins to be excessive. The publishers criticized for making excess profit argue that the revenue is needed to maintain quality, improve services, and help support online publishing.

The value-added services publishers provide are very real and vital to the usefulness of serials literature. Publishers have not done a very good job of explaining their legitimate costs of business to librarians and readers. Reports of the high profits enjoyed by a few publishers have distracted attention from the legitimate economic needs of publishers of serials as a group. More open dialogue is needed between publishers and librarians, based on more forthright explanations of actual costs on both sides.

ECONOMICS OF SUBSCRIPTION PRICES

Time and money are scare, so choices among scarce resources create tradeoffs. The willingness of people to pay is based on those tradeoffs, which economists call "opportunity costs." The opportunity cost of a serial subscription is whatever else could have been bought with the same money. Earlier in this chapter, the example was given of an individual choosing a $25 subscription to *Scientific American* over going out for dinner. The subscription cost the individual the opportunity of buying dinner with the $25.

Trading one dinner for a year's worth of reading is reasonable. The other part of the example earlier in this chapter was a subscription to the *Journal of Personality and Social Psychology*, which happens to cost a library $1,069 per year. The price of that scholarly journal is not unusual and many cost far more. A librarian's willingness to pay for this journal is based on the tradeoff of choosing it over other journals, or over books, videos, or other materials. But a college that offers a degree in psychology needs to provide psychology journals. Trading off the $1,069 to buy 50 novels or videos would not be acceptable to the Psychology Department. That tradeoff would be quite acceptable for most public libraries, though, which is one reason why few public libraries collect scholarly journals.

A person subscribing to the *Journal of Personality and Social Psychology* would not likely be willing to trade a mortgage payment for 12 issues of the journal, no matter how well produced it is. The publisher, the American Psychological Association (APA), knows that, and sets a separate price for individuals. A subscription is still real money, costing $382 per year to nonmembers of the APA or $190 to members (the discount is a benefit of membership). Individual willingness to pay is increased by the fact that many individual subscribers are practicing professionals who can count the subscription as a business expense or have it covered by professional development funds. The APA, like all publishers, balances their need for revenue with their subscribers' willingness to pay when setting subscription rates.

Willingness of librarians to pay for serials is based on the opportunity costs among titles capable of meeting collection development goals. Which titles are chosen in the first place is based on selection criteria and budgetary constraints. As been discussed earlier, the inflation rate for periodicals is higher than the general inflation rate and typically exceeds increases in library budgets, and the reason why inflation for journals has continued year after year is rooted in willingness to pay and the closely related economic concept called elasticity of demand.

Elasticity of Demand

Elasticity of demand is the degree to which changes in price influence buyers' willingness to pay for a product. In general, luxury items have high elasticity of demand, and necessities have low elasticity of demand. Soft drinks sold in grocery stores tend to have highly elastic demand. It is not necessary to buy large quantities of soda at once, and there are many alternatives to any one particular flavor or brand. The producers of soft drinks keep prices low relative to competing soft drinks because they know that increasing the price will cause many people to buy something else.

People may pay higher prices for soft drinks in convenience stores than they are willing to pay in grocery stores since they go to a convenience store to satisfy a need for a cold one at the moment. The convenience factor creates a lower elasticity of demand, the customer will go ahead and buy a soda even though it is 20 cents cheaper somewhere else. Lack of alternatives in the context gives the seller greater leeway to raise prices and still make sales.

For serials, individual subscriptions have relatively high elasticity of demand, and institutional subscriptions have low elasticity of demand. Individuals are much more likely than libraries to not renew their subscription when the price increases noticeably. Individuals are aware of their opportunity costs, and subscriptions are not usually considered necessities. Individuals may conclude, after all, that they will just read it at the library.

As described before, librarians operate a gift economy, purchasing serials at subscription prices generally unknown to patrons. While a librarian can make choices among titles, collection development policies and institutional missions call for subscriptions to certain types of serials. The most important journals in a discipline tend to be considered "must haves." Being deemed necessary, the librarian sees little choice but to pay for the subscriptions to these titles, even if their prices are escalating rapidly. Jean-Claude Guedon (2001) has argued that a primary reason certain journals have become indispensable is their ranking in ISI's Journal Citation Reports (*JCR*) database. Selection of titles for inclusion in the ISI citation indexes gives them a high profile. If they also have high impact factors, the titles become sacred cows; very difficult to cancel even if priced much higher than competing titles. The "must-have" journals with high impact factors have very inelastic demand.

Dividing the Market (Price Discrimination)

Sellers can take advantage of elasticity of demand and maximize profits by implementing price discrimination. Sellers can choose to divide the market into segments based on each target group's sensitivity to changes in price. For the purpose of explaining the principle of dividing the market based on elasticity of demand, consider the soft drink example. Assume that there are three types of soft drink buyers: discount seekers, brand name buyers, and soda snobs. The discount seekers will buy whatever is cheapest. The brand name buyers seek out well-known flavors and brands. The soda snobs are willing to pay more for something special, unusual, or produced in a socially conscious way. The Bubbled Sugar Water Company, armed with this information about their customers, can create three product lines. Discount-seeking consumers of "Guzzle Soda" have highly elastic demand, so the product is priced lower than the competition. "Big Brand

Soda" has a middling price in line with competitors, but is marketed on features other than price such as free prizes in bottle caps and celebrity endorsements. "EcoFresh Effervescent Fructose Splash" has a designer label and costs much more than the other two. The wealthier buyers are willing to pay a higher price and thus have inelastic demand even though the contents of the bottles could be exactly the same. Since the consumers in each market segment have a different elasticity of demand, the Bubbled Sugar Water Company divides the market and charges different prices for essentially the same product.

Of course, serials are different from soda. Each issue of a serial is usually packaged exactly the same for all subscribers. Occasionally, publishers create different versions, for example, a newsstand version and a subscriber version, or a U.S. version and a U.K. version. Fortunately, the practice of publishing different versions of the same serial is not very common. In most cases, the issues received by libraries are identical to the issues received by individuals. Despite identical packaging of most serial issues, the principle of dividing the market works the same. Different segments of the market are identified, their elasticity of demand estimated, and different prices charged to subscribers in each segment. Dividing the market into segments allows price discrimination among segments. Serials are sold at different prices to different groups based on their different levels of will-ingness to pay, their elasticity of demand.

Price discrimination for popular magazines exists in that librarians pay the full price while individuals can take advantage of discounts. For scholarly journals, it is standard practice to charge one price to individuals, and another, much higher price for institutions. It is not unusual for a publisher to divide the market into additional segments. For instance, different prices may be set for type of institu-tion (e.g., research library, college library, corporation, nonprofit organization) or professional status (e.g., student, professor, practitioner, retired). Some societies even charge different subscription rates for different self-reported income levels.

Publishers charge libraries higher subscription rates and are able to raise prices because librarians have relatively inelastic demand. The perpetuation of the serials crisis and the growing availability of resources online are making librarians less willing to pay ever higher subscription rates. The more elastic demand among librarians for serials is beginning to show signs of affecting publishers' pricing. If librarians, as a whole, are more sensitive to increases in subscription prices, publishers will either have to reduce annual price increases or accept sales of fewer subscriptions.

Inflation

Inflation has two distinct but interrelated causes. Cost-push inflation is caused by increases in the costs of production. For instance, if the salaries of editors and the price of printing increase, a publisher will need to cover the higher costs, probably by raising the subscription price. Cost-push inflation affects serials when publishers increase the number of pages published per volume and increase the quality of printing and binding. The costs of salaries, offices, and postage are examples of other areas where increases push inflation of subscription rates.

Demand-pull inflation occurs when there is an increase in buyers' willingness to pay, or when money is available to buy more of a product than can be readily delivered. Demand-pull inflation played a significant role in the entry of commercial, for-profit publishers into scholarly publishing. Soon after the Second World War, a combination of factors sharply increased the demand for scholarly journals. In 1950, there were fewer than 7,000 Ph.D.s in the United States. By 1970, there were almost 30,000. This rapid increase in the number of Ph.D.s meant a rapid increase in researchers who needed outlets for their publications, and who needed to read about the research of their peers. The launch of Sputnik in 1957 created a political furor and strident calls to invest resources for the United States to catch up to the Soviet Union. Funding for research increased sharply, and with it, increases in library budgets to subscribe to the serials that published research findings. The combination of more people and more funding for research created more demand for journal articles than scholarly societies were able to supply.

Commercial, for-profit publishers saw the demand and took the opportunity to launch new journals. Many of the commercially produced journals begun in the 1960s became leaders in their disciplines. Since researchers needed to read these prestigious journals, the librarians paying for them had very inelastic demand. Publishers could and did raise prices from year to year because librarians were willing to pay. Rapid increases in library budgets to cover the new serials slowed dramatically in the early 1980s. Despite librarians' budgetary constraints, publishers recognized that librarians' demand for scholarly journals was inelastic, and continued raising subscription prices at rates significantly exceeding overall inflation.

These inflationary factors were described in Chapter 1 as causes of the "serials crisis." The cumulative effect of serials inflation outstripping library budgets has led librarians and other observers of serials publishing to contemplate alternative ways to fund scholarly periodicals. One perspective is to highlight the public goods characteristics of scholarly publications.

SCHOLARLY JOURNALS AND THE THEORY
OF PUBLIC GOODS

Market forces alone are failing to adequately fund the social value of scholarly publications. The ongoing serials crisis has created a situation where scholars have inadequate access to the periodical literature in their fields. It is the opinion of the author that the stakeholders in scholarly publishing would all benefit if better ways could be found to create an adequately funded, equitable system that efficiently and effectively serves all scholars. A possible way to improve the system would be for the stakeholders to choose to treat scholarly serials as public goods. No technical reason stands in the way of this occurring, as online scholarly periodical literature naturally lends itself to be treated as a public good.

Public goods are consumer goods that when supplied to one person can be made available to others at no extra cost. A pure public good, as defined by Paul Samuelson, is

1. non-rival in consumption—one person's consumption of the good does not reduce its availability to anyone else, and
2. has the characteristic of nonexcludability—once the good is provided, the producer is unable to prevent anyone from consuming it (Sandmo 1987, p. 1061).

Practically nothing in the real world totally fits the definition of a pure public good. A typical limitation to a public good is geography, because access is restricted to a limited area. Examples of public goods limited by geography are fireworks displays and radio broadcasts. Public goods can also be limited by congestion. A roadway is non-rival and non-excludable if traffic is not heavy, but congestion reduces the road's availability to drivers. The print serials in a library are public goods, but are limited by physical access to the collection and the fact that a volume cannot be used by more than one person at a time.

It is critical to recognize that "public good" refers to non-rivalrous, non-excludable consumption attributes, and NOT to whether a good is produced by the public sector. For instance, a broadcast radio program is a public good. One person listening to the broadcast does not lessen another's ability to listen (non-rivalrous), and within its range the radio station cannot limit who can listen (non-excludable). Whether a station's broadcast is paid for by public funds or by advertising or by government is a separate issue from it being a public good. Since the source of funding is not a defining characteristic of public goods, one can accept the premise that scholarly journals should be treated as public goods without assuming anything about how or by whom the production of journals is financed.

Also worth emphasizing is that a public good need not have the same benefit to all, even though the availability is the same to all. A radio broadcast is a public good even though some people do not listen to it. So although not everyone has an interest in scholarly journals, they can still be public goods.

Collective choice to treat something as a public good makes sense when the costs of creating the first unit are very high, but the cost of making one more unit available is very low. Public goods tend to need a great deal of funding initially and relatively less to produce additional units or to maintain the good. Journals have this characteristic, since a large portion of the cost of production lies in the initial costs of producing the first copy.

Pareto Optimum

According to an economic principle called the Pareto optimum, society as a whole derives the greatest benefit from a good when no possible reallocation of the good can make anyone better off without making someone else worse off

(Lockwood 1987, p. 811). The optimal, most efficient allocation of a public good is achieved at the Pareto optimum when the total marginal cost to all consumers is equal to the total marginal cost of production. In other words, the ideal level of spending on a public good is to cover the costs beyond the initial cost of creating the product or service. Publishers create online articles with basically all initial costs in creating the first copy and trivial marginal costs of providing additional copies. To provide articles at the Pareto optimum would be to provide them practically for free and providing journals for free will not cover publishers' costs of production. Some mechanism(s) must be found to pay for the publishers' initial first copy costs. At least one example now demonstrates serials provided at the Pareto optimum and the accompanying issue of how to fund first copy costs.

The Example of Open Access Journals

Current technologies enable online journal articles to be treated as public goods. For example, the titles linked from the Directory of Open Access Journals (DOAJ) at http://www.doaj.org are essentially non-rival in consumption and non-excludable. A journal article retrieved from a site linked from the DOAJ is non-rival in consumption because one's viewing and downloading of an article does not affect another's ability to read or download. Some limits caused by congestion on a server might occur, but would not likely create any significant barrier to access. Articles linked from the DOAJ are non-excludable because anyone with a connection to the web has free access. In contrast, print journals in libraries are more likely to cause rivalries and are excludable in consumption since only one person can use an issue at a time, and use is limited by physical access to the library. The journals listed in the DOAJ are being treated as public goods. How are the publishers' costs being paid for?

Without subscription revenue, publishers of Open Access (OA) journals rely on some combination of author fees, grants, and subsidies. Whether OA journals can be self sustaining over the long run is an outstanding question. Regazzi (2004) argues that author fees alone are probably not enough because the cost of producing each article is higher than authors are willing or able to pay. He cites the Wellcome Trust (2004) estimated cost of $1,950 per article for a high-quality journal and notes that the Public Library of Science (PLoS) charges authors $1,500 (Regazzi 2004, p. 277). The Wellcome Trust (2004) suggests that OA journals could charge authors fees not only for accepted papers but also charge for submitting a paper, thus helping to spread the cost of peer review. Costs of producing journals may be funded with subsidies from sponsoring organizations and grants from government agencies or private foundations. OA journals will have to find adequate funding to replace subscription revenue.

Publishers whose content is linked from the DOAJ have chosen to make their content freely available to all. Other journal articles accessible online are made excludable to the degree chosen by the publisher. Free access to journal articles on the web is technologically simpler to administrate than creating a system to limit access to subscribers. Since posting content for free does not pay for costs of production, necessity forces publishers who rely on subscription revenue to spend effort and resources to limit access to subscribers. Limiting access requires effort that creates costs for the publisher beyond the costs of producing the serial, thus contributing to a gap between the price subscribers pay and the revenue publishers receive.

Serials and Deadweight Loss

A deadweight loss is the gap between the price buyers pay and the revenue received by sellers (e.g., manufacturers, transporters, retailers). A market is optimally efficient when consumer surplus and producer surplus are maximized. That is, when buyers feel they are getting a good deal and the sellers make acceptable profits. Deadweight loss reduces market efficiency. The classic example of a deadweight loss is a sales tax. The price consumers pay for a taxed good is higher than the price received by the producers, so the tax hangs like a dead weight on the producers' income and the consumers' willingness to pay. This causes consumers to buy less, thereby reducing producers' ability to set prices as high as they would prefer. For serials, costs beyond producing the content and making it available to readers can be considered to be deadweight losses.

The deadweight losses in the serials supply chain are mostly in the time and effort spent to distribute, organize, and access journals. Unlike a sales tax, these deadweight losses are not immediately apparent, and some are so diffuse as to be easily overlooked. Since librarians operate a gift economy, a typically ignored deadweight loss is the enormous amounts of time readers spend accessing journal literature. Patrons spend time getting to the library, identifying holdings, and retrieving articles. Data gathered at the author's library indicate that patrons use the online version of a serial about six or ten times as frequently as they use the print. Although no study has been conducted to confirm the disparity in use, the time patrons save accounts for much of the dramatic difference in the online and print use of the same serials. Patrons' time has a real and meaningful value that is not directly accounted for in the present system.

The funds librarians spend on serials acquisition, organization, and maintenance reduces funds available to pay for subscriptions. The nonsubscription costs of managing a serials collection represent a deadweight loss in the system of linking authors of serials content with their readers. Nonsubscription costs of providing serials are substantial. The Council on Library and Information Resources' research report *The Nonsubscription Side of Periodicals* reports total nonsubscription costs of print periodicals in a range of about $30–$300 per subscription (Schonfeld et al. 2004). The same report shows nonsubscription costs of electronic serials in the range of about $7–$47. Having scholarly journals online will not eliminate overhead costs for libraries, but the per-title cost of maintenance may be reduced by offering journals online. Over time, the shift to online access may allow librarians to shift resources from binding, re-shelving, and processing to paying publishers' subscription or license fees.

The portion of publishers' total expenses for marketing, invoicing, responding to claims, and handling physical volumes also represent deadweight losses. For online publishing, the cost of restricting access to subscribed users is also a deadweight loss. For scholarly journals, the deadweight losses basically consist of all the costs not directly related to editing, peer review, and first copy production. Treating journals as public goods can potentially reduce deadweight losses in serials publication.

The Public Goods Choice

If the stakeholders in serials work together and employ current technologies, a system could be created that could dramatically reduce the deadweight losses in publishers' overhead, libraries' nonsubscription costs, and patrons' time. Treating something as a public good is usually a choice made by groups of people who recognize the importance of supporting the social value of a good. It is taken for granted that roads and schools will be publicly funded so all can benefit from efficient transportation and an educated populace, but long ago both roads and schools were exclusively available to those individuals willing to pay for their use.

It is logical for society to choose to treat something as a public good when it would be under produced without group intervention. That choice is typically made when the social value of something is recognized as being worth paying for. Information found in journals has both a primary value and a social value. The primary value is the gain individuals enjoy from using the information. The social value is the benefit to society derived from the education gained from use of the information. Unless an organization able to act in the public's interest becomes involved, the social value of information is not funded. Librarians can organize consortia to help fund the social value of information published in serials.

Club Goods and Consortia

Consortial purchasing of online content represents a *de facto* move from a market of private, excludable goods to quasi-public "club" goods. A club good is a quasi-public good made available to a defined group of users who pay a fee to partake in the benefits of club membership (McGuire 1987, pp. 454–455). An example of journals being treated as club goods is Elsevier's ScienceDirect contract with the Pi Squared consortium of private colleges located mostly in New York State. This contract allows authorized users at institutions in the consortium access to all the journals subscribed to by any member institution. Every library in the consortium is treated as one customer, so all the students, faculty and staff are members of the club. Membership in the club is typically verified with a current library card or student ID. Each member library gains access to significantly more titles than could be afforded before, the publisher benefits by reducing the number of contracts to administer, and scholars save time formerly spent requesting and waiting for articles via ILL. The price Elsevier charges for ScienceDirect and the limits they have placed on libraries' ability to cancel have been criticized by some librarians. But by treating the journals in ScienceDirect as a club good, scholars have online access to many, many more journals than individual libraries could provide acting alone.

Statewide consortia are actively working in many states to increase the online journal content available to library patrons. These statewide consortia effectively make all citizens of the state members of the club. One example of statewide funding of a full-text database is the Health Reference Center, a Gale database provided to all libraries in New York State. Access to journal content is funded through the Library Services and Technology Act (LSTA) grant to the New York State Library by the Federal Institute of Museum and Library Services (IMLS). A second example is Pennsylvania's Power Library project funded by the Pennsylvania legislature for all citizens of Pennsylvania through their public library card. These efforts in New York and Pennsylvania are not unique, as many states have similar initiatives to provide statewide access to full-text databases through libraries.

The distinct advantage of the club goods version of treating scholarly journals as public goods is that it helps control the "free rider" problem of people taking advantage of the service without paying their fair share. Given the instant and borderless transmission of information on the web, some way to control access to members of a club is needed, even if the club were to be all citizens of a state, country, or alliance of countries. The theory of club goods summarized by McGuire (1987) has been intensively analyzed by economists, whose work on the most efficient ways to employ clubs for optimum allocation of goods deserves greater attention by the stakeholders in the journal market.

Challenges. While it appears that the journal market may be moving towards a quasi-public goods model in the form of club goods, important needs of stakeholders are not being adequately addressed. Since there is no direct support for publishers' first copy costs, uncertain revenue to publishers threatens the stability of content in aggregated full-text databases. EBSCOhost, a leading vendor of aggregated full-text databases, holds the position that these databases complement, but should not replace, individual journal subscriptions. EBSCOhost's rationale behind the position that aggregated full-text databases are not a replacement for individual subscriptions has been described by Sam Brooks (2002). The gist of his argument is that since the royalties EBSCOhost pays to publishers for full-text content is a small fraction of their production costs, and publishers have ultimate control over what content they provide to the database, EBSCOhost cannot guarantee future coverage of particular titles. So if a library definitely wants access to a journal, they need to subscribe to it, and not rely on an aggregated database.

At present, payments by full-text aggregators to publishers are not sufficient to cover their first copy costs of production. If librarians do choose to replace individual subscriptions with contracts for aggregated full-text serials, publishers will have to receive substantially more money from the aggregators. Reductions in overhead may help reduce overall costs to publishers, but the price to libraries for aggregated databases will inevitably increase, probably quite dramatically.

Smaller libraries lack the resources needed to adequately support subscriptions to individual online journals. While it is feasible for a smaller library to administer an aggregated database of a few thousand titles, it is not feasible to administer access and logins through dozens of publishers for access to a few thousand separate online subscriptions. Similarly, small publishers may not have the resources to provide online content in a competitive manner. The fixed costs of administering online content may be too great for smaller publishers to cover through available revenues.

Potential Benefits. A club goods model could reduce the costs to publishers not related to the first copy costs of creating content. Large contracts for online access to journals would reduce marketing and subscription management expenses, and could ease the transition away from also having to produce print issues. Libraries' nonsubscription expenses could be greatly reduced if online serials are provided via stable aggregated databases. A club goods model might facilitate the implementation of standards and provide more consistency across user interfaces. Each interface and method of linking to content may be rational, but library patrons currently face a very complicated system filled with potential for failed connections. To be able to assist patrons, librarians need a stable, predictable, explainable system for retrieving journal articles online. Libraries also need to minimize the administrative overhead associated with managing access to online journals.

Scholars clearly desire access from a convenient location to as much information as possible via understandable, navigable systems that allow efficient searching. Scholars also have a stake in maintaining, and perhaps even improving, the quality of journal content. Another important audience is independent and young scholars. Giving prodigies and curious laymen broad access to scholarship thus allowing them to feed their curiosity with good information could be a great social benefit. After all, what good is it to tell students the great value of being life-long learners, but then tell them they have to be at a university to keep in touch with research found in publications?

With respect to technology, online access to scholarly periodicals easily allows serials to be treated as a public good. Aggregations of journals into large databases and organization of libraries into consortia are moving us in the direction of treating scholarly journals as club goods. However, we are in danger of creating an oligopoly that fails to adequately serve the information needs of all stakeholders. Market forces alone will not provide enough funding to support the social value of scholarly journals. Publishers, librarians, and all organizations responsible for published scholarship should choose to treat journals as public goods or club goods, and create an adequately funded, equitable system that serves all scholars as efficiently and effectively as possible.

How scholarly journals are paid for is one important piece of a range of issues surrounding the publication of scholarship. Chapter 7 expands on discussion of economics and addresses issues of quality of content, ethics, and incentives. The next chapter also presents more alternatives to traditional publishing models.

SUGGESTIONS FOR FURTHER READING

Bruce R. Kingma's *The Economics of Information: A Guide to Economic and Cost-Benefit Analysis for Information Professionals* (Englewood, CO: Libraries Unlimited, 2001) provides a broad treatment of economic principles as they apply to serials. A compilation of classic papers is Donald Ward King, Nancy K. Roderer, and Harold A. Olsen's *Key Papers in the Economics of Information* (White Plains, NY: Published for the American Society for Information Science by Knowledge Industry Publications, 1983). More thorough, authoritative definitions of the economic terms discussed in this chapter, with bibliographies of classic articles on each topic, are in the *The New Palgrave: A Dictionary of Economics* (New York: Macmillan, 1987).

Recommended research studies on the costs of creating scholarly journals are Todd A. Carpenter, Heather Joseph, and Mary Waltham, "A survey of business trends at BioOne Publishing Partners and its implications for BioOne," *portal: Libraries and the Academy,* 4(4), 2004, 465–484, and *Costs and Business Models in Scientific Research Publishing: A Report Commissioned by the Wellcome Trust* (April 2004, available online at http://www.wellcome.ac.uk/doc_WTD003185.html).

Several issues discussed in this chapter are treated in greater depth by Jean-Claude Guedon in his *Oldenburg's Long Shadow: Librarians, Research Scientists, and the Control of Scientific Publishing* (Annapolis Junction, MD: ARL Publications, 2001, http://www.arl.org/arl/proceedings/138/guedon.html). Guedon's report analyzes the role of ISI's databases in the creation of "must-have" journals, the rise of commercial publishers, and the Open Archives Initiative, among other things.

An early overview of potential cost savings and a possible model for electronic publication may be found in Hal R. Varian, "The future of electronic journals" (presented at the Scholarly Communication and Technology Conference at Emory University, April 24–25, 1997, http://arl.cni.org/scomm/scat/varian.html). For a more recent analysis of the potential cost savings to libraries of online access versus housing volumes on shelves in the library, see president of JSTOR, Kevin Guthrie's "Archiving in the digital age: There's a will, but is there a way?" *Educause Review,* 36(6), 2001, 57–65, http://www.educasue.edu/ir/library/pdf/erm 0164.pdf.

A broad view of the issue of more open access to information is contained in Nancy Kranich's *The Information Commons: A Public Policy Approach*, online at http://www.brennancenter.org/resources. An excellent treatment of the various flavors of public goods and how they might apply to remote access scholarly serials is Charlotte Hess and Elinor Ostrom, "Ideas, artifacts, and facilities: Information as a common-pool resource," *Law and Contemporary Problems,* 66(11), 2003, 111–145, and online at http://www.law.duke.edu/journals/lcp/articles/lcp66dWinterSpring2003p111.htm.

REFERENCES

Brooks, Sam. 2002. Issues facing academic library consortia and perceptions of members of the Illinois Digital Academic Library. *portal: Libraries and the Academy* 2: 43–57.

Guedon, Jean-Claude. 2001. *Oldenburg's Long Shadow: Librarians, Research Scientists, and the Control of Scientific Publishing.* Annapolis Junction, MD: ARL Publications.

Lockwood, B. 1987. Pareto efficiency. In *The New Palgrave: A Dictionary of Economics*, ed. John Eatwell, Murray Milgate, and Peter Newman, vol. 3, pp. 811–813. New York: Macmillan.

McGuire, Martin C. 1987. Clubs. In *The New Palgrave: A Dictionary of Economics*, ed. John Eatwell, Murray Milgate, and Peter Newman, vol. 1, pp. 454–455. New York: Macmillan.

Regazzi, John. 2004. The shifting sands of Open Access publishing, a publisher's view. *Serials Review* 30(4): 275–280.

Sandmo, Agnar. 1987. Public goods. In *The New Palgrave: A Dictionary of Economics*, ed. John Eatwell, Murray Milgate, and Peter Newman, vol. 3, pp. 1061–1066. New York: Macmillan.

Schonfeld, Roger C., King, Donald W., Okerson, Ann, and Fenton, Eileen Gifford. June 2004. *The Nonsubscription Side of Periodicals: Changes in Library Operations and Costs between Print and Electronic Formats.* Washington, DC: Council on Library and Information Resources, http://www.clir.org/pubs/reports/pub127/pub127.pdf.

Van Orsdel, Lee, and Born, Kathleen. 2005. Choosing sides. *Library Journal* 130(7): 43–48.

Wellcome Trust. 2004. *Costs and Business Models in Scientific Research Publishing.* Histon, UK: Wellcome Trust, http://www.wellcome.ac.uk/doc_WTD003185.html.

Chapter 7

Issues in Scholarly Journal Publishing

Serials librarians must be interested in issues related to scholarly journal publications because these issues are very familiar to their primary users, faculty, students, and other researchers in academic, public, and special libraries. Serials librarians have no direct and very little indirect influence on the content of scholarly journals. Their indirect influence comes through decisions on which subscriptions to continue, add, or drop. The issues that will be discussed in this chapter include strengths and weaknesses of the peer review process, the profit motive in scholarly publishing, incentives for publishing research, and alternatives to traditional ways of reporting scholarship in serial publications.

A serials librarian needs to be familiar with issues in scholarly journal publishing in order to be informed when conversing with scholars who use the serials collection. Faculty and other researchers need to trust the librarian to make wise decisions concerning "their" journals. Researchers at academic institutions and special libraries are intimately familiar with peer review and "publish or perish," and may be concerned about the rapid changes in scholarly publishing. It is much easier for librarians to gain researchers' trust when they are knowledgeable about issues surrounding serials publishing.

ACCURACY OF CONTENT

Scholars, writing in scholarly publications, publish the results of their research in order to advance human knowledge. The content of magazines and newspapers is produced by journalists with different standards of research. These two approaches are discussed in terms of the ethics of the writers and scholars who review the content before it is published.

Ideally, published research articles written by scholars are unbiased, objective reports of original research conducted with no conflicts of interest and motivated by an altruistic desire to share knowledge with anyone interested in the topic. Research should be reported according to professional standards established in the discipline, including appropriate and accurate application of accepted research methods. Academic disciplines typically follow codified standards that describe correct research and publishing practice. Examples of standards may be found in the American Historical Association's *Statement on Standards of Professional Conduct* http://www.historians.org/pubs/Free/ProfessionalStandards.cfm and the American Psychological Association's (APA) Ethical Principles of Psychologists and Code of Conduct. Editors of journals strive to uphold principles described in their discipline.

The content of magazines and newspapers is produced by journalists with different standards of research. While journalists are also dedicated to advancing human knowledge, their approach to research is somewhat different from a scholars' approach. The intended audience is usually broader, the methods of seeking truth are not based on laboratory work, and are not as heavily based on what has been previously written on a topic. The Code of Ethics of the Society of Professional Journalists stresses the public's right to know the truth, and requires journalists to write with objectivity, accuracy, and fairness http://www.spj.org/ethics_code.asp. Accountability is rooted in readers' feedback and ability to complain. Responsibility for accuracy in magazines and newspapers lies with the author, the editor, and the publisher. To evaluate the content of scholarly publications, a peer review process may be used.

PEER REVIEW

Peer review is the process by which highly qualified experts in a field, known as peer reviewers or referees, review research articles for accuracy before they are published. Peer review is expensive for the publisher due to the costs of organizing and administering the process. High-prestige journal editors, many of whom reject a significant percentage of submitted papers, pay relatively more because they have administrative costs for the rejected papers. Software that streamlines the process is available but is expensive to implement.

The editor of a scholarly journal chooses a group of reviewers with knowledge of the topic area to critique papers before they are published. They may be asked to read a single paper or they may be given a term on the editorial staff of a publication. Their names may be on the masthead, they may be acknowledged annually, or they may lack public recognition. Three is a common number chosen to review a single article, but some journal editors use two or four referees; editors may expand the number of reviewers if the research being reported might be controversial. Copies of the manuscript are sent by the editor to each reviewer and this person may or may not know the author of the paper. Best practice calls for double-blind peer review.

Double-blind review helps reviewers critique articles on their own merits, without influence of familiarity with the author's other work, institutional affiliation, or professional relationships. The author does not know who the reviewers are, and the referees do not know who the author is. Double-blind review helps authors objectively consider reviewers' feedback separate from their familiarity with the reviewers' research interests and professional associations.

Critics of double-blind peer review have argued for an open process, so that authors', editors', and reviewers' identities and affiliations are known by everyone. One proponent of open peer review is Fiona Godlee, who has argued that an open process would increase the accountability of the reviewers, help expose any biases or conflicts of interest, and give reviewers due credit for the work they put into critiquing manuscripts (Godlee 2002). A few journals, including the *British Medical Journal* and the medical journals in BioMed Central have gone to an open review process, whereby readers not only know who the peer reviewers are, but can also read their feedback. A related approach is to share reviewer's comments, but retain confidentiality. For example, The *Journal of Educational Research* includes some reviewers' comments at the end of articles, but does not identify the reviewers. A potential drawback to open review is that the reviewers may be less frank than they would be in a confidential process. Referees must return manuscripts within a schedule.

The time given to reviewers to return feedback to the editor varies, as some disciplines place a higher value on timeliness of reporting research than do others. A range of two to eight weeks is a rough guide to the time allowed for peer reviewers. Manuscripts, because they undergo peer review, are thought to be of higher quality when they are published.

Reviewers respond to the manuscript with several types of feedback. They give an overall impression of the major strengths and weaknesses of study design and methods, as well as the quality of the writing, judging both the research and how it is presented. They also give specific feedback on the author's interpretation of the data. This is critical, as a major value of peer review is challenges to the author's conclusions before the article is published. Feedback in the peer review process gives the editor suggestions for an author to make improvements.

Feedback from reviewers to the editor gives context and perspective on the manuscript as it relates to other research on the topic, helping the editor make a decision whether to accept the manuscript, require revisions, or reject it. Feedback to the author is written in a constructive and professional manner. When peer reviewers do a good job, the published article can be relied upon to meet research standards set by the discipline and be free of major errors.

Benefits of Peer Review

The benefits of substantive feedback from multiple experts are many. Authors are forced by the process to consider alternate points of view, examine their assumptions, refer to all the relevant research, and assess their work in the context of existing research. The result of this process is published research that can be trusted to contain accurate information created in accordance with established standards. Peer review and competent editing help minimize unethical data manipulation and plagiarism. When the peer review process works, it provides excellent quality control, and in the scientific and medical areas, the user of this research for later research or application certainly wishes to know that results are accurate and trustworthy.

The need for accuracy and trustworthiness is amplified by the ease with which self-appointed "experts" can disseminate their work via websites and blogs. Also of concern are news reports of preliminary research results that have yet to be reviewed. Schwartz, Woloshin, and Baczek (2002) found that a quarter of studies presented at conferences and reported in the news remained unpublished after three years. Unsuspecting readers may not distinguish unreliable opinion disguised as scholarship or news reports of preliminary findings from reliable information published in peer-reviewed sources. Librarians selecting serials for a library collection can exclude publications that are not peer reviewed, but the open nature of the web prevents them from performing this important gate-keeping function. The best librarians can do is teach readers how to recognize reputable information using methods described in Chapter 9. Faculty and researchers have learned the importance of this skill.

Faculty members who wish to confirm their research competence rely on publishing in peer-reviewed publications, and this represents a major benefit of peer review. Faculty members also confirm their reputation as researchers by serving as peer reviewers. Recognition for this work is evident when editors annually publish a list of reviewers' names, and reviewing activity does count for rank and tenure at some academic institutions.

Not everyone is pleased with peer review. Alternatively, critical views present several potential weaknesses in its means to ensure accuracy and trustworthiness.

Criticisms of Peer Review

Unfortunately, peer review is not always as effective as intended. In an editorial published in *JAMA*, the Journal of the American Medical Association, Drummond Rennie wrote:

One trouble is that despite this system, anyone who reads journals widely and critically is forced to realize that there are scarcely any bars to eventual publication. There seems to be no study too fragmented, no hypothesis too trivial, no literature citation too biased or too egotistical, no design too warped, no methodology too bungled, no presentation of results too inaccurate, too obscure, and too contradictory, no analysis too self-serving, no argument too circular, no conclusions too trifling or too unjustified, and no grammar and syntax too offensive for a paper to end up in print. (Rennie 1986)

Critiques of the peer review process have addressed problems including inadequate compensation for the work of reviewing, lack of timeliness, lack of rigor, and bias. Research reports on problems with peer review have focused mostly on biomedical research due to the very real stake everyone has in the accuracy of medical research and efforts by the editors of leading medical journals; however, the problems presented here also occur to varying degrees within other disciplines.

Inadequate Compensation for the Work of Reviewing. Inadequate compensation may lie at the root of most of the problems with peer review. Refereeing a paper is a difficult, time-consuming job that requires objectivity and great intellectual energy. Seldom is compensation given for refereeing articles, and training is virtually nonexistent. Rather peer reviewing is expected of professionals as a normal part of their duties. The only benefit of being a peer reviewer is the honor of official recognition of the reviewer's valuable informed opinion. Peer reviewers are not directly compensated; and they have little extrinsic motivation to devote energy to peer review. They do it out of their individual sense of responsibility and dedication to the advancement of knowledge. Such altruism may wane in the face of other duties making the timing of peer review a concern to editors.

Lack of Timeliness. Allowing referees sufficient time to do their work unavoidably slows down the publication of research results. Since peer reviewers voluntarily donate their time to the task of giving feedback on manuscripts, it is difficult for editors to induce them to do the work promptly. Pitkin and Burmeister (2002) studied methods for inducing tardy reviewers of articles submitted to *Obstetrics & Gynecology* to review and return the manuscripts. In the 15-month time span of their study, 378 reviewers out of an unreported total number of reviewers failed to return manuscripts to the editors on time. Since that journal publishes 200–300 peer-reviewed articles a year, and some articles are reviewed but not published, late returns of manuscripts are obviously a problem. Unpublished data on reviewers for the *Bulletin of the American Meteorological Society* show that in 2005, 20 percent of reviews were a week or more late, and another 20 percent of reviewers never returned their review (Melissa Fernau, personal communication, January 17, 2006). Experience in other journals may vary from these examples, but delays in peer review are common.

Lack of Rigor. Given the voluntary nature of peer review and the time pressures referees undergo to return comments, it is not surprising that some reviewers may spend less energy on reviewing than is needed. Not only does it require very close attention to the details of a manuscript to catch mistakes, but editors assume that the referees will be aware of the related research and can relate the text with other published research. However, busy scholars can miss relevant works. A common complaint regarding lack of rigor is in review of statistical analysis. Errors in statistics that appear in published studies, despite peer review, include discrepancies between the numbers in tables and interpretation of them in the text. Other errors that can slip undetected by reviewers include incorrect citations and misinterpretations or distortions of cited works. Another problem comes with bias.

Bias. Publishers and editors of scholarly journals are responsible for upholding the integrity of their publications, without bias. To accomplish this, they must possess a quality described by the rather old-fashioned term "disinterestedness." That is, they must act so that knowledge is disseminated for the benefit of all and not for the pursuit of personal interests. Professional standards in each discipline support and encourage disinterested, professional behavior. Researchers are well aware of the essential role of trust in the process. The system of scholarship fails if published research cannot be trusted to have been properly conducted and presented without conflict of interest.

As with any system based on trust, abuses occur. Biased research can be honest self-deception although fraud can and does occur in the recording of data, the reporting of data, and in the use of other people's work. Hopefully, reviewers can determine this as reality and not as their bias for the results.

Opportunity for bias in the review process includes reviewers' and editorial or publication bias. Reviewers' bias toward the content of the manuscript may undermine their ability to objectively assess the quality of the work. Some bias is the natural outcome of research standards current in a discipline. Accepted truths can become so entrenched that challenges to them are deemed unworthy of publication, a tendency dubbed "the iron law of disciplines" (Fleck 1935). Campanario (1996) found that about 10 percent of the authors of the 400 most cited articles in science had difficulty getting their research published, and he concluded that editors and referees sometimes wrongly reject important papers, mostly because it is difficult to distinguish between the innovative and the wrong or insignificant. Prejudice or resistance to new ideas can prevent important findings from reaching readers. It can also work in the opposite way.

Conversely, bias towards accepting some ideas over others can slowly become a part of a discipline when prejudices or predilections cause reviewers to see certain viewpoints in a positive light. Kuhn's (1962) classic work on scientific paradigms emphasized the way an accepted theory or method can hinder the acceptance of new ideas. A theory that ultimately turns out to be false can be perpetuated for years when peer reviewers in a discipline have accepted the theory as fact.

Publication bias is a term that refers to the greater likelihood that studies with positive results will be published than studies with negative results. Some observers of scholarly publishing have expressed concern that research reporting techniques, treatments, or methods that did not support the research hypothesis are less likely to be published than studies that report successful outcomes. In one example, Easterbrook and Berlin (1991) found that studies with statistically significant results were more likely to be published. Editors of *JAMA* responded to potential concerns regarding publication bias by systematically examining publication in *JAMA*. They did not find a statistically significant difference in publication rates between papers on controlled clinical trials with positive versus negative results (Olson et al. 2002). The *JAMA* editors comment that "researchers are more likely to write and submit manuscripts for studies with positive results" (Olson et al. 2002, p. 2828). Due to the special importance of negative findings in medicine, the International Committee of Medical Journal Editors (2004) calls for special careful consideration of research findings that refute the efficacy of a treatment. Researchers continue to study publication bias and editors are working to improve the trustworthiness of published data (Hampton 2005).

If there is a publication bias for studies reporting positive results, a reason may be the desire by editors and publishers to publish important findings of interest to readers. If a researcher tries out an idea or technique and the research indicates it was not true, or did not work, editors may be more likely to conclude that the research is not of interest. This type of publication bias is criticized for unfairly punishing researchers with the misfortune of concluding with negative findings. The broad problem with not publishing negative findings is that other researchers will not be aware of the failure and may unnecessarily follow the same unfruitful path. The specific problem for individual researchers is that negative findings may hinder their ability to fund further research, which in turn affects their ability to advance their careers.

PUBLISH OR PERISH

Knowledge of the tenure and promotion process in academic institutions is useful for understanding faculty demands for the scholarly literature needed for the research that advances their careers. Tenure is the granting of a continuing contract. When a professor is granted tenure, they can expect to continue working for the institution as long as they do their job, behave ethically, and the institution exists. Since the institution is bestowing lifetime job security, tenure is a commitment not to be taken lightly.

Academic promotion is the separate process of moving in rank through three and sometimes four steps, from Instructor to Assistant Professor to Associate Professor to Professor. The exact titles of academic ranks vary among institutions. The rank of full professor is usually the most demanding of a distinguished record of publication, and what constitutes "distinguished" is a decision in the process. In most colleges and universities, a committee of faculty peer reviews portfolios of evidence of scholarly work and makes recommendations to the administration on whether to grant tenure or promotion in rank. While details of the process vary a great deal among institutions, examination of published work by a committee of peers is standard practice for research institutions, but may not be a requirement for smaller colleges and community colleges when teaching is emphasized over research.

Incentives to Publish

For academics, publication of research in well-respected peer-reviewed sources is the coin of the realm. Research publication in the sciences and social sciences is primarily in serials. The humanities tend to place more emphasis on the publication of monographs, at least to attain the rank of full professor, but publication in serials is still important. At research universities, publishing a certain number of articles in peer-reviewed journals is a requirement for tenure and promotion. The system of publishing research to gain tenure is thus known as "publish or perish." If newly hired professors cannot get the required number of articles published within the first five to seven years on the job, the usual period for consideration for tenure, they will need to find other positions.

The record of publication required for attaining tenure and being promoted in rank is judged primarily on the number of articles published, the quality of the journals in which the articles were published, and how often others have cited those articles. In practice, tenure and promotion committees recommending promotion count articles published, consider the impact factors of the journals in which the articles were published, and count the number of times the published articles have been cited. The ISI citation databases record the journal impact factors and frequencies of citation often used by rank and tenure committees to assess the quality of a candidate's publications. ISI consistently appeals for rational, balanced use of ISI data, and has never advocated using their data alone for evaluating the quality of a scholar's work.

In institutions where librarians are granted faculty status, they also are given promotion and tenure through a similar peer review process. Some institutions do hire librarians as staff and administrators. Librarians who wish to work in an academic library but who would rather not be required to publish research may prefer a college without that requirement.

Quantity and Quality

Counting the number of articles published and using ISI data have important consequences for serials publishing and collection development. One consequence is that authors have a powerful incentive to publish as many articles as they can. This leads them to submit articles in what has been called the "least publishable unit" or reporting the smallest amount of information possible to have their article accepted in a reputable journal. Instead of publishing one long article describing an entire research project, several articles will be submitted describing individual stages or facets of the project. This is an entirely rational and intelligent strategy, especially given the emphasis on numbers of publications counted in the tenure and promotion processes. However, it results in several articles published in multiple journals where one may have sufficed. The problem with this is "publishing to get more items on one's vita adds to the escalating costs of journals, and therefore leads to the cancellation of more journals" (Gherman 2004). As the number and cost of scholarly journals rise, the portion of serial literature a library can subscribe to shrinks.

The use of journal impact factors and citation rates by tenure and promotion committees has consequences for serials collection development. Scholars want to publish in the journals in the ISI databases because otherwise their work will have no journal impact factor, no count of the number of times cited. For some tenure and promotion committees, one might as well write a book review as publish research in a journal not covered in the citation databases. Either way, it probably will not count. The publishers whose journals are covered in the ISI citation indexes are very well aware of this phenomenon, making it a powerful incentive for publishers to create high-quality journals that will be included in the ISI database. The problematic part is that publishers of journals with high impact factors know that the journals are considered essential. They may feel justified in raising subscription prices because they know the market will bear a high price for well-regarded titles in high demand by scholars.

Scholars' need to publish their research creates a need for outlets of good repute. As the topics studied by scholars grow in number and in specialization, new serial titles are published to meet the scholars' needs. This natural development of scholarship drives a proliferation of journals. Belief in the value of the dissemination of knowledge encourages publishers and librarians to take the financial risk on new niche journals, even though many will not break even for the publisher or have a favorable cost per use for the librarian. This has led to the creation of new journals to meet the needs of a sub-specialty within an existing discipline, a practice known as "twigging."

Twigging has risks. In the early years of a new topic of inquiry, it can be difficult to judge whether titles on the new twig of a branch of knowledge will grow into branches or fade away. Publishing new "twigs" is risky, as is subscribing to them. The money and effort publishers invest in the new titles may not pay off, and an added subscription may get little use or cease in a short time. On the other hand, groundbreaking scholarship published in a new "twig" may lead to important advances in knowledge that benefit society, and the new journal may turn a profit for the publisher. Despite the risk, publishers routinely solicit editors to launch new journals. Once a new journal is announced, faculty and other patrons often respond to its advertising by pressuring the librarian to subscribe.

Serials librarians should recognize the strengths of peer-reviewed scholarly serials and be aware of criticisms of the process. Knowledge of pressures to publish and the need for new outlets for publication can help the academic librarian anticipate faculty needs. Pressures sometimes lead individuals to act inappropriately. Another criticism of the process of conducting research and publishing findings is that the individuals responsible for research may have conflicts of interest.

CONFLICTS OF INTEREST

The funds to conduct research come mostly from university budgets, grants from government, foundations and other organizations, and direct corporate funding. Corporate funding of research has led to serious concerns with financial conflicts of interest, especially in medicine. Individual researchers may have financial interest in the funding source through employment, consulting work, or stock ownership. The financial interest might be for themselves or for immediate family members. Having a financial interest gives the researcher a personal stake in the outcome of the research. The concern is that having a financial stake in the outcome of research inevitably biases the process. Risk of conflicts of interest can exist for authors, referees, editors, and publishers. Some journals require full financial disclosure of any possible conflict of interest by everyone involved in the research process, as described by the International Committee of Medical Journal Editors (2004).

Sponsors of research may exert control over publication of results and therefore be able to suppress publication of negative findings. This practice is strongly discouraged but may still occur. The International Committee of Medical Journal Editors (2004) recommends that editors consider any restrictions sponsors may have placed on authors when deciding whether to publish a study. All of the possible pitfalls inherent in scholarly publishing add to the challenge of being a serials librarian.

As participants and stakeholders in the scholarly publication process, serials librarians also have an obligation to be ethical in the acquisition and maintenance of journal collections. This includes avoiding their own personal biases or conflicts of interest. The previous discussion of peer review and conflicts of interest is relevant to collection development because it directly relates to the reputation of journals and publishers. A competent serials collection development librarian will be alert to unprofessional practices and take them into account during renewal time.

Issues surrounding the trustworthiness of the content of serials are observed by librarians and impact the reputations of serial titles. A separate issue from the ethics of content creation is the economic relationship between librarians and publishers. The next section addresses subscription revenue as an issue relevant to the vitality of scholarly communication.

PROFIT MOTIVE IN SCHOLARLY PUBLISHING

The issue of a profit motive in scholarly publishing was discussed in Chapter 6 in the context of the serials crisis and costs to libraries and publishers. This issue remains a current one and additional information is presented here in the context of how this issue affects the publication of and access to scholarly journals. A great deal has been written and discussed about the pursuit of profit in scholarly publishing. Librarians have complained that some publishers make excessive profits. Some publishers counter that the real problem is university administrators allowing runaway growth of administrative expenses while under funding libraries (Henderson 1996). Discussion about profits in journal publishing on the SERI-ALST listserv discussion group for serials librarians has at times been rather shrill and does not always acknowledge all stakeholders' legitimate needs and interests. For example, exchanges between Stevan Harnad, champion of authors making their works freely available, and Albert Henderson, former editor of *Publishing Research Quarterly*, highlight the needs of scholars and large research institutions (Henderson 2000). This author has found their exchanges sometimes lack full consideration of the needs of college libraries and students (Black 2000). The context is serials prices rising more rapidly than library budgets. Libraries often have materials budgets that are flat or decrease from one year to the next. Regardless of the publisher's legitimate costs, when subscription prices rise, librarians managing budgets increasing at a slower rate than those increases cannot spend money they do not have.

The hottest issue among librarians has been the high profits made by a few of the largest publishers. Critical discussion of high profits has been in the literature and on conference programs for at least a decade. One focal point for librarians' criticism was revealed by Crispin Davis, CEO of Reed Elsevier. In a *Business Week* interview, Davis stated, "A key priority is consistent, above-average growth. That means above-market revenue growth and double-digit earnings growth" (O'Connell 2002). The context of Davis' comment was improvement in Reed Elsevier's stock price after the company's acquisition of publisher Harcourt General. One must be realistic that publishers must make some profit for their shareholders. Double-digit profit growth may appear excessive to some circles, but may be expected by shareholders. Librarians have been quick to point out that annual budget increases are rarely, if ever, in double digits. The reality of library budgets is that librarians are forced to buy less when publishers are pushing revenue growth.

According to Davis' statement, Reed Elsevier, publisher of all the journals in *ScienceDirect* and in the business of providing high-quality journals, mostly in the sciences, prices and markets their products to achieve the desired double-digit earnings growth. The prices also allow Elsevier to provide innovative online services and maintain quality in peer review, editing, and production standards, and also support intensive marketing and ample representation at conferences.

Representatives from Elsevier counter librarians' complaints about unfairly high subscription prices with general descriptions of the legitimate costs involved in publishing. Librarians remain distrustful, in part because publishers' publicly available financial data does not list actual costs in sufficient detail to see exactly where the money goes, and in part because the profit-maximizing goal of the company is well known. Elsevier has made double-digit profits in years that most libraries faced flat or shrinking budgets (Odlyzko 2003). It is important to note that Elsevier is not the only publisher criticized by librarians for pursuing profits too aggressively. They are presented as the example here because Elsevier is frequently mentioned in the context of this discussion.

Librarians' complaints about journal prices have sometimes framed the issue as good society versus bad commercial publishers. That is, society publishers have fair prices and are the good guys, while commercial publishers are just out to maximize profits and are the bad guys. This framing of the issue only holds true if one selects particular publishers of each type. Many commercial publishers price journals at a level that just allows them to survive, and some society publishers use significant portions of subscription revenue to finance activities other than publishing. Those activities typically help fulfill the societies' missions of disseminating knowledge through conferences, education programs, scholarships, and the like. Whether libraries should subsidize these types of society activities through serial subscriptions is debatable.

Albert Henderson, editor of *Publishing Research Quarterly* and a regular contributor to the SERIALST discussion group, has argued with dogged consistency that the serials crisis is a funding crisis, not a pricing crisis. His main point is that administrative costs and reserve funds at universities have drawn away funds that should go to the education of students in general, and to library materials in particular. Henderson (1996) claims that if academic institutions paid the same proportion of revenue for library materials they did in the 1970s, there would be adequate funds for serials. He may have a point, but the relatively flush library funding of the 1970s is highly unlikely to return.

The level of distrust that has developed among librarians toward at least some publishers is very unfortunate. Publishers have legitimate costs. Going online is costly, competition is fierce, the business is risky, and the whole publishing process is expensive. On the other hand, serials publishers seem to feel that librarians do not appreciate these costs. Publishers have done a poor job of informing librarians of just where the money goes, and detailed information on publishing costs could help librarians justify budget increases to administrators. If publishers could be more forthcoming, collaboration between publishers and librarians might replace the current adverse situation. Keith Seitter (2004) of the American Meteorological Society (AMS) has described the finances of AMS journal publishing in great detail at a NASIG conference. More of that kind of openness would support trust and cooperation. In the meantime, groups and individuals have proposed alternatives to traditional journals sold by subscription.

ALTERNATIVE MODELS FOR SCHOLARLY JOURNALS

The serials crisis directly affects scholars when librarians' cancellations in ever-increasing numbers can reduce the availability of scholars' work and thus reduce how often their articles are cited. The availability of journals online subscribed to by consortia of libraries may mitigate the impact of librarians canceling individual subscriptions. A risk remains that having fewer titles in serials collections will diminish scholars' access to literature, making research more time-consuming and reducing their ability to make serendipitous finds while browsing the collection. Any solution to the serials crisis must preserve the integrity of scholarly communication. The system of scholarly communication is officially defined as "the system through which research and other scholarly writings are created, evaluated for quality, disseminated to the scholarly community, and preserved for future use" (Association of College and Research Libraries 2003). Each of the four elements of the definition are necessary for the health of the system: (1) creation, (2) evaluation, (3) dissemination, and (4) preservation. Issues surrounding creation and evaluation were discussed earlier in this chapter. The dissemination aspect is being shaken by the serials crisis, which is denying many scholars timely access to serial literature. Scholarly communication published online is also at risk of being inadequately preserved, an issue discussed in the chapter on online journals. A proposed solution with challenges to overcome is posting scholarly works on preprint servers.

Preprint Servers

The serials crisis led creative people to envision solutions to the problem of inadequate access. One proposed solution, championed by Stevan Harnad, is a preprint publishing process. In Harnard's (1990) plan, scholar authors retain copyright for their works and post them on the web, free for all to view and provide informal peer review. Using this method, authors gain feedback on early drafts of research papers.

Harnad backed his idea with action and created *Psycoloquy*, a discussion group designed to allow open peer review of draft papers. In the publication's words, "Authors of accepted manuscripts assign to *Psycoloquy* the right to publish and distribute their text electronically and to archive and make it permanently retrievable electronically, but they retain the copyright, and after it has appeared in *Psycoloquy* authors may republish their text in any way they wish—electronic or print—as long as they clearly acknowledge Psycoloquy as its original locus of publication" http://www.cogsci.ecs.soton.ac.uk/psycoloquy/. The articles posted in *Psycoloquy* are screened before posting and are reviewed by any reader who chooses to post a response. The papers are preprints, not the final draft shaped by formal peer review and editorial guidance. Preprints may exist in several versions. Although very useful for sharing information, the *Psycoloquy* model lacks formal evaluation of research, and the existence of multiple versions complicates citation and preservation.

Posting preprints as a way to share scholarly information caught on most completely in high-energy physics. In 1991, a listserv discussion group was established by Paul Ginsparg at Los Alamos National Laboratory. Its popularity as a medium for exchanging current research findings grew rapidly, and the e-mail forum grew into a full-fledged preprint server. Ginsparg moved to Cornell in 2001 with what is now called the e-print arXiv. The arXiv.org server gets over 100,000 hits per weekday, and now includes preprints for not only physics, but also mathematics, computer science, and other disciplines. Another successful preprint server is RePEc for economics at http://repec.org/.

Despite the success and usefulness of preprint servers, the validation of published research still occurs through traditional peer review and publication in recognized journals. Papers posted and discussed on preprint servers excel at serving scholarly communication purposes of creation and dissemination, but do not offer sufficient evaluation. Posting preprints counts for little, if anything, in tenure and promotion. Preservation of research posted by authors on preprint servers or other websites is problematic because multiple versions of papers may exist, and URLs tend to change or disappear.

Whitfield (2004), an editor of *Nature*, found that links to about 20 percent of websites mentioned in abstracts in Medline fail, and 12 percent of links cited in some top medical and science journals were no longer available just two years after publication. Whitfield states in the same article, "We do what we can to ensure that formal citations will stand the test of time, and we wouldn't let a significant part of a paper depend on a website." The problem of poor preservation of online sources undermines research and should give any scholar pause before choosing to publish online, particularly if the online publication is not an established, reputable journal. One solution to this problem is the Open Archives Initiative (OAI).

The OAI

The OAI is an organized effort to provide standards for posting and preserving preprints. The OAI's work is explained at http://www.eprints.org/self-faq/. The "Open" in OAI means open for linking via standard tags and formats, including the use of Digital Object Identifiers (DOI) to link to individual articles. The "Open" does not mean free of charge, although in practice many of the preprints are freely available. Professional archivists accurately point out that the use of the word "archives" for self-archiving of papers and the OAI is an imprecise use of the term. An "archive" in the preprint and OAI sense just means accessible files stored online. OAI is not the same as Open Access (AO) discussed in Chapter 6 or the Budapest Open Access Initiative described next. OAI can be used by authors who obtain their publisher's permission to post versions of articles published in traditional journals.

Lower-Cost Alternative Serials

Proposed solutions to the serials crisis include strategies to reduce the cost of journals. One strategy is to create lower-cost alternatives to high-priced commercial journals. Sometimes, the editors of a commercially published journal quit to create a new journal intended to offer similar content at a lower price. For example, editors of *The Journal of Academic Librarianship* objected to a sharp increase in the subscription price of the journal when it was taken over by a commercial publisher. Believing there was a need for a more affordable alternative, the editors established the new journal *portal: Libraries and the Academy*, which is included in subscriptions to Project MUSE (St. Clair 2001).

The most prominent organized effort to provide lower-cost alternative journal titles is the Scholarly Publishing and Academic Resources Coalition (SPARC, online at http://www.arl.org/sparc). SPARC is a coalition of research libraries and scholarly organizations has worked on several fronts to create a more competitive marketplace for scholarly journals. Their efforts include forming partnerships with publishers to create lower-priced alternatives to some very prestigious and expensive journals. For example, SPARC partnered with the American Chemical Society (ACS) in 1998 to support the new journal *Organic Letters*, priced at $2,300. It was intended to compete directly with Elsevier's $8000-year *Tetrahedron Letters*. A few other lower-priced alternative titles have been successfully supported by SPARC. After the introduction of *Organic Letters*, annual percentage price increases for *Tetrahedron Letters* moderated to single digits (SPARC 2001).

Around 1999, SPARC began to support affordable journals published online. Several projects were funded by SPARC grants, including *BioOne*, an aggregation of biology journals published by scholarly societies. SPARC supported the participating societies to offer them some financial stability during the transition from print-only to online publishing. SPARC's competitive grants have also supported several other online publishing projects, including *Stanford Encyclopedia of Philosophy*, *Optics Express*, published by the Optical Society of America, and *Academic Serials in Communication-Unified System* (ASCUS), and *Labor: Studies in Working-Class History of the Americas*, published by Duke University Press (http://www.arl.org/sparc/about/act2004.html). As these activities continue, SPARC's advocacy for change now includes strong support for OA.

Open Access

The Office of Scholarly Communication of the Association of Research Libraries (ARL) defines Open Access (OA) to scholarly communication as "works that are created with no expectation of direct monetary return and made available at no cost to the reader on the public Internet for purposes of education and research," making clear that "open access does not apply to materials for which the authors expect to generate revenue" (Office of Scholarly Communication 2004). As was described in Chapter 6, the idea behind OA is to fund the online publication of scientific and research texts by means other than subscriptions, so that the work can be freely available to any reader with an Internet connection and browser software.

John M. Unsworth, Dean of the library science program at the University of Illinois at Champaign-Urbana, argues for OA by saying, "In a better world, high-quality, peer-reviewed scholarship would be freely available soon after its creation; it would be digital by default, but optionally available in print for a price; it would be easy to find, and it would be available long after its creation, at a stable address, in a stable form" (Unsworth 2004). His better world marries searchable, properly archived digital information with free access for anyone interested in reading the material.

A force driving scholarly communication toward this better world is the Budapest Open Access Initiative sponsored by the Open Society Institute, established by George Soros in 1993. The Budapest initiative's mission statement reads,

> An old tradition and a new technology have converged to make possible an unprecedented public good. The old tradition is the willingness of scientists and scholars to publish the fruits of their research in scholarly journals without payment, for the sake of inquiry and knowledge. The new technology is the Internet. The public good they make possible is the world-wide electronic distribution of the peer-reviewed journal literature and completely free and unrestricted access to it by all scientists, scholars, teachers, students, and other curious minds. Removing access barriers to this literature will accelerate research, enrich education, share the learning of the rich with the poor and the poor with the rich, make this literature as useful as it can be, and lay the foundation for uniting humanity in a common intellectual conversation and quest for knowledge. (Budapest Open Access Initiative 2002)

The Initiative goes on to "recommend two complementary strategies" for accomplishing this: "self-archiving," in which scholars "deposit their refereed journal articles in open electronic archives," and "open-access journals" which "use copyright and other tools to ensure permanent open access to all the articles they publish. Because price is a barrier to access, these new journals will not have subscription or access fees, and other methods will be used for covering their expenses (ibid.)." As to how these journals will happen, the Initiative offers some business plans and suggests that there are many alternative sources of funds. These include the foundations and governments that fund research, the universities and laboratories that employ researchers, endowments set up by discipline or institution, friends of the cause of OA, profits from the sale of add-ons to the basic texts, funds freed up by the demise or cancellation of journals charging traditional subscription or access fees, or contributions from the researchers themselves (Budapest Open Access Initiative 2002).

Since OA is intended to minimize barriers to information access, it fits quite well with the missions of scholarly societies whose mission statements include a goal of disseminating the results of research to the widest audience possible. The problem lies in how to pay for the costs of producing and maintaining well-edited and properly peer-reviewed journals.

One way of paying for high-quality production of scholarly journals is being pursued by the Public Library of Science (PLoS), a "non-profit organization of scientists and physicians committed to making the world's scientific and medical literature a freely available public resource" http://www.plos.org/. Their business model calls for the bulk of costs to be paid for by page charges. That is, the authors of the articles pay the journal to have their work published. This is not a new idea, as many journals have author page charges. The unusual part of the PLoS business model is that authors are charged $1,500 per article. PLoS has a much higher page charge than journals that also rely on membership dues and/or subscription fees for revenue. Commentary on the sustainability of this model was reported in Chapter 6.

The inaugural issue of the first PLoS journal, *PLoS Biology*, was published in October 2003. Print subscriptions are available for $160 per year. A second title, *PLoS Medicine*, began publication in Fall 2004. Both journals are free online at www.plos.org. The success of these journals and the evolution of the PLoS business model are being closely watched by those interested in OA.

The DOAJ at http://www.doaj.org covers free, full-text, quality-controlled scientific and scholarly journals in all subjects and languages. According to the Directory's home page, there were 2,000 journals in the directory as of January 2006. Involvement by publishers in the DOAJ is all well and good. But there remains an access problem, since people have to know that the OA journals exist, and need to find the articles in them when they search in citation databases. The directory at http://www.doaj.org provides a list of journals, which can be browsed by title or subject area, but it does not provide a searchable database of the articles in those journals. Some of the OA journals are not indexed in any database. The OA titles need to be fully integrated into citation databases and library catalogs to be viable alternatives to traditionally funded journals.

The combined effect of activities by SPARC, the OAI, the Budapest initiative, PLoS, and all the other publishers and organizations striving to provide alternatives to traditional serials publishing will continue for the immediate future and the size of the gap between subscription prices and library budgets will continue to impact the outcome. Which models will succeed, or rather which parts of which models will succeed, is an open question. The ongoing debate, experimentation, and research on the relative successes of the various approaches will be worth watching. The unfolding process of new ways to fund and provide access to serials will impact the use of serials, the topic of Chapter 8.

SUGGESTIONS FOR FURTHER READING

Problems with peer review, and lack of research into the causes and possible solutions to the problems, led to creation of the International Congress on Peer

Review and Biomedical Research first held in 1989. This Peer Review Congress has stimulated research on the process, and helped bring commentary on it beyond opinion pieces and informal commentary. Information about the Congress, with some text of research, is available online at http://www.ama-assn.org/public/peer/peerhome.htm.

JAMA published a theme issue on the Fourth Peer Review conference on June 5, 2002, v. 287, no. 21, pages 2745–2871. This issue is an excellent source for research on the peer review process, scholarly publication, and the uses of scholarly biomedical literature. The fifth peer review conference was scheduled for September 15–17, 2005, in Chicago, Illinois. A detailed example of peer reviewers' responsibilities may be found online at http://www.greenjournal.org/misc/rev guide.pdf, the reviewer's guide for the journal *Obstetrics & Gynecology*.

For a full but concise treatment of ethical considerations in the publication of biomedical research, see the International Committee of Medical Journal Editor's *Uniform Requirements for Manuscripts Submitted to Biomedical Journals: Writing and Editing for Biomedical Publication*, online at http://www.icmje.org/index.html.

Nature, the science journal, regularly publishes news about Open Access (OA). Their forum on access to scientific literature is online at http://www.nature.com/nature/focus/accessdebate/.

A thorough but concise introduction to OA is Peter Suber's *Open Access Overview: Focusing on Open Access to Peer-Reviewed Research Articles and their Preprints* at http://www.earlham.edu/~peters/fos/overview.htm. Peter Suber also edits a monthly *Open Access Newsletter* on current developments; issues from March 2001 to the present are online at http://www.earlham.edu/~peters/fos/newsletter/archive.htm. *Serials Review* (30(4), October 2004) published a special issue entitled "Open Access 2004" co-edited by David Goodman and Connie Foster. Thirteen articles representing a broad range of viewpoints thoroughly address the issues surrounding OA at that time.

REFERENCES

Association of College and Research Libraries. 2003. Principles and strategies for the reform of scholarly communication, approved by the ACRL Board of Directors on June 24, 2003, http://www.ala.org/ala/acrl/acrlpubs/whitepapers/principlesstrategies.htm (accessed February 3, 2006).

Black, Steve. May 15, 2000. Harnad vs. Henderson: A view from the bleachers. SERIALST Archive, http://list.uvm.edu/cgi-bin/wa?A1=ind0005&L=serialst (accessed January 17, 2006).

Budapest Open Access Initiative. 2002. http://www.soros.org/openaccess/read.shtml (accessed February 3, 2006).

Campanario, Juan Miguel. 1996. Have referees rejected some of the most-cited articles of all times? *Journal of the American Society for Information Science* 47(4): 302–310.

Easterbrook, P.J., and Berlin, J.A. 1991. Publication bias in clinical research. *Lancet* 337(8746): 867–876.

Fleck, Ludwik. 1935. Genesis and development of a scientific fact. In *Ludwik Fleck*, ed. Thaddeus J. Trenn and Robert K. Merton, foreword by Thomas S. Kuhn. Chicago: University of Chicago Press.

Gherman, Paul M. 2004. Faculty members and publishable units. *Chronicle of Higher Education* 50(29): A47.

Godlee, Fiona. 2002. Making reviewers visible. *JAMA, The Journal of the American Medical Association* 287(21): 2762–2765.

Hampton, Tracy. 2005. Biomedical journals probe peer review. *JAMA, The Journal of the American Medical Association* 294(18): 2287–2288.

Harnad, Stevan. 1990. Scholarly skywriting and the prepublication continuum of scientific inquiry. *Psychological Science* 1: 342–343, http://cogprints.ecs.soton.ac.uk/archive/00001581/00/harnad90 .skywriting.html (accessed February 3, 2006).

Henderson, Albert. 1996. Publishing and the productivity of R&D. *Publishing Research Quarterly* 12(2): 3–9.

Henderson, Albert. May 15, 2000. Re: Economist article + Faustian bargain. SERIALST Archive, http://list.uvm.edu/cgi-bin/wa?A1=ind0005&L=serialst (accessed January 17, 2006).

International Committee of Medical Journal Editors. 2004. *Uniform Requirements for Manuscripts Submitted to Biomedical Journals: Writing and Editing for Biomedical Publication.* Philadelphia: Author, http://www.icmje.org/ (accessed February 3, 2006).

Kuhn, Thomas S. 1962. *The Structure of Scientific Revolutions.* Chicago: University of Chicago Press.

O'Connell, Patricia. June 26, 2002. Managing Reed Elsevier's about-face. *Business Week Online,* http://www.businessweek.com/technology/content/jun2002/tc20020626_6092.htm (accessed February 3, 2006).

Odlyzko, Andrew. March 30, 2003. Re: Elsevier profit. Liblicense-L Archive, http://www.library.yale .edu/~llicense/ListArchives/0303/msg00071.html (accessed February 3, 2006).

Office of Scholarly Communication, Association of Research Libraries. 2004. *Framing the Issue: Open Access.* Washington, DC: Association of Research Libraries.

Olson, Carin M., Rennie, Drummond, Cook, Deborah, Dickersin, Kay, Flanagin, Annette, Hogan, Joseph, Zhu, Ai, Reiling, Jennifer, and Pace, Brian. 2002. Publication bias in editorial decision making. *JAMA, The Journal of the American Medical Association* 287(21): 2825–2828.

Pitkin, Roy M., and Burmeister, Leon F. 2002. Prodding tardy reviewers: A randomized comparison of telephone, fax, and e-mail. *JAMA, the Journal of the American Medical Association* 287(21): 2794–2795.

Rennie, Drummond. 1986. Guarding the guardians: A conference on editorial peer review. *JAMA, The Journal of the American Medical Association* 256(17): 2391–2392.

Schwartz, Lisa M., Woloshin, Steven, and Baczek, Linda. 2002. Media coverage of scientific meetings: Too much, too soon? *JAMA, The Journal of the American Medical Association* 287(21): 2859–2863.

Seitter, Keith. June 17–20, 2004. Economics of society publishing: Through a glass, darkly. Paper presented at the 19th Annual NASIG Conference, Milwaukee, Wisconsin.

SPARC. 2001. SPARC E-News, http://www.arl.org/sparc/pubs/enews/aug01.html (accessed January 17, 2006).

St. Clair, Gloriana. 2001. Through portal. *portal: Libraries and the Academy* 1(1): v–vii.

Unsworth, John M. 2004. Presentation on "Open Access, Open Archives, and Open Source in higher education," Southern Illinois University at Edwardsville, February 12, http://www3.isrl.uiuc.edu/~unsworth/siue.2-04.html (accessed February 3, 2006).

Whitfield, J. 2004. Web links leave abstracts going nowhere. *Nature* 428: 592.

Chapter 8

Use of Serials

To paraphrase the first of Ranganathan's (1931) five laws of library science, serials are for use. To inform readers, they disseminate more up-to-date knowledge, and provide a fixed record of current research findings and current events. This chapter will explore the role of copyright in the use of serials, patrons' use of serials, libraries' measurement of use, and patterns of serial use. The discussion will focus on both traditional print and online journals.

COPYRIGHT AND FAIR USE

Publishers are understandably keen to protect the copyright of their serials because they wish to sell as many periodical subscriptions as possible. When patrons choose to read issues in the library instead of paying for personal subscriptions, potential sales are lost. This is part of any publisher's rationale for charging libraries more for subscriptions than individuals pay. An even greater loss comes when copyright is violated and multiple copies of the content are made without permission. All librarians are responsible to see that copyright and fair use are not violated. This is not always easy.

Librarians follow The American Library Association Code of Ethics, which includes the statement "We recognize and respect intellectual property rights" (ALA Council 1995). While copyright gives control of reproduction of intellectual property, the principle of fair use allows reproduction without permission under limited circumstances. Fair use, as described in Section 107 of title 17 of the U.S. Code, allows individuals to make photocopies of articles for their personal use, teaching, scholarship, and research. Whether reproduction of copyrighted works counts as fair use depends upon the interpretation.

Interpretation in general relies on several factors including whether the use is for monetary gain, how much of the work is used, and the impact the copying has on the market for the copyrighted work. Interpretations of what counts as fair use in specific circumstances can vary, but disagreements between publishers and librarians have not been decided in court. Summaries of court cases addressing fair use at Stanford's Copyright and Fair Use website http://fairuse.stanford.edu/ Copyright_and_Fair_Use_Overview/chapter9/9-c.html include copying for educational purposes and are relevant to libraries, but librarians are not parties in the cases. Differing opinions and the lack of judicial decisions leaves librarians and publishers to struggle with gray areas in the precise definition of fair use. Since there is room for interpretation of copyright law, policies concerning the enforcement of copyright and the scope of fair use will vary among institutions.

Years ago when copiers were first installed in libraries, the copyright implications of photocopying within libraries were somewhat controversial. Today, patron copying from serials is a universally accepted practice. Librarians are required to post a notice at copiers to inform patrons of copyright restrictions and the limits of fair use. The fundamental principle of fair use in copying from serials is that photocopying must be for individual use at the time of need. Making multiple copies for distribution at a future time is considered publication and is not allowed. For serials, copyright rules and fair use need to be interpreted for and applied to course reserves, interlibrary loan (ILL), and patron access to full-text databases.

Course Reserves

The rules for course reserves reflect the principle of individual use at time of need. Instructors may place one copy of an article on reserve for a section of a course for one semester. If the same article is placed on reserve for more than one semester, the instructor must obtain permission from the rights holder. This one semester limit is fairly new, based on a reasonable interpretation of the Digital Millenium Copyright Act of 1998 (U.S. Copyright Office 1998). Some academic librarians offer faculty assistance in obtaining permission to reproduce articles. Librarians may also budget funds to pay copyright fees when necessary. These fees are typically handled through the Copyright Clearance Center (CCC) online at www.copyright.com. This website includes an easy-to-navigate title search. It should be noted that not all publishers participate in the CCC. Rights from a nonparticipating publisher must be made directly with the publisher.

Interlibrary Loan

Publishers recognize that ILL may undercut their sales of institutional subscriptions. A librarian who retrieves an article for a patron might have been, and maybe should have been, a subscriber to the journal containing the requested article. Librarians have forcefully and consistently argued that since no library can own everything, collaboration and sharing are legitimate library functions. In 1976, in response to publishers' concerns about the impact of ILL on their sales, the U.S. House of Representatives held hearings to look into the meaning of "systematic reproduction" in the context of ILL. They charged an *ad hoc* committee, the National Commission on New Technological Uses of Copyright, better known by the acronym CONTU, to create guidelines for ILL. The publishers wished to disallow "such aggregate quantities as to substitute for a subscription to or purchase of such work" (Coalition for Networked Information 2004). This was a reasonable demand, in line with guidelines for fair use.

While some in the library community preferred no limits on ILL, participants in the commission were able to work out an agreement. CONTU defined an unreasonable quantity as more than five article requests per year from any one serial, and the "Rule of Five" became the guideline for ILL. An important piece of the "Rule of Five" is that only serial issues published within the last five years count. Loans of articles from journal volumes more than five years old are not limited. While more CONTU guidelines exist, the Rule of Five is the part directly applicable to serials and ILL.

The CONTU guidelines are guidelines, without the force of law, and they have never been challenged in court. Nevertheless, CONTU is the standard by which librarians operate. They comply by annually tracking how many requests are made for articles from each serial. If more than five requests are made from the current five years of a title, the librarian must either deny the request or pay the copyright fee to the publisher to obtain the copy. Librarians may choose to pass on the cost of the copyright fee to patrons or absorb it as a cost of providing service. The lists of the titles that exceed five requests per year are important serials collection development tools because titles appearing on the "closed copyright" list are prime candidates for adding to the collection. This is especially true when the maximum number of requests is exceeded for more than one year.

Remote Access Serials and Copyright

Online availability of remote access serials has created new challenges for interpretation and protection of copyright. A principle of copyright is that a library cannot act as a publisher. If a librarian provided unrestricted access to a full-text database, anyone in the world could log in and use the library's serials. In theory that single subscription to an online database could supply all the serials housed there to the whole world. Publishers and vendors of full-text databases are well aware of this potential.

To protect their product, publishers and vendors insist that use of their serials and full-text databases be restricted to authorized users. An overarching issue surrounding limiting access to only authorized users is the principle that patrons have the right to access to information acquired for their library making it important that limits on access create minimal inconvenience to patrons. Three stakeholders factor into this process, the publisher or vendor, the librarian, and the patron.

How publishers and vendors choose to restrict access varies, and the terms of control to access are key factors in contract negotiation. The two choices here are access to restricted computers or access by authorized users. Some publishers and vendors insist that access be restricted to a physical location such as a college campus. To limit to a physical site, the Internet Protocol (IP) addresses for all the computers on site are registered with the content provider. Computers linked via a wireless network are managed as extensions of the entire network so they will be within the registered range of IP addresses. If users wish to access the content from a computer "off-site" they are out of luck, because only the computers with registered IP addresses can gain access.

Strong demand by patrons and libraries has induced most vendors to allow off-site access by authorized users. Two options are available here, login name and password or proxy server technology. The first option for off-site access is to give authorized users a login name and password they can use from anywhere. While off-site access by password works, patrons may have trouble keeping track of the login, and the librarian may have little control over unauthorized use. Although patrons have to sign user agreements promising not to share the login, they are on their honor to respect that limitation.

The second option for off-site access is proxy server technology. The IP address of the proxy server is registered with the publisher or vendor as an authorized user. When patrons attempt to connect to a database, a login screen pops up, and the patron enters a personal code determined by the institution. The login information is compared to a database of authorized users kept on the proxy server. If the login matches, the proxy server gives the patron's browser a cookie that makes it look on the web as if they are working from the proxy server's IP address. The patron may then use any database that registers the proxy server's IP as a valid user. The cookie works for the duration of the patron's session online, so they only have to login to the proxy server once per session.

Two limitations for using a proxy server are using cookies and the publisher or vendor's permission. In the case of cookies, patrons must have cookies enabled in their browser for the proxy server to work and network administrators sometimes block cookies. Publishers or vendors can also prohibit the use of a proxy server to access a database. If the license does not allow off campus access, the librarian cannot register the proxy's IP address as an authorized user.

Expanding availability of remote access serials makes it important that the serials librarian negotiate with the publisher or vendor for the widest possible use of technology in retrieving serial content. Computers with web connections are essential tools in libraries today. The negotiation of licenses to provide patrons the best possible access to online serials increases the urgency to have more collaboration among libraries in consortium arrangements. The benefits of consortia for licensing were discussed in Chapter 2. Libraries can also benefit from collaboration by pooling resources to build and maintain the computer networks necessary to efficiently provide remote access serials to all patrons.

PATRON PSYCHOLOGY AND THEIR USE OF SERIALS

Most library mission statements include a commitment to providing services equitably to all patrons. Since patrons have diverse attitudes, motivations, and levels of skill in finding and using collections, meeting their diverse needs can be challenging. The task of teaching skills to users, including how to address various levels of comfort with libraries, will be treated in some detail in the chapter on teaching patrons to use serials. This section will introduce a few perspectives patrons bring with them as they seek and use serial literature. The purpose of presenting these psychological perspectives is to enhance understanding of patron behavior. Enhanced recognition of patrons' attitudes and motivations only indirectly influences collection development or the arrangement of the serials collection, but it may illuminate causes of patron responses to serials collections.

Patrons finding and using serials make choices whether to browse, search in a database, or use works cited. If patrons browse, they choose call number ranges, titles, and articles that might best meet their needs. If they use a database, they pick which one(s) to use. Once they have results, they choose which articles to actually acquire. If they follow a citation trail by using works cited in books, articles, or other sources, they have to interpret which citations are most likely to lead to useful information. Those are just a few of the choices to be made; the whole process of finding literature in serials is a succession of choices. So the psychology of choice is directly relevant to understanding patrons' behavior.

Patron Satisfaction with their Choices

Psychologist Barry Schwartz studies the psychological effects of the opportunity to choose. While it is commonly assumed that greater freedom of choice is a good thing, he has found that there are psychological costs to making choices. Schwartz (2004) has written that in general, people tend to be satisficers or maximizers. A satisficer accepts whatever is good enough, and is not overly concerned with what may have been missed or passed over. A maximizer is an individual who is not comfortable until all possible choices have been explored. Interestingly, his research indicates that maximizers are less likely to be satisfied with their choices, in part because they are nagged by the sense that something better may have been chosen. This greatly affects the potential satisfaction of each type of user.

Patrons who are satisficers tend to print or copy articles that appear to be good enough for their need and not worry about what else may be available. As long as adequate sources are in the collection, these patrons will be unlikely to complain. The maximizing patrons will be less willing to accept only readily available serials, and will tend to be more dogged in pursuit of cited articles. For librarians, this means that some patrons will seem content and some will complain, in no apparent relation to the completeness of the collection. It is important to note that the nature of advanced studies forces doctoral students to be maximizers in their pursuit of literature. Doctoral students who are satisficers by nature will need to become maximizers if they are going to be able to graduate. Collections intended to support advanced studies are as comprehensive as possible for many reasons and fulfilling the maximizing attitude is one of them. Helping patrons gain access is another challenge.

Helping the Patron Make Choices

The purpose of reference service is, after all, to match every reader with the best information to meet their needs. Although librarians provide data in catalogs and offer database instructions go help patrons make good choices, this is difficult for most patrons because of significant mental effort involved in deciding what one wants and in then deciding what best meets one's needs.

Patrons vary widely in how precisely they know what they are looking for. For someone new to a topic or new to a discipline's methods of conducting research, it is very difficult to know what will best meet one's needs. In academic settings, novice researchers are unlikely to know the most important researchers or journals or know what the hot lines of inquiry are. In a public library, anyone approaching a topic new to them faces similar hurdles. Special librarians may encounter fewer patrons uncertain of their needs since many special libraries primarily serve experienced professionals. Yet, even well-educated professionals may need to research topics new to them. Recognizing that patrons often do not know what they want is a central assumption of good reference interviewing. So when patrons select periodical literature they have two challenges: to decide what they need, then to select from the collection something that meets that need. Librarians help patrons decide their needs through the reference interview and then help them choose appropriate resources. Serials are often appropriate resources.

An implication of patrons' difficulty in making choices is that less can be more. A highly selective collection of appropriate materials can be of great help to the people fresh to a topic. Library collections are not usually tailored to meet only the needs of novices. Meeting their needs can be supported by creating pathfinders and by providing selective online full-text databases. Pathfinders are guides to available information resources published by librarians on topics of interest to patrons. These are well suited for frequently encountered information needs and typically include suggestions for appropriate serials and databases in the topic area. Selected serials may be in print or online. A pathfinder with suggestions of print resources should include classification numbers or other instructions for locating the information. The defined list of resources in a pathfinder effectively reduces options to a more manageable range of choices.

Selective online full-text databases also define a range of choices. For example, the PsycARTICLES database containing the full text of a few dozen journals can be less taxing for patrons to use than the full PsycINFO. The subset of content from PsycINFO one finds in PsycARTICLES meets research standards in psychology and is immediately accessible. A patron who just needs one appropriate article on a topic may spend less time and get better results using the smaller, more focused full-text database. Librarians can help patrons choose by providing selective databases and helping patrons use them. To paraphrase Ranganathan's (1931) second law of library science, "every reader his or her serial." If a serial meets a patron's information need the patron should be able to find and use it.

MEASURING USE IN LIBRARIES

Knowing how often each serial is used is fundamental to making wise collection development decisions and will help with decisions concerning both print and online subscriptions. Counts of use combined with subscription price data provide an objective measure of the value of a serial to the patrons of a particular collection. This discussion of measuring the use of serials in libraries will concentrate first on print serials and conclude with issues concerning the use of remote access serials.

Serials librarians have two major approaches to measuring the use of print serials: counting how often they are cited and counting how often they are removed from shelves. Other approaches include counting circulation, surveying patrons, and counting uses in particular circumstances.

Counting Citations

Counting serials citations, more useful for the academic or special librarian, can be done globally by sampling citations in published literature, or locally by sampling citations in papers produced within an institution. The global approach indicates the use of serials by all authors in a selected topic area. The rationale and methods of the global approach are described in the section "Citation Analysis" later in this chapter. The local approach indicates the use of serials by selected patrons of the library. A strength of counting citations is that a citation indicates a concrete, verifiable use. A weakness is that counting citations misses any uses that do not become incorporated into publications. Local citation counts concretely indicate uses, but cannot measure all uses.

Local citation counts in the academic setting can be of student papers, theses and dissertations, or professors' publications. The basic method is to gather the sample of papers and enter the serial title in every work cited into a spreadsheet or database. After all the works cited in the sample of papers are entered, frequency counts can be calculated for each cited serial. Doing this analysis with student papers is valuable because it indicates which journals' articles are actually incorporated into their academic work. It conveniently excludes items that were removed from shelves, printed off, or checked out, but not actually used as works cited.

A challenge with using student papers is that it is difficult to obtain a sample large enough to accurately represent use. Gathering the papers is time-consuming and requires effort on the part of instructors. Effort in gathering and entering data may be reduced by having students submit papers electronically. When students follow the standard practice of submitting copies of their theses and dissertations to their institution's library, a sample can be drawn from the library's collection. It is still as laborious to enter the data, but at least the sample of research papers may be easier to acquire. Local citation studies provide an important perspective on serials use despite the labor involved and difficulty obtaining a robust sample. Sylvia and Lesher's (1995) analysis of psychology students' thesis citations and Leiding's (2005) analysis of undergraduate honors thesis bibliographies report gaining valuable insights on the use of serials collections.

Counting citations in the articles published by professors and researchers using academic libraries or special libraries is done in a similar fashion, except the sample is drawn from published books and journal articles. The ISI citation databases can be used for this kind of citation count because their Web of Knowledge records authors' affiliations. Since the Web of Knowledge does not include all scholarly journals, some researchers' publications will be missed if ISI data alone are used. The serials librarian uses ISI data differently than for the process for tenure and promotion described in Chapter 7. The librarian compares what the local researcher cited with the library's serials to see how well the collection is meeting their needs (Burright, Hahn, and Antonisse 2005). If the librarian also measures citations of the researchers' work, the purpose is to identify publications important to the researcher. Locally kept bibliographies can be employed if the institution keeps records of faculty's publications. If a new serials librarian finds that no bibliographies of locally written papers are kept they may consider keeping one. The primary advantage of doing a citation study of local authors is that the results will reflect the research interests of the library's patrons who publish. A potential disadvantage is that individuals' published research may not accurately reflect the needs of the academic or special library patron population as a whole. One way to overcome this might be to count the removal of serials from library shelves.

Counting Removal from Shelves

Counting removal of serials from library shelves is easier when stacks are closed. In that setting, it is relatively easy to control and count when items are removed from shelves. The use of each serial can be tracked by recording requests for items. Open stacks provide a greater challenge.

Open stacks, more commonly used in libraries, make counting the use of print serials more difficult. In this instance, frequency of use of print journals in open stacks can be measured by the "sweep method," counting the number of times items are re-shelved. A librarian choosing to use the sweep method must count how often each serial is used. Major decisions need to be made including the length of the study, how volumes and issues will be identified, and the method of recording what is re-shelved. Unless library staff members always measure the use of serials, a use study necessarily relies on a sample of total uses. A good sample accurately represents the entire population, which for journal use in a library includes all uses by all patrons over the life of the library. To accurately reflect the population of uses, the study's sample needs to encompass patrons' likely uses of the collection. In academic libraries, that means choosing a period of time that includes the courses typically offered. Since many courses are only offered once per year, measuring use for two semesters or a calendar year is often needed to adequately sample use. Public and special libraries may also have seasonal variations of use to be considered when choosing the length of a study. Given changes in courses offered and other variables, continuous measurement of all journals' use is the sampling method most likely to accurately measure the actual use. Once the time frame of a serials use study is determined the serials librarian will plan how to record uses.

How volumes and issues are identified depends mostly on how and if the librarians barcode serials. If every issue receives a barcode, then it makes sense to use a hand-held scanner to record issues being re-shelved. Some librarians only barcode bound volumes, so in that case only volumes would be scanned. Unbound issues would either not be included in the count or would be recorded by another means. One option for using barcodes is to put the barcode labels on the shelves. Workers then scan the shelf label, which can be faster than opening every volume to find the barcode. However, the use data will then be for the full run of the title, and data on which years are being used is not collected. Having data on which years of a serial are being used is valuable information when a librarian needs to move volumes to storage or weed unused volumes.

For libraries which do not barcode serials, titles are usually used for recording use. Titles are recorded by marking the volumes, or labels, or a list of titles. The following method has been used by the author with satisfactory success. Shelf labels can be made with blank space on one or both sides of the title. Workers can be trained to put a dot on the label for each item re-shelved. Other librarians record use on a list of titles rather than on shelf labels, which has the advantages of being invisible to patrons and providing a convenient record of use.

The sweep method assumes that an issue or volume removed from the shelf has been used once. This assumption is inaccurate because a patron may have removed the serial and not used it at all or may have, particularly if a serial is bound, used multiple citations in the volume. Other considerations concern measurement errors in the process of recording the count of re-shelved volumes. Circulation, surveys, and other methods may be considered as alternative measures of use.

Other Counting Methods

A summary of methods used in journal use studies published through 1997 may be found in Nisonger (1998). Circulation statistics can be used to measure use in libraries that allow patrons to check out serials. Automated library systems make data collection and reporting easy, but many libraries do not circulate serials. Circulation counts do not measure in-house use, although use in the library may correlate with serials' circulation rates. Other methods employed to measure use include observing behavior of patrons in the stacks, forcing patrons to request volumes purposely removed from the shelves, and inserting surveys into volumes. These methods suffer from more problems with validity and reliability than counting removal from shelves or circulation statistics, primarily because it is so difficult to obtain an adequately large sample. Challenges to validity and reliability are inherent in all serials use studies.

Validity and Reliability

All serials use studies face challenges with validity and reliability of the use data. Validity is the degree to which gathered data measures what it intends to measure. The validity of the sweep method for counting uses is based on the assumption that volumes or issues found on carts and tables have, as stated earlier, been used once (and only once), and that volumes and issues still on the shelves have not been used. Since an unknown number of patrons with unknown frequency pull items but do not read them, and re-shelve items they have read, the sweep method is not a perfectly valid way to count use. Trying to measure the variability of use counts from actual use suffers from the so-called "reference problem." That is, no omniscient observer exists to indicate a true level of use against which measured use can be compared. With no reference point, the validity of the use counts cannot be accurately measured. This inability to test the internal validity of use counts is true of any use study relying on the sweep method.

Reliability is the degree to which data consistently measures whatever it is supposed to be measuring. High reliability for a measurement of the use of serials relies on use counts consistently measuring which serials are actual read, a measure difficult to attain for the use of serials. Problems with reliability come from three areas: variability in counting (use study data gathering behavior), variability in use (patron behavior), and variability in what is being counted (volumes and issues of serials). Variability in counting is not amenable to controlled measurement. As with validity, no true reference points exist against which counts can be compared, since there is no omniscient observer. No way exists to confidently verify that every re-shelved volume is properly recorded. Reliability of use study data gathering is supported by careful training and close oversight.

Variability in use is a particular problem at the level of individual titles. A single research project of class assignment can dramatically change the use of a serial title from one year to the next. Patron use of online journals instead of print is disrupting use trends. The author has found that online availability impacts print use differently among disciplines (Black 2005).

Variability in the serial titles being counted is a fundamental challenge to serials use study reliability. Print serials vary in content, frequency, and title. In an endless stream of variability, they cease, split, arrive late, grow, shrink, change names, and otherwise create problems for serials librarians and confuse patrons. Further problems are created when librarians add and cancel titles. Variability in number of articles published and delays in publication also impact use and the calculations for use. Changes in editorial boards or publishers responsible for titles can shift the focus or prestige of a journal. All these potential changes in serial titles cause variability in measured use.

Statistical Analysis of Use

Measures of use are difficult and cannot be considered for most statistical analysis. Statistical measures of variability are appropriate for an entire collection, but are not appropriate for individual titles because of the challenges to validity and reliability discussed previously. Should it be necessary to provide statistical analysis of use for administrators, it would be well to consult with a statistician to help design the research, analyze the data collected, and confirm the appropriateness of the vocabulary used in the report. When questioned about any such study, it is important to understand each step of the research process. Implementing the analysis shown next may help convey the danger of applying statistical analysis to measured serials use.

It is important to recognize the degree of variability in use of titles from one year to the next. An appropriate tool to measure year-to-year variation is the coefficient of variation, which is the standard deviation divided by the mean. It measures the spread (variation) in use counts, taking into account the number of uses. To illustrate how the coefficient of variation works, take this example of local use counts at the author's library for the *Journal of Educational Psychology* and *Science News*.

Title	2003 uses	2000 uses	1996 uses	Standard deviation	Average uses	Coefficient of variation
Journal of Educational Psychology	283	348	324	26.8	318	8%
Science News	10	51	154	60.6	72	84%

The use counts for the *Journal of Educational Psychology* remained fairly stable in the three years of the study. The coefficient of variation of 8 percent quantifies the relatively little variation in use from year-to-year. [The 8 percent is calculated by dividing the standard deviation (26.8) by the average uses (318), and multiplying by 100]. In contrast, *Science News* experienced large changes in use from one year to the next, as indicated by the coefficient of variation of 84 percent.

When choosing titles to cancel, it is helpful to know which titles have a relatively high coefficient of variation (and thus a low reliability of measured uses). If reliability is low for a title, the use counts should be given relatively less weight when considering canceling. Conversely, a title with a low coefficient of variation has reliably measured uses indicative of actual use over time. Use counts are only one of several important tools for the serials selection process described in Chapter 3. Calculating the coefficient of variation for each title helps keep the use count for each serial title in proper perspective. Determining the precise role of measured use in serials collection development is further complicated by coexistence of remote access serials with the print collection.

Measuring Use of Remote Access Serials

Some of the measures discussed here can be applied to measuring use of remote access serials. One of the advantages of providing serials online is that the database vendors can track and record how many times articles are accessed. To access a full-text article means to view it on screen, print it, save it, or e-mail it. Since accessing a full-text article serves the same function as pulling a printed volume from a shelf, it is reasonable to equate access with use, remembering that access and actual use present measurement problems. Having found an article does not mean it was used.

Use data for remote access serials suggest two interesting phenomena. First, patrons access the online full text of a periodical far more frequently than they use the print. Morse and Clintworth (2000) found a 15-fold increase in viewings of the corresponding electronic versions of print serials. A study at the University of California (UC) found digital use exceeded print use by at least a factor of ten to one (Collection Management Initiative 2003). Serotkin, Fitzgerald, and Balough (2005) concluded that the majority of users appreciate the convenience and efficiency of electronic forms of information. The author's study of print and online use found that on average, titles online get accessed almost five times as frequently as titles get used in print (Black 2005). Perhaps the greater rates of viewing online versus using print are due to the convenience to patrons of online access. Some portion of the difference may be due to undercounts of print use. The obvious question is, "If five, ten, or fifteen times as many articles are being used, where are they going"? It would be interesting to investigate the impact of the quality of work done by students who view more articles online than they are willing to read in print. It may simply be that patrons click on many more articles than they read, and the difference is due to the ease of clicking relative to the effort of pulling volumes from shelves. But the difference in frequency of use of print and online serials deserves careful study.

The second interesting phenomenon is that patrons use many titles in aggregated databases that are not in the print collection. Sanville (2001) reported a fourfold increase in the number of serial titles used by patrons of Ohio's academic libraries when remote access serials were made available via OhioLINK. The use of titles never held in a library's print collection may include titles seemingly irrelevant to local academic programs or research activities. Since it is impossible to predict everything patrons will read, having access to more titles is beneficial to patrons who have a clear sense of what they seek.

The study of the relationships between online and print use is made possible by combining data on use within the library with data on frequency of access to remote access serials. It is potentially much easier to track use of online periodicals than it is to count uses of print periodicals. The details of running use reports vary, but vendors typically allow authorized users to get reports on monthly and annual use of titles. Use can be defined as abstracts viewed, articles viewed in HTML, articles viewed in PDF, or articles printed. Unfortunately, vendors do not count and report uses in the same way. The COUNTER project is working to establish standards for counting and reporting the use of databases and full-text content. In their words, "Librarians want to understand better how the information they buy from a variety of sources is being used; publishers want to know how the information products they disseminate are being accessed. An essential requirement to meet these objectives is an agreed international Code of Practice governing the recording and exchange of online usage data" (COUNTER 2004). "The COUNTER Code of Practice specifies: the data elements to be measured, definitions of these data elements; usage report content, format, frequency and methods of delivery; protocols for combining usage reports from direct use and from use via intermediaries" http://www.projectcounter.org/code_practice.html. Despite COUNTER's excellent work, as of 2006, not all vendors follow their code of practice. Consequently, it is difficult to compare online use statistics across databases. Despite that difficulty, the use statistics within vendors' suites of databases can be enlightening and are relatively easy to acquire and interpret. Comparing the use of remote access and print serials is an important component of decision processes to shift resources from print to online access.

Serials librarians measure use to create valuable data to inform librarians responsible for collection development. As described, a librarian can count citations in a local patron's publications to see what is being used. A global approach may also be taken to analyze the use of serials by all users.

CITATION ANALYSIS

Citation analysis is the systematic, quantitative study of works cited. It is part of the broader field of bibliometrics, the application of mathematical and statistical methods to study the use of documents and patterns of publication. Citation analysis has been used to rank publications according to their importance, to identify core collections, measure the impact of publications, rank the output of

authors and institutions, and study subject interrelationships. The underlying premise is that citations to literature more or less accurately represent the influence of
that literature. The logic is that the more an author or periodical is cited, the more
influential that author or periodical is in the applicable discipline. Potential flaws in
this assumption are that influences are not always cited, authors may have bias in
citing works, authors often cite themselves, types of citation are not consistent, and
citation rates vary considerably among disciplines, nations, and times (MacRoberts and MacRoberts 1989, p. 343).

Many citation analyses are based on data provided by published citation indexes, notably the ISI *Journal Citation Reports* (*JCR*), which is based on data in
the *Science Citation Index* (*SCI*) and *Social Science Citation Index* (*SSCI*). These
databases are now offered in ISI's Web of Science, which also incorporates the
Arts & Humanities Citation Index (*A&HCI*). The *A&HCI* is not included in the
JCR because, in arts and humanities, citations to journals (as opposed to books and
primary sources) are too infrequent to justify using citation rates to measure
journal quality. The ISI databases include the citations to all works cited in the
journals selected for coverage. Citations are counted the same whether journals
are published in print, online, or both. Each citation for every research article in the
covered publications is parsed into author, date, source, volume, pages, and others,
and entered into the ISI databases. ISI does this with electronic copy or scanned
page images using optical character recognition and special software to parse the
fields and check for errors. ISI's end user product allows one to search on the data
in these fields. The technique of using the author affiliation field to study local
researcher's citations was described previously as a method to measure serials use.

Measuring the use of serials is only one of many types of citation analysis. A
value for researchers of the ISI citation indexes is that they allow one to identify all
the articles that have cited another article. The logic is that if one article cites
another, they are related. Using the citation indexes allows researchers to find more
related articles than could be identified by following works cited alone. Works
cited can only point back in time, while the citing works recorded in the Web of
Knowledge point forward in time from an article's publication date. This is a very
powerful way for users to locate related articles.

An error rate in the citation data is inevitable (as is the case in any bibliographic
database), and the citation databases suffer from lack of consistency in many
citation styles required by serials publishers. For example, authors and periodical
titles vary in the database because names and titles are abbreviated differently. But
ISI strives to make the data as accurate as they can. The Web of Knowledge is
intended to facilitate searches for articles on a topic. ISI data can also be used to
study serial titles.

The *JCR* citation analysis tool for evaluating serials is based on data in the ISI
citation indexes, and this information is used to create rankings of journals. The
top-ranked journals have the most frequently cited articles. Journals publish
varying numbers of articles per year, so it would be unfair to compare a citation
count for a journal publishing a thousand articles per year to the count for one

publishing forty. The *JCR* adjusts for number of articles published with what they call the impact factor, which is the frequency of citation divided by the number of articles published in the last two years. The higher a journal's impact factor, the more frequently articles in that journal have been cited. A high impact factor implies that the journal publishes important articles, and is thus important to have in a library's collection. As discussed in Chapter 7, rankings in the JCR have conferred "must-have" status on those journals with relatively high impact factors.

The JCR is not a perfect record of citation, despite the effort ISI puts into creating an accurate database. The most important shortcoming of the JCR is that it does not include all of the journals for which works cited appear in the database. That is, articles in the works cited in journals included in the JCR may be to journals not covered in the JCR. Many periodicals are thus left out, so important authors and publications fall through the cracks. Rice et al. (1989) found problems in the reliability of data in the ISI databases due to title changes, aberrant title abbreviations, and incomplete coverage. Despite potential weaknesses, citation analysis is the most objective quantitative method for identifying the relations among publications, including the most frequently cited journals, and the JCR is the most accessible and complete record available. Independent citation analyses are occasionally published, but finding one on a particular discipline is difficult.

Since many journals are not included in the ISI citation indexes and the JCR does not include data for every discipline, there remains a need for independently conducted citation analyses, particularly in interdisciplinary fields. Any serials librarian finding a need to conduct and publish research could choose a topic and do a citation analysis; however, given the burgeoning interest in interdisciplinary studies, using citation analysis to indicate the most important serial titles and types of materials (i.e., periodicals, books, dissertations, and government documents) for topic areas is a fertile area for future research. Citation analysis can also be used to study patterns of journal use.

PATTERNS OF JOURNAL USE

The rates of use of serials vary by title, age of publication, disciplines, and types of users. In every serials collection, rates of use range from a few very heavily used titles to many that get moderate use and to many more that get very little use. This holds true for print and online serials collections, although patterns of online use may be different from print collection use. Understanding patterns of use help the serials librarian match the collection to patrons' needs. Patterns of use by title can help a librarian choose serials within a defined scope of a collection.

Patterns by Title

As stated, in every serials collection there is a range of rates of use from a few very heavily used titles, to many that get moderate use, to many that get very little use. The broadest concept of the phenomenon of use concentrated in relatively few titles is called the Matthew Effect. The classic formulation by Merton (1968) described how the reward system in science concentrates attention on publications that have already received attention. The concept was formally applied to the use of serials by Price (1976) and applied concretely in citation databases by Garfield (1979). The term comes from the passage in the book of Matthew, "For unto every one that hath shall be given, and he shall have abundance: but from him that hath not shall be taken away even that which he hath—Matthew 25:29." In other words, the rich get richer and the poor get poorer. In scholarly publishing, the more often a work is cited, the more likely it is to be cited again. Highly cited journals attract the best work because the authors want to be published in a highly cited journal. Universities with highly cited researchers attract the best researchers, because they want to be well recognized for their work. Journals that get most heavily used become the most prominent, and therefore continue to attract the most use.

Perhaps the most frequently mentioned and most widely applied model for concentration of use is the so-called 80/20 Rule described by Trueswell (1969). It is only a "rule" in the sense of being a rule of thumb, but as a rule of thumb it is impressively, if crudely, predictive of concentration in a remarkable number of human endeavors. For example, it has been said that 20 percent of the workers do 80 percent of the work, and that 20 percent of inventory accounts for 80 percent of sales. For serials, the formulation is that 20 percent of the subscriptions will account for 80 percent of the use.

A more sophisticated model of the distribution of journal use is known as the Bradford Distribution. This distribution of use, also known as Bradford's law of scatter, is recognized as fundamental to bibliometrics and information science and has received significant attention since its publication. To determine Bradford's distribution for a set of journals, the journals are ranked in use order with the journal receiving the highest number of uses ranked first. The mathematical formula expressing the concentration of use among the ranked list of titles is stated as $1 : n : n^2 : n^3 : n^4 \ldots$, which Bradford originally derived by examining the use of print journals within the specific disciplines of applied geophysics and lubrication (Bradford 1953, p. 154). The Bradford multiplier, n, is equal to how many journals on the ranked list it takes to achieve the same number of uses as the highest-ranked journal. Thus, if the first journal receives 1,000 uses, and the next three ranked journals together receive approximately 1,000 uses, the Bradford multiplier n is 3. Bradford's formula then predicts that it will take the next n^2 journals, or nine journals in this case, to receive the next 1,000 uses; the next n^3, or 27 journals, to receive the next 1,000 uses, and the next n^4, or 81 journals, to receive the next 1,000 uses.

Bradford's work was with journals in a single discipline. Patterns of journal use in aggregated databases may follow a different pattern (Black and Sisson 2003/2004). During Bradford's day, it was prohibitively time-consuming to collect data on the use of large collections of serials. Today, however, use statistics that are easily reported from aggregated databases make it relatively easy to list and rank titles by the number of hits received for abstracts, text, and/or page images. Very little research has been published on the patterns of use in these databases, and it is an area ripe for exploration.

The study of patterns of use is primarily of academic interest, but it can be helpful for collection development in any library that defines the scope of its collection after the Carnegie classification based model described in Chapter 1. The concentration of use in a collection or disciplines within a collection suggests how many titles are needed to collect at a given level. The 80/20 rule is only a rough guide. Some collections may have a steeper drop-off in use, meaning that very few titles get most of the use. In those cases, a smaller collection may adequately meet patrons' needs. Conversely, a collection with a gradual decline in use from the most-used to the seldom-used titles indicates demand for more titles to collect at a chosen level.

However, none of these models take into account the value of seldom-used titles to the individuals who read them. It must be remembered that for the patron giving a title its only two uses in a year, that title is an important part of the collection. Since all patrons should have their serials, the librarian should try, as much as possible, to maintain the breadth of serials in the collection. When cuts are necessary, knowledge of patterns of use can inform deselection decisions.

Patterns by Age of Publication

Serials typically experience a distribution of use by the age of the volumes. Magazines intended to convey current events tend to get their heaviest use when they first arrive in the library. Scholarly journals can have a somewhat delayed distribution of use driven by the time lag that can exist between publication and inclusion in bibliographic databases. While some users want to browse recent issues, many library patrons only seek articles when they find citations in databases or in works cited in published articles. Concentration of use by age of publications varies by discipline, but peak use of scholarly journals in a library tends to be about two years after the journals' publication dates. Citations to journals in published articles peak at about three years after publication. If one were to record the dates to all the works cited in the 2005 volume of a journal, one would typically see the most citations to works published in 2002.

After that peak, use and citation of journals typically drop off at a steady rate. Use drops off fairly rapidly in some disciplines, and more gradually in others. The ISI's *JCR* reports the rate of drop in use over time as the cited half-life of the journal, the number of years that account for half of the citations to the journal. For example, one could record one year's worth of all journal articles' citations for *Communication Quarterly* and list them in chronological order. Draw a line at the halfway point on the list. The publication date at the halfway point marks the cited half-life of *Communication Quarterly*. The *JCR*'s calculation of half-life is more involved and is expressed to one decimal place, but the principle is the same. A serial's half-life expresses its pattern of use by publication date. The half-life of a journal is an important consideration when volumes need to be weeded or moved into remote storage. If a title has a short half-life, say two or three years, older volumes can be expected to get little use and are good candidates for removal from the stacks. Conversely, a title with a half-life of ten or more years would not be a good choice for removal from the shelves.

Patterns by Disciplines

Rates of serial use vary by discipline, especially as measured by citations in published literature. For example, it is the norm in psychology to cite all relevant sources. Published research articles in psychology commonly cite over a 100 journal articles (among other sources), while historians often cite many primary source documents and relatively few articles from history journals. This makes citation rates and citation impact factors much higher in psychology than in history. Given the difference in citation rates, it makes little sense to rank history and psychology journals together. Similarly, use within a particular academic library can vary by discipline because of enrollments in disciplines and the nature of work assigned in those disciplines. In some topic areas, one individual's use of a title can dramatically increase measured use. Since the otherwise rarely used serial may be of critical importance to that individual researcher, use statistics alone may not accurately reflect the value of that title. Variations in use by disciplines are thus important to consider for collection development.

Patterns by Type of User

Patterns of use within a discipline also vary by whether the patrons are undergraduate students, graduate students, staff, professors, or members of the generalpublic. Unfortunately, periodical use studies based on the sweep method cannot indicate this variation. One way to measure variations in use by patron type is to conduct local citation analyses of papers, theses, or publications as described previously in the section "Counting Citations to Measure Use." It is also possible to survey users about their academic status and intended use of articles during their process of accessing full text (Connell, Rogers, and Diedrichs 2005). Awareness of varying patterns of use by different portions of a library's patron population informs collection development. The emphasis placed on serving the needs of each type of user is a policy decision.

This chapter has addressed copyright in the use of serials, patrons' use of serials, libraries' measurement of use, and patterns of serial use. The issues and practices described help librarians effectively and efficiently develop serials collections well suited to local patrons. Even an ideally selected collection will be underutilized if patrons do not know how to access the serials. Chapter 9 will describe challenges and techniques of teaching patrons to find serials that meet their needs.

SUGGESTIONS FOR FURTHER READING

A reliable and concise treatment of copyright and fair use is Janis H. Bruwelheide, *The Copyright Primer for Librarians and Educators* (Chicago, Washington, DC: American Library Association; National Education Association, 1998). Bruwelheide enhances a detailed discussion of copyright and fair use for materials in various formats with question and answer sections addressing specific, realistic problems encountered by librarians and teachers.

The complete CONTU report on copyright and interlibrary loan (ILL) has been posted online by Lee A. Hollaar at http://digital-law-online.info/CONTU/PDF/index.html. The CONTU guidelines on photocopying for ILL begin on page 54 of the report.

A succinct treatment of maximizers and satisficers, along with Barry Schwartz's argument for why more choice is not necessarily better, may be found in "The Tyranny of Choice" article in *Scientific American* cited previously. For a more in-depth treatment, see Schwartz's *The Paradox of Choice: Why More Is Less* (New York: Ecco/HarperCollins Publishers, 2004). See also Patrick Wilson's *Two Kinds of Power: An Essay on Bibliographical Control* (Berkeley: University of California Press, 1968), in which the same concept is addressed in the context of bibliography.

For more on measuring the use of print serials in libraries, start with Chapter 6, "Study of Periodical Use" in Nisonger's *Management of Serials in Libraries*, which includes comprehensive references to published library periodical use studies. Several alternatives to the sweep method are discussed and cited by Nisonger. Reba Leiding's "Using citation checking of undergraduate honors thesis bibliographies to evaluate library collections," *College & Research Libraries*, 66(5), 2005, 417–429, includes a literature review of local citation studies. Studies of online journal use have only recently begun to appear in the literature. One interesting recent study by Tammy R. Siebenber, Betty Galbraith, and Eileen E. Brady found that patrons' switch from print to online formats is not occurring across the board ("Print versus electronic journal use in three sci/tech disciplines: What's going on here?" *College & Research Libraries*, 65(5), 2004, 427–438). A report of the author's own work in this area with a literature review of related studies may be found in Steve Black, "Impact of full text on print journal use at a liberal arts college," *Library Resources & Technical Services*, 2005, 49(1), 19–26. For a more comprehensive review of recent research on the use of remote access serials, see Carol Tenopir with the assistance of Brenda Hitchcock and Ashley Pillow, *Use and Users of Electronic Library Resources: An Overview and Analysis of Recent Research Studies* (Washington, DC: Council on Library and Information Resources, 2003).

A good introduction to the literature on citation analysis is Osareh's "Bibliometrics, citation analysis and co-citation analysis: A review of the literature," *Libri*, 46, 1996, 149–225. Osareh surveys applications of citation analysis and provides abundant references to other works in this area. For a more recent example of citation analysis, see Juris Dilevko and Keren Dali, "Improving collection development and reference services for interdisciplinary fields through analysis of citation patterns: An example using tourism studies," *College & Research Libraries*, 65(3), 2004, 216–241. Thomson ISI provides rather extensive information about citation analysis and the ISI Web of Knowledge on their website at http://www.isinet.com/. See especially the essays at http://www.isinet.com/essays/ covering a variety of topics including the history of citation indexing and using the impact factor.

Appropriate entry points to the literature on concentration of use are Mary W. Lockett's "The Bradford Distribution: A review of the literature, 1934–1987," *Library and Information Science Research,* 11, 1989, 21–36, and Stephen J. Bensman, "Journal collection management as a cumulative advantage process," *College & Research Libraries,* 1985, 46(1), 13–29. See also Paul Metz, "Bibliometrics: Library use and citation studies" in Mary Jo Lynch and Arthur Young, eds., *Academic Libraries: Research Perspectives* (Chicago: American Library Association, 1990). Of the many studies that have applied citation analysis to assess the value of journals, one of special interest is Henry Barschall's "The cost effectiveness of physics journals: A survey," *Physics Today,* 41, July 1988, 56–59. The publisher Gordon & Breach sued Barschall's organization in the case *Gordon & Breach v. American Institute of Physics and American Physical Society,* claiming that Barschall's study constituted false advertising. Gordon & Breach lost the lawsuit described in detail with primary source documents at http://barschall.stanford.edu/.

REFERENCES

ALA Council. June 28, 1995. *Code of Ethics of the American Library Association.* Chicago: American Library Association Council, http://www.ala.org/ala/oif/statementspols/codeofethics/codeethics.htm (accessed February 3, 2006).

Black, Steve. 2005. Impact of full text on print journal use at a liberal arts college. *Library Resources & Technical Services,* 49(1): 19–26.

Black, Steve, and Sisson, Amy. 2003/2004. Bradford's Distribution, the 80/20 Rule, and patterns of full-text database use. *Against the Grain* 15(6): 20–24.

Bradford, S.C. 1953. *Documentation.* London: C. Lockwood.

Burright, Marian A., Hahn, Trudi Bellardo, and Antonisse, Margaret J. 2005. Understanding information use in a multidisciplinary field: A local citation analysis of neuroscience research. *College & Research Libraries* 66(3): 198–210.

Coalition for Networked Information. 2004. *Information Policies: CONTU. Highlights of the Final Report of the National Commission on New Technological Uses of Copyrighted Works,* July 31, 1978. Washington, DC: Library of Congress, 1979, 54–55.

Collection Management Initiative. 2003. *Collection Management Initiative Preliminary Findings from the Journal Use and User Preference Studies.* Oakland: University of California, Office of the President, http://www.ucop.edu/cmi/findings.html (accessed January 20, 2006).

Connell, Tschera Harkness, Rogers, Sally A., and Diedrichs, Carol Pitts. 2005. OhioLINK electronic journal use at Ohio State University. *portal: Libraries and the Academy* 5(3), 371–390.

COUNTER. 2004. *Counting Online Usage of Networked Electronic Resources*. Edinburgh, UK, http://www.projectcounter.org/ (accessed February 3, 2006).

Garfield, Eugene. 1979. *Citation Indexing: Its Theory and Application in Science, Technology, and Humanities*. New York: John Wiley.

Leiding, Reba. 2005. Using citation checking of undergraduate honors thesis bibliographies to evaluate library collections. *College & Research Libraries* 66(5): 417–429.

MacRoberts, M.H., and MacRoberts, B.R. 1989. Problems of citation analysis: A critical review. *Journal of the American Society of Information Science* 40(5): 342–349.

Merton, Robert K. 1968. The Matthew Effect in science. *Science* 159(3810): 56–63.

Morse, David, and Clintworth, William A. 2000. Comparing patterns of print and electronic journal use in an Academic Health Science Library. *Issues in Science & Technology Librarianship* 28, http://www.library.ucsb.edu/istl/00-fall/refereed.html (accessed January 20, 2006).

Nisonger, Thomas. 1998. *Management of Serials in Libraries*. Englewood, CO: Libraries Unlimited.

Price, Derek J. de Solla. 1976. A general theory of bibliometric and other cumulative advantage processes. *Journal of the American Society for Information Science* 27: 292–306.

Ranganathan, S.R. 1931. *The Five Laws of Library Science*. Madras: Madras Library Association; London: E. Goldston.

Rice, R.E., Borgman, C.L., Bednarski, D., and Hart, P.J. 1989. Journal-to-journal citation data: Issues of validity and reliability. *Scientometrics* 15: 257–282.

Sanville, Thomas J. 2001. Use of electronic journals in OhioLINK's Electronic Journal Center. In *Libraries and Librarians: Making a Difference in the Knowledge Age. Council and General Conference: Conference Programme and Proceedings* (67th, Boston, MA, August 16–25, 2001).

Schwartz, Barry. 2004. The Tyranny of Choice. *Scientific American* 290(4): 70–76.

Serotkin, Patricia B., Fitzgerald, Patricia I., and Balough, Sandra A. 2005. If we build it, will they come? Electronic journals acceptance and usage patterns. *portal: Libraries and the Academy* 5(4): 497–512.

Sylvia, Margaret, and Lesher, Marcella. 1995. What journal do psychology graduate students need? A citation analysis of thesis references. *College & Research Libraries* 56: 313–318.

Trueswell, Richard W. 1969. Some behavioral patters of library users: The 80/20 Rule. *Wilson Library Bulletin* 43: 458–461.

U.S. Copyright Office. December 1998. *The Digital Millenium Copyright Act: U.S. Copyright Office Summary*. Washington, DC: Author, http://www.copyright.gov/legislation/dmca.pdf (accessed February 3, 2006).

Chapter 9

Teaching Patrons to Use Serials

Many of the challenges librarians face in the management of serials also affect patrons. Title changes, availability in multiple formats, failed links, missing issues, and cancelled subscriptions all make patrons' work of finding what they seek more difficult. While librarians help patrons find what they need by making the system as intuitive, seamless, and user-friendly as possible, the complexity of serials makes it impossible to build a system that is completely transparent to users. Even the best designed system will be intuitive to some people but not to others. The cynic's view is that no system can be idiot-proof because one can never underestimate the ingeniousness of idiots. In any case, to use serials effectively and efficiently, patrons need to learn the characteristics of serials, how to search for serial literature, and how to navigate links. Librarians' task of teaching these skills to patrons is an essential complement to a well-managed serials collection. This may be done through the reference interview process, bibliographic instruction, or by providing finding aids. Serials librarians may not be directly responsible for teaching patrons, but familiarity with the issues and practices of reference and instruction help them manage serials to best meet patrons' needs. The expertise of serials librarians may be called upon to help answer questions, plan instruction, or create finding aids.

MEANS OF TEACHING PATRONS

Instruction is most effective when it occurs at a teachable moment, that moment when a patron is ready, willing, and capable of perceiving information and integrating it into their existing knowledge. To take advantage of teachable moments, librarians need to provide appropriate instruction at the point of need. One highly effective way of doing this is at the reference desk.

Teaching Patrons at the Reference Desk

Patrons seldom approach the reference librarian at anything other than a teachable moment. A patron approaching the reference desk may be unaware of the amount of new information they need or are able to absorb is limited, but the fact that they are there with a question provides an excellent teaching opportunity. The basic principles of effective reference service described in the Reference and User Services Association (RUSA) Guidelines for Behavioral Performance of Reference and Information Service Providers (RUSA 2004) apply equally to teachable moments in person, by telephone, or online. However, when the reference transaction is not face-to-face visual cues that a patron understands are lost. Effective communication without visual clues requires special effort and the process of teaching the patron may be more difficult.

Teaching patrons to find information in serials via telephone requires the ability to describe processes without the benefit of nonverbal clues that the patron understands. If the information sought is in a print serial, the librarian should be able to provide a citation and directions for finding it in the library. If the information sought is in a remote access serial, the librarian should determine the patron's ability to access it and give appropriate instructions. Patrons who call a librarian while using library resources online can be talked through the process of finding the information they seek.

Online or virtual reference can include communication by online chat, e-mail, or instant messaging (IM) and if implemented, should be viewed as integral to a library's overall reference service (MARS Digital Reference Guidelines Ad Hoc Committee 2004). Reference transactions via e-mail are without verbal or visual clues of patron's level of understanding and often require several messages back and forth to accomplish a rudimentary reference interview. More complex questions sent by e-mail often need to be followed up with a phone call or by asking the patron to come to the library. In cases where a patron's need can be quickly determined and it can be met by an article in a remote access serial, the librarian can send the citation or document directly to the patron.

Reference service, provided online by the librarian with chat or IM, add the pressure of real-time communication to the challenges of e-mail reference. Ronan (2003) has described the skills needed to provide virtual reference via chat or IM to the RUSA (1996) standard. These include being familiar with chat's norms and conventions, marketing the service, and being aware of patrons' comfort levels (Ronan 2003). Woodward (2005) argues that instructing patrons is an essential aspect of reference service and advocates including more instruction in virtual reference, while acknowledging the difficulty of doing so in a new medium lacking nonverbal communication clues.

Reference service by appointment is also an effective way to teach patrons. One-on-one appointments with patrons are similar to transactions at the reference desk except they are designed to provide in-depth help without interruptions. Campbell and Fyfe (2002) developed a list of best practices for one-on-one instruction that include taking stock of the teachable moment, respecting the patron's perspective, taking time with each step of the process, and encouraging the patron in their learning process. While effective for individual patrons, one-on-one instruction is time-consuming for librarians. Librarians can teach more patrons for their invested time by addressing groups.

Teaching Patrons through Library Instruction

Another way to reach patrons is through library instruction, until recently called bibliographic instruction. Library instruction sessions are conducted for groups of people, typically either as a workshop open to anyone or for students in a class. The advantage of library instruction over reference is that more people are reached at one time. The disadvantage of group instruction is that it may not occur at the audience's immediate point of need, so they may lack the focus needed for genuine learning. Including hands-on practice during a session or immediately afterwards encourages genuine learning. Offering group instruction is standard practice in most college and university libraries and for those public libraries where students come for school visits. For those groups, students' interest in the presentation is improved when the teacher or professor has timed the session to coincide with an assignment. This process will more likely be improved if teachers and faculty understand serials.

Communicating information about serials to teachers and faculty is another good way to spread knowledge of serials in academic and public library settings. Memos and conversations to instructors about title changes, new database offerings, new linking services, and changes in full-text coverage not only help teachers and higher education faculty, but communication also helps spread the word to students. In academic libraries, keeping faculty informed of price changes and developments in remote access serials is important to managing the serials collection. Regular communication is vital to be able to adapt the collection to the budget and to curricular needs. All patrons can be informed of the serials collection and methods for finding information in serials via finding aids.

Teaching Patrons with Finding Aids

Finding aids are guides to resources or procedures created to help library patrons find what they need. These concise descriptions show what is available, how to link to information or how to evaluate information both in print or online. Some patrons avoid using reference service, perhaps because they had past negative experiences with librarians, do not understand what the librarian can do for them, or have a personal reluctance to ask for help. Finding aids displayed prominently in the library and on the library's web site help teach these patrons to use the library on their own. Finding aids are also useful tools during reference transactions, as one may succinctly answer a patron's question. Some patrons may overlook finding aids, but the patrons who use them appreciate the help they provide. Serials librarians might create finding aids that describe how to determine if a serial is available in full text, list serials worth browsing for particular topics, or explain how to find a print journal in the library.

The serials librarian should know what to teach about serials whether they are responsible for the actual library instruction or they participate in the instructional planning process. Planning instruction may be based upon what has been taught before, but past instruction should always be reviewed in terms of new serials, new databases, and new searching methods.

TEACHING ABOUT SERIALS HOLDINGS

Librarians may have only a few minutes to teach at the reference desk or may have a few hours during freshmen orientation. Knowing what to cover is essential, especially when it is uncertain what a patron already knows. Initial orientation to the library typically includes links to databases and the library's serials holdings. Patrons may also need to learn about the availability of serials beyond the institution's holdings and the interlibrary loan (ILL) process. These mechanics of finding serials meet patrons' primary need to find articles by browsing, searching databases, and following citations. Finally, students need to be helped to learn how to correctly cite information.

Database Links and Serials Holdings

Teaching patrons the difference between using a database and using the library catalog is a first priority. They have to learn that databases are for finding individual articles and that the catalog is for finding a library's serial holdings. If the library uses an A-to-Z list of online serials, its purpose and function must also be taught. Novice researchers with a citation in hand often need to be taught how to distinguish the article title from the serial title. Distinguishing titles is fairly easy because the serial title in a citation is almost always in italics. Patrons also need to learn to tell the difference between a citation to a book and a citation to a periodical. The easiest way to convey the difference is to point out that book citations have a place of publication and periodicals do not. An effective class exercise is to give students a list of works cited and have them mark whether each is to a book or periodical (or conference among others).

Series are more difficult, since they can be cited, as a book can, with a place of publication but may be shelved with periodicals. Details to teach about how to find series depends on how the librarian catalogs and shelves them, since volumes in a series may be cataloged and classified individually as monographs or together under the series title.

Teaching patrons how to determine if a cited article is available in the library is also a high priority. An article may be in a print serial in the library or accessible online in a remote access serial. It should be simple to answer the straightforward question, "Is this cited article in the library?" Unfortunately, despite librarians' best cataloging and linking efforts, the question is not always easy to answer. The fact that many full-text databases cite more articles than are available in full text confuses some patrons. They have to learn on their own or with the help of teachers, faculty members, or librarians that some full-text databases link to a mix of complete articles and abstracts only. Once they have learned that lesson, they then must learn to look in the catalog or A-to-Z listing of serials holdings to see what can be accessed beyond full-text links in the database they first used. Patrons must learn that some titles are in print only, some are available only online, and some will not be accessible in the library at all.

Helping patrons navigate links to full text is made more difficult by the co-existence of the several categories of remote access serials delivery methods described in Chapter 2: individual titles, provider platforms, society publisher packages, commercial publisher packages, and index- and abstract-based aggregated databases. While patrons have no reason to care about which method is used, the methods influence how links are made. Various implementations of these methods across vendors and publishers further complicate location and retrieval. Details of what patrons will be taught depend on each library's vendors and databases.

If all publishers and vendors used OpenURL metadata or DOIs, link resolvers would be able to connect patrons to every article from every database, but implementation of OpenURL and/or DOIs is inconsistent. Spotty implementation means connections work for only some titles. Patrons who have favorite databases or publishers soon learn which publications connect to full-text articles. Unfortunately, there is no blanket solution for teaching the patron population as a whole which databases link to which serials. However, it can help to teach them how OpenURL works in principle and to explain that implementation is spotty. Patrons will then at least have some understanding of why some links connect directly to full text and others do not. Perhaps some day all bibliographic databases and remote access serials will be OpenURL compliant. Then links from every database should work for every subscribed serial article. But seamless integration of remote access serials is not yet reality.

Serials Beyond the Local Collection

It may not be necessary to explain that patrons need to go beyond the local collection. Patrons learn quickly enough on their own that their library does not own or have online access to every serial. While large research institutions are more likely to have most of the journals indexed in bibliographic databases, even they do not own every serial. It should be explained to patrons that, since no library has everything, going beyond the local collection is a normal part of doing library research. If the library participates in a local, regional, or statewide union catalog, how to use that union catalog should be a part of the library's instruction program. Functions in the union catalog for requesting items should be included in finding aids, instruction sessions, and reference encounters. Librarians should also explain any requirements for using the libraries represented in the union catalog. Patrons may discover that the item they seek is not in a local library.

Items from other libraries may be requested by ILL. Librarians should first make patrons aware that ILL is the method for getting copies of articles not in the library or accessible online. Patrons wishing to request an item must learn how to request an item. Instructions on where and how to fill out requests should include a clear explanation that the library can only request items not owned. Some patrons may need to be disabused of the notion that ILL can be used as a free photocopying service. The relative ease of identifying potentially useful articles has increased demand for ILL because it takes less time now to gather citations to periodical articles in bibliographic databases than it formerly took to find citations in printed indexes or works cited. Frivolous requests and impatient complaints may be reduced by explaining to patrons the effort that goes into processing requests, the work that must be done by the lending libraries, and the lack of control the requesting library has over the speed of fulfillment. An approach to teaching appropriate use of ILL is "Link? Library? Loan?" Taught in that order, patrons learn to first look for a link to the serial article. If there is no link, they then check the library catalog or A-to-Z list for serial holdings. Only when there are no holdings and no online access is an ILL request appropriate.

In some cases, librarians will need to explain to patrons the CONTU "Rule of Five" copyright restriction described in Chapter 8. A patron whose ILL request has been unfulfilled due to the CONTU restriction naturally deserves a clear explanation. Whether librarians should routinely include CONTU guidelines in library instruction and finding aids should be decided locally. The Rule of Five is in the category of myriad ifs, ands, and buts of library materials and procedures that can be more confusing than clarifying to include in instruction sessions and finding aids. Librarians must also decide how much to emphasize finding serials or other materials outside the library's collection.

A widely available tool for identifying materials beyond a library's collection is WorldCat, the public interface of the OCLC database. WorldCat includes a "Libraries Worldwide" link in each bibliographic record. Patrons can be shown how WorldCat displays summary holdings for libraries that have provided their holdings to OCLC in MARC Format Holdings Data (MFHD). Reference librarians should check that patrons know about ILL, but patrons may prefer to make a trip to a library. They should be warned that the summary holdings do not show gaps, so it is wise to check a library's catalog before traveling to a library for an item.

Patrons who become familiar with looking up holdings in WorldCat commonly misperceive that holdings information should be included in their ILL requests. So it is important to instruct patrons there is no need to identify holdings for their ILL requests because library staff handles that task. The version of the OCLC database used in ILL has more detailed holdings for each library than displays in WorldCat.

Teaching patrons the mechanics of database links and serials holdings is essential for them to find serials once citations have been identified. Librarians also have a role in teaching patrons how to identify articles on topics of interest.

STRATEGIES FOR FINDING ARTICLES

Experienced researchers use three basic strategies to find information from periodical articles or other sources of information: browsing, database searching, and following citation trails (Bates 2002). Since all three methods have their particular strengths, patrons should understand how to do each. The principles of the methods can apply to any class of patrons seeking any type of information, but this discussion will focus on students finding articles in periodicals.

Browsing

Browsing works well for finding information in periodicals when one or a few titles are focused on the research topic. For instance, if a student is doing research for a paper on stuttering, it will be quite efficient for them to browse through recent issues of the *Journal of Fluency Disorders*. One of the strongest arguments for classifying periodicals (rather than arranging them alphabetically by title) is that it facilitates browsing. Professors are well aware of the focused journals in their disciplines, but students usually need to be directed to them by their professors or a reference librarian.

Another reason to teach patrons to browse through specific periodicals is because some databases have significant time lags between the publication of an issue and the loading of the citation in the database. Browsing recent issues of relevant serials is a way to find articles not yet covered in the databases. A good rule of thumb to teach about browsing titles is "Saw it three times? Seek it out." That is, when using the works cited in articles on one's research topic, if the same journal appears in three or more relevant citations it is probably worthwhile to browse the current years of that journal. This practice has the side benefit of helping students learn which journals are the most important for their topic area.

Students may be taught to do subject searches to find journals on a specific topic. Students need to be aware that LC Subject Headings may be different from what they would imagine, so they must learn how to find the correct subject for their topic. For instance, the subject heading for the *Journal of Fluency Disorders* is "Speech disorders—Periodicals," not "Stuttering—Periodicals." An easy thing to teach is that the subject heading for every journal, magazine, or newspaper ends with "—Periodicals." Teaching how to identify and use correct subject headings is also an important skill for effective database searching.

Database Searching

Effective teaching requires a balance of instruction in specific skills with attempts to impart an understanding of general concepts. One aspect of teaching patrons how to find articles in serials is to show, tell, and guide them in which databases to use and how to use them. Instruction should be supported with handouts for students' reference. The content of instruction and handouts will vary, but in general they should address the types of information needs the database can fulfill, the types of material covered, dates of coverage, how to enter search terms, how to use the thesaurus or subject headings, and options for limiting the search. Instruction and the supporting handouts can highlight noteworthy search features or coverage of the databases being taught. The level of detail presented should match the student's levels of expertise. Appropriate instruction for using PsycINFO is very different for freshman taking introductory psychology course than for graduate students in a research seminar. The freshmen need to learn basic search strategies and how to navigate the user interface, while the graduate students need to learn how and why to use an array of searchable fields.

At any level, teaching specific, detailed information is not enough. Patrons also need a conceptual understanding of the systems they are using. Once a patron understands that database records are composed of fields and that searches can be limited to certain fields, they can apply their knowledge to widely disparate interfaces. The remaining task is to identify and exploit the searchable fields in each database. When they understand in principle how databases work they will adapt more easily to changes in search interfaces and be able to transfer their skills from one database to the next.

A fundamental concept to teach is the structure of bibliographic databases. Patrons should know that database records are citations to units of information, and that records are divided into fields (e.g., author, article title, source title, subject headings, publication date, and the like) Database search interfaces are programmed to find information in these fields. Database structures and search engines vary, so which fields are searched and how they are searched differ from one database to the next.

A special problem with periodicals and bibliographic databases arises when patrons want to search a database for articles on their topic in a specific periodical. This requires knowing which database(s) index the publication. Creators of the cooperative project called Jointly Administered Knowledge Environment (JAKE) compiled a free resource on the web listing database coverage of thousands of periodicals. The JAKE database is online at http://jake.med.yale.edu/index.jsp. It is proving to be difficult to maintain, and the future of this all-volunteer resource is in doubt.

Information on which indexes and databases cover periodicals may also be found in the serials reference resources described in Chapter 3. *Magazines for Libraries*, *The Serials Directory*, and *Ulrich's International Periodicals Directory* all list the databases and indexes covering each periodical. Since *Magazines for Libraries* has selective coverage of serials, it is the least comprehensive of these three sources. The online versions of *The Serials Directory* and *Ulrich's International Periodicals Directory* provide the most current and comprehensive records of which indexes and databases cover periodicals. Once identified, the patron will know which index or database they can search for articles on their topic. When articles are found, they may then employ the third strategy for finding articles.

Following Citations

Following a citation trail means using the works cited in one publication to find more relevant information. As each source is found, more citations can be followed. Knowledge of why and how to follow a citation trail correlates highly with a researcher's experience level. Seasoned researchers understand that the works cited in a published study on their topic are likely to be well selected and relevant. They recognize the intellectual effort that goes into selecting citations and the value of the descriptions in the articles of the cited works. Novice researchers need to be taught that following the citations in relevant articles is one of the most efficient ways of finding more research on their topic. They can be resistant to this at first, and may be slow to realize the true value of citations in articles. Seeing for themselves the interrelationships among research studies is an important step toward becoming an effective researcher.

Following a citation trail is an effective method for finding relevant articles, but works cited can only look back in time. Every book or article cited was, of course, written before the article in hand was published. The ISI publishes the three citation indexes described and discussed in Chapter 7. A benefit of citation indexes is that records link to articles subsequently citing an article. A researcher can thus follow a citation trail forward in time from when the article in hand was published. ISI's Web of Science not only integrates the three citation indexes, it also includes a "find relevant articles" feature. "Find relevant articles" retrieves citations to other articles that cite the same works, based on the logic that studies citing the same papers will be on related topics.

The cited reference and relevant articles searches are powerful tools for following citation trails for those serials covered by the citation indexes. However, not every periodical citation can be found using the Web of Science, because links within the Web of Science only work for the journals covered by the ISI citation indexes. Although articles from journals not indexed in the Web of Science are listed in the works cited of every article included in the database, the excluded journals are missed in searches for cited references or relevant articles. Users of the Web of Science need to be aware of this limitation to avoid the erroneous belief that this powerful tool has comprehensive coverage. ISI's Web of Science is expensive, making it difficult for many librarians to include it in their serials budget; however, it is an extraordinarily powerful way to follow citations.

Some database vendors other than ISI now include links in database records to indicate which articles cite other articles. Two examples are the EBSCOhost company's version of the PsycINFO database and Elsevier's Science Direct. As with the Web of Science, the "cited by" links only work for publications covered within the databases. The links to citing articles are thus not comprehensive, but are still quite useful. Patrons can be taught that the "cited by" feature can help them find the most often cited and presumably most important articles on their topics. For instance, a patron can do a search in PsycINFO and get a list of results. The EBSCO version of the database includes notes showing how many times each article in the result list has been cited by other articles indexed in PsycINFO. Students can be taught to give priority in their retrieval of articles to those with a relatively high number of times cited, since the highly cited articles are probably important to include in their research.

IDENTIFYING SCHOLARLY PUBLICATIONS

It is very common in college and university settings for faculty to require students to use and cite scholarly sources in their research papers. Professors have found from experience that if they do not require scholarly sources, student papers will have citations to articles from popular magazines such as *People* or *Reader's Digest* and to websites that are inappropriate for college work. Librarians are often called upon to help teach the students how to tell if a source is scholarly. Some vocabulary typically needs to be covered initially to clarify that "scholarly," "peer reviewed," "refereed," and "professional" are essentially synonymous. Next, it can be helpful to describe the peer review process and emphasize the quality control imparted by the editor, peer experts on the topic, and copy editor. The principle that peer review is intended to make published articles conform to the discipline's research standards should be emphasized. Once these points are made, the peer review process for journals can be compared to the publication process for magazines. With magazines, quality control is up to the editors and authors with no outside review of accuracy before publication.

Once students understand the principle of peer review, the challenge is to teach them how to tell whether a particular publication is scholarly. The most consistent characteristic of scholarly articles is that they include references or works cited. An advantage of using citations as the criterion is that it can be applied to individual articles rather than whole issues of journals. Many serials publish a mix of peer-reviewed articles and other content like news, letters to the editor, book reviews, and opinion pieces. If students are taught to use only those articles with works cited, they can recognize content in peer-reviewed journals that has not been reviewed. This is especially useful with online journals accessed via databases, where one typically sees the article isolated from other journal content.

Two other characteristics of scholarly articles are worth teaching. One is that contact information for the author(s) is typically listed. Explaining that contacting an author to ask serious questions or make substantive comments is a normal part of scholarly communication makes the point that scholarship is a collaborative, iterative process. The second characteristic worth teaching is that scholarly articles in sciences and social sciences will include descriptions of methods used. Describing the method is essential to science because pursuit of truth relies on replication of results. Other general characteristics of scholarly periodicals that can be taught include the nature of advertising, the price of the publication, and the existence of a board of editors. But those characteristics are less universally present in scholarly journals and may not be discernable in individual articles from remote access serials. Once articles have been selected and used in research papers and reports, it is important that users know how to cite them properly.

CITING SERIALS

Patrons need to learn the proper citation of serials so they can, after they find the articles, cite them correctly in their written work. Commonly used citation styles are prescribed in the *Publication Manual of the American Psychological Association*, the *MLA Style Manual and Guide to Scholarly Publishing*, and *The Chicago Manual of Style*, but many other citation styles are also in current use. "Cheat sheets" for citation styles are popular with students and are offered in many academic libraries. Two dangers with handouts summarizing citation styles are that librarians must use great care that their instructions are current and accurate, and that a cheat sheet can oversimplify and lead users to make mistakes when citing materials that require additional information beyond examples on the handout.

The details of how to properly cite periodicals vary, but there are some basic principles worth teaching whenever the opportunity arises. This may seem too obvious to explicitly teach, but it is important to be sure patrons understand the difference between the title of the article and the title of the publication. The general rule to teach is that the article title comes first and may appear in quotation marks, and the source title follows and is usually in italics. One should teach this principle when teaching patrons to search for the title in italics in an online catalog or A-to-Z list of periodicals holdings. Searching an article title instead of a periodical title is a common mistake.

Another skill to teach is how to translate bibliographic records as they appear in databases into citations in specific styles. A good exercise is to give students database records and have them write the citations in a chosen style. This exercise forces students to discern each required element of the citation in the database records, which has the added benefit of reinforcing their understanding of the concept of database fields. More than one database should be used for the exercise because fields display differently in different databases. This is a good time to also teach proper citation of full-text articles retrieved from databases.

The abbreviations of journal and magazine titles used in Medline and other databases present a challenge that calls for some instruction. Patrons need to know that abbreviated titles in one database may not work as search terms in catalogs, A-to-Z lists, or other databases. They also need to use full titles when making ILL requests. Librarians can explain that when indexes such as *Index Medicus* were produced in print, the sheer volume of citations forced publishers to abbreviate information to reduce the bulk of printed volumes. The publisher of *Index Medicus* reduced *Drug Development and Industrial Pharmacy* to *Drug Dev Ind Pharm*. Many journals still use abbreviations for works cited. The teaching tasks are to make sure patrons know to use the unabbreviated titles when looking up holdings and to direct them to sources to look up full titles.

EVALUATING THE QUALITY OF SOURCES

Before the Internet, librarians had a fair amount of control over the information available to patrons. Books and serials were selected for their quality and appropriateness to patrons' interests. They still are, and so are aggregated databases and other subscribed full-text content. Good collection development is as important as ever. However, the web has created a new information environment, easily accessed and full of accurate and inaccurate if not misinformation. Teaching patrons to evaluate the quality of information has gained greater urgency and has attracted more attention from librarians who teach. The criteria that have been developed for evaluating the quality of websites are equally applicable to serials or any other sources of information. Five fairly standard criteria have been developed after Kapoun (1998) for evaluating the quality of sources: authority, accuracy, objectivity, currency, and coverage.

Authority

Authority refers to who is responsible for publishing the information. For serials, the authority responsible for the whole publication is the corporate body, and for individual articles, the authority is the author. Since the corporate body is not apparent on copies of individual articles, patrons need to be taught to look at the serial record in the online catalog to see who is responsible for publishing the journal. When a professor or other experienced researcher reads an article on a topic within their specialty, they will probably recognize the corporate body responsible for the publication. Students and other readers new to a topic area will not have this prior knowledge and will have to seek additional sources of information to discern the authority of the publisher. Information about society publishers can be found in the *Encyclopedia of Associations* and on the web.

Most scholarly articles include information about the author's affiliation along with their contact information. Professors and researchers may recognize authors, and students can be taught to search on the author(s) in appropriate databases to see what else they may have published. If the Web of Science is available to them, they can also see how often the authors' works have been cited by others. In library instruction sessions, students should be taught to seek a librarian's help to determine the authority of a publisher and to use citations in databases, and to seek their professors' help to determine the authority of authors.

Accuracy

Accuracy is at once one of the most important criteria of quality and one of the most difficult to determine. One approach to teaching how to determine accuracy is to emphasize the role of the peer review process. Since that process is intended to ensure the quality of work, the accuracy of articles from good scholarly sources is more trustworthy. It is worth pointing out to patrons that no source is the last word and that the progress of knowledge includes correction of published mistakes. Novices do not begin with enough prior knowledge to recognize conflicting facts among publications. But they can be taught to be alert to conflicts and to look for the methods and reasoning that lead the authors to come to their conclusions.

Objectivity

Since objectivity is so much in the eye of the beholder, it may be better to teach awareness of point of view than to promote guidelines for determining objectivity. The primary teaching task for this criterion of quality is to convey that every source of information is created from a point of view. In academic settings, students should be instructed to actively seek out a variety of points of view on a research topic. If students use websites, zines, blogs, or similarly opinioned sources in academic work, they should be taught to compare the information they find in alternative sources with information they can find in the library's collection. When there are discrepancies between the alternative view and the information published in books and journals, the author(s) of the alternative perspective should acknowledge and offer reasoning for the discrepancy.

Patrons should be taught that contrary viewpoints are healthy and to be encouraged, but not to be accepted without comparing them to other sources. If a patron complains that serials representing a point of view should be or should not be in the collection, the librarian can explain that libraries develop a collection intended to represent a variety of viewpoints, but that no library can have everything.

Currency

Currency is one of the easier criteria of quality to determine, especially with serial literature. Of course what counts as current depends on the topic, but patrons are generally able to determine currency or timeliness on their own. The most important concept to teach about currency is to make patrons aware of the time lags between when research is conducted, published, and cited. Since writing a research report and ushering it through peer review takes time, newly published articles report data collected several months (or even years) beforehand. Databases may have delays in creating index records for articles, and it takes time for published research to be cited in other articles. It depends on the discipline, but it typically takes a few years for citations to works to appear as references in other articles. On average, research reports are most frequently cited about two to five years after publication. Teaching about these delays gives patrons a better sense of what counts as current in scholarly publishing.

Coverage

Finally, the breadth and depth of topic coverage can be used to judge the quality of information. The key point to teach here is that the coverage has to be what the author claims for the publication. It is all right to provide a broad overview or a study of a tightly focused topic. What is not alright is for an author to claim more comprehensive coverage than an article or website actually provides. Serials present a particular coverage problem to undergraduate students. Students searching in databases often find either superficial news reports or highly specific research, but little in between. Few articles in scholarly journals present broad context balanced with specific research findings. Whatever context is provided is normally found in the literature review section of articles, which will not be apparent from citations in databases. Students should be taught (warned?) that the peer-reviewed journal articles they are required to use may not give them much context, but they may find a broader approach in the articles' introductions and literature reviews. They can also be taught to look in monographs and reference books for treatments of the broader context of a research topic.

INFORMATION LITERACY

Knowing how to find serial literature and evaluating the quality of articles is a part and parcel of information literacy. A thorough discussion of information literacy lies outside the scope of this book, but the foregoing discussion of teaching patrons how to use serials is directly relevant to advancing information literacy. An information literate person can:

- Recognize the need to find information
- Determine the extent of information needed
- Access the needed information effectively and efficiently
- Evaluate the information and its sources
- Incorporate the information into one's knowledge
- Use information to accomplish specific purposes
- Use information ethically and legally (Association of College and Research Libraries 2000).

The Association of College and Research Libraries' (ACRL) (2000) *Information Literacy Competency Standards for Higher Education* include student learning outcomes for each standard. The issues and practices discussed in this chapter are directly relevant to several of the desired learning outcomes. Students should be able to distinguish between scholarly and popular sources according to Standard 1, Performance indicator 2, Outcome 4 (ACRL 2000 1:2:4). They should determine the availability of information and broaden their search beyond the library and use ILL if necessary (ACRL 2000 1:3:1). They select appropriate subject headings (ACRL 2000 2:2:3) and use appropriate search strategies for selected databases (ACRL 2000 2:2:4). The information literate student differentiates between the types of sources in citations (ACRL 2000 2:5:3) and uses an appropriate citation style to consistently cite sources (ACRL 2000 5:3:1).

All the issues and practices discussed in this chapter affect patrons' abilities to efficiently and effectively access serial literature. Whether at the reference desk, in instruction sessions or with finding aids, librarians need to teach patrons how to identify and find information published in serials. Techniques for finding articles include browsing, database searching, and following citations. Librarians can help patrons learn to cite sources correctly and to evaluate the quality of the information they have found. All these skills for finding and using serials are integral to becoming information literate.

SUGGESTIONS FOR FURTHER READING

Much has been written on teaching patrons to use libraries and become information literate, but little focuses exclusively on serials. Some books on teaching information literacy include exercises on teaching patrons to use serials. Trudi E. Jacobson and Timothy H. Gatti's *Teaching Information Literacy Concepts: Activities and Frameworks from the Field* (*Active Learning Series*, no. 6. Pittsburgh, PA: Library Instruction Publications, 2001) includes activities on proper citation and database searching techniques. Joanna Burkhardt, Mary MacDonald, and

Andrée Rathemacher's *Teaching Information Literacy: 35 Practical, Standards-based Exercises for College Students* (Chicago: American Library Association, 2003) includes exercises on finding periodicals.

The American Library Association (ALA) has done extensive work on information literacy, much of which is directly related to teaching patrons to use serials. The Information Literacy Competency Standards may be found online at http://www.ala.org/ala/acrl/acrlstandards/informationliteracycompetency.htm. This document includes detailed learning outcomes and an appendix of Information Literacy initiatives. The ALA has also published *Guidelines for Instruction Programs in Academic Libraries*, online at http://www.ala.org/ala/acrl/acrlstandards/guidelinesinstruction.htm.

For the background and rationale behind making information literacy the primary goal of library instruction, see Patricia Senn Breivik and E. Gordon Gee's *Information Literacy: Revolution in the Library* (New York: American Council on Education, 1989). Theory and techniques of teaching information literacy are described in Esther Grassian and Joan Kaplowitz's *Information Literacy Instruction: Theory and Practice* (New York: Neal-Schuman, 2001).

REFERENCES

Association of College and Research Libraries. 2000. *Information Literacy Competency Standards for Higher Education*, http://www.ala.org/ala/acrl/acrlstandards/informationliteracycompetency.htm (accessed January 27, 2006).

Bates, Marcia J. 2002. Speculations on browsing, directed searching, and linking in relation to the Bradford Distribution. In *Emerging Frameworks and Methods: Proceedings of the Fourth International Conference on Conceptions of Library and Information Science (CoLIS 4)*, ed. Harry Bruce, Raya Fidel, Peter Ingwersen, and Pertti Vakkari, pp. 137–150. Greenwood Village, CO: Libraries Unlimited.

Campbell, Sandy, and Fyfe, Debbie. 2002. Teaching at the computer: Best practices for one-on-one instruction in reference. *Feliciter* 1: 26–28.

Kapoun, Jim. 1998. Teaching undergrads WEB evaluation. *College & Research Libraries News* 59(7): 522–523.

MARS Digital Reference Guidelines Ad Hoc Committee. 2004. Guidelines for implementing and maintaining virtual reference services. *Reference & User Services Quarterly* 44(1): 9–13.

Ronan, Jana. 2003. The Reference interview online. *Reference & User Services Quarterly* 43(1): 43–47.

RUSA. 1996. Guidelines for behavioral performance of reference and information services professionals. *RQ* 36: 200–203.

RUSA. 2004. Guidelines for behavioral performance of reference and information service providers. *Reference & User Services Quarterly* 44(1): 14–17.

Woodward, Beth S. 2005. One-on-one instruction: From the reference desk to online chat. *Reference & User Services Quarterly* 44(3): 203–209.

Glossary

80/20 Rule. Rule of thumb that 80 percent of use is concentrated in 20 percent of items in a collection

AACR2. Anglo-American Cataloguing Rules, Second Edition

acquisitions. Process of selecting, purchasing, and receiving materials

aggregation. Grouping together, as in providing the full text of many publisher's journals in one database

allocation. Division of budget into portions, for example, by department, topic area, or division

A-to-Z list. Alphabetical listing of all periodicals available to patrons of a library, usually maintained by a company outside the library on a subscription basis

bibliographic instruction [BI]. Process of librarians teaching people how to find information, often by making presentations to groups of students

bibliometrics. Science of studying the use and interrelationships of published works

Big Deal. Large packages of journal content offered under contracts that restrict libraries' choice of terms for accessing individual titles

Blog. Web log created by an individual or group used to chronicle and comment upon topics of interest to the author, known as a "blogger"

Bradford Distribution. Formula (n: n^2: n^3) expressing a theory of concentration of journal use, where the number of titles accounting for a portion of use rises exponentially

cancellation. Halting a subscription before its term is complete. "Cancel" is commonly but imprecisely used to describe choosing to not renew a subscription

Carnegie classification. A system of describing institutions of higher learning by degrees offered and other characteristics

CCC. Copyright Clearance Center, provider of copyright licensing and compliance that acts as an intermediary between copyright holders and content users, facilitating the exchange of reuse rights and royalties through a wide range of licensing services [copyright.com]

chronology. Dates that identify issues of serials. *See also* enumeration

citation analysis. The study of references (works cited) in scholarly literature, for purposes including identifying trends, ranking output, and characterizing interrelationships among publications

coefficient of variation. Standard deviation divided by sample size

CONSER. Cooperative Online Serials Program of the Library of Congress, which publishes the *CONSER Cataloging Manual*, the authoritative guide for cataloging serials

consortium. A group of organizations that cooperates to achieve a common purpose

continuing resource. A bibliographic resource that is issued over time with no predetermined conclusion. Continuing resources include serials and ongoing integrating resources [AACR2]

CONTU. [National] Commission on New Technological Uses of Copyright, which established guidelines in 1978 for the copying of materials for interlibrary loan. *See also* Rule of Five

cookie. A packet of information sent by a web server to a user's browser

COUNTER. Counting Online Usage of NeTworked Electronic Resources, a nonprofit project organization of libraries, publishers, and other interested parties seeking to implement a code of practice for measuring online use of remote access publications

DCMA. Digital Millennium Copyright Act of 1998, legislation intended to clarify application of copyright for online materials that affects the licensing and use of remote access serials

direct access electronic serial. Serial retrieved from portable carriers of computer files, for example, discs, cassettes, CD-ROMs

direct subscription. Library subscription for a serial placed directly with the publisher, not through a subscription agent

document delivery. Purchase from a supplier of copies of articles or other documents that includes payment of applicable copyright fees

DOI. Digital Object Identifier, encoded identifier of online information in a standard format, used to uniquely identify individual articles in remote access serials

e-journal. Electronic journal a.k.a. online journal. *See also* remote access serial

embargo. Period of time when recently published issues of a serial are not available in full text in an aggregated database

enumeration. Designation of issues of a serial with a numbering scheme, for example, volume and issue

fair use. Legally allowed use of copyrighted material without payment to the copyright holder for personal, research, or educational purposes

GIF. Graphic Interchange Format, used for image files. *See also* JPG

half-life. In citation analysis, the period of time during which half of the citations to a publication occur

holdings. For serials, the volumes and issues of a serial owned and maintained on the shelves by a library

HTML. Hypertext Markup Language, the coded format language for documents created to be accessed on the web

ICOLC. International Coalition of Library Consortia, a group of approximately 150 library consortia from around the world that facilitates discussion on issues of information resources, pricing policies, and related matters

ILL. Interlibrary loan, the process by which a library requests material from, or supplies material to, another library

index- and abstract-based aggregation. Collection of remote access serials based on titles covered in a periodicals index and produced by various publishers

IP. Internet Protocol, basic standard for communicating on the Internet. An IP address consists of four numbers separated by periods, and uniquely identifies a certain computer on the Internet

ISBN. International Standard Book Number, a machine-readable unique identifying number for books

ISSN. International Standard Serial Number, an eight-digit number used to identify periodical publications, including electronic serials

ISO. International Organization for Standardization, a nongovernmental network of 158 national standards institutes that facilitates creation of common frameworks of specifications and criteria

item. Document or set of documents in any physical format given a single bibliographic description in the catalog, including barcode identification of serial issues

journal. A periodical that publishes content intended to be used for research and scholarship

JPEG (also abbreviated as JPG). Joint Photographic Experts Group, a format for image files that allows compression of images. *See also* GIF

JSC. Joint Steering Committee responsible for coordinating changes to Anglo-American cataloging rules

latest entry cataloging. Creation of bibliographic records with the current title of a serial as the main entry, with information about preceding titles contained in the record for the current title. *See also* successive entry cataloging

link resolver. Software that checks the URL of an online document in a database to verify that a user is authorized to view the document, and provides link(s) to the document

LOCKSS. Lots of Copies to Keep Stuff Safe, a method of archiving copies of online documents such as remote access serials in multiple locations

magazine. A periodical intended for an audience without specialized training who generally read the content for personal use, rather than for professional development

MARC. Machine Readable Cataloging, standard formats for representing and communicating bibliographic and related information

monograph. A bibliographic resource that is complete in one part, or complete or intended to be completed in a finite number of parts [AACR2]

multimedia serial. A serial incorporating visual and/or audio content

newspaper. A serial containing news on current events, with numerical designation, usually published at least once a week on paper larger than 8 ½ × 11

NISO. National Information Standards Organization, producer of a wide range of library standards

nonsubscription costs. Expenses libraries incur for the management of serials beyond the prices paid to publishers

NSDP. National Serials Data Program, agency at the Library of Congress responsible for administering ISSN in the United States

OCR. Optical character recognition, software that converts a scanned image of text into text characters

OpenURL. A protocol for interoperability between an information resource and a link resolver

PDF. Portable Document Format, a file format developed by Adobe Systems that captures formatting information from a variety of desktop publishing applications and makes them appear as created with only Adobe Reader software

peer review. Process whereby articles submitted for publication in scholarly journals are critiqued by qualified experts prior to publication

periodical. A serial published or intended to be published indefinitely at stated intervals

platform provider. Organization that supplies servers, Internet connections, and administration of remote access serials produced by various publishers, usually those too small to efficiently provide Internet access on their own

proxy server. A computer that acts as a gateway that users have to go through before accessing information on the Internet, used to authenticate patrons and identify them to database providers as authorized users

publication pattern. A periodical's intended enumeration and chronology

publisher package. Aggregation of remote access serials provided by one publisher

reliability. Consistency of measurement

remote access serial. A serial delivered online via a network

Rule of Five. CONTU guideline stating that a library may borrow each year no more than five articles from the current five years of a serial

serial. A continuing resource issued in successive or discrete parts, usually bearing numbering, that has no predetermined conclusion [AACR2]

serials crisis. Commonly used term for the combination of rapidly inflating journal prices and relatively stagnant academic library budgets that has occurred since 1980

series. A group of separate items, each with its own title, with a title that applies to all items in the group

SGML. Standard General Markup Language, a standard for how to specify a document markup language or tag set. HTML is an example of a SGML-based language

SICI. A code used to uniquely identify serial items and/or individual articles, typically affixed to serial items as a barcode

SISAC. Serials Industry Systems Advisory Committee, which developed a system to encode serial information. *See also* SICI

stakeholder. Person or group with an interest in an organization, process, or activity, and who is affected by it and defines its success

subscription agent. Company that acts as an intermediary between publishers and libraries, providing services to facilitate efficient serials ordering, payment, delivery, and recordkeeping

successive entry cataloging. Creation of separate bibliographic records for each title of a serial, containing a linking relationship with the previous title when the title has changed. *See also* latest entry cataloging

sweep method. Measuring the use of serials by counting how often items are re-shelved

validity. The degree to which a measure accurately measures what it intends to

vendor. A company that sells access to or services supporting the acquisition of serials, databases, or other products

XML. Extensible Markup Language, a subset of SGML used to define the kind of information contained in data elements, and provide metadata for online documents

zine. A self-published periodical, usually addressing a narrow scope of interest

Index

About the Author

STEVE BLACK is Reference, Instruction, and Serials Librarian, The College of Saint Rose/Adjunct Lecturer, School of Information Science and Policy, University at Albany/SUNY.